GF

£3 -
gen

Brookman

Cambridge ½ 61

18/50 .

LONGMANS' LINGUISTICS LIBRARY

THE LINGUISTIC
SCIENCES AND
LANGUAGE TEACHING

The Linguistic Sciences and Language Teaching

M. A. K. HALLIDAY
Reader in General Linguistics
University College London

ANGUS McINTOSH
Forbes Professor of English Language
University of Edinburgh

PETER STREVENS
Professor of Applied Linguistics
University of Essex

 LONGMANS

LONGMANS, GREEN AND CO LTD
48 Grosvenor Street, London W.1

Associated companies, branches and representatives
throughout the world

First published 1964
New impression 1965

Made and printed in Great Britain by
William Clowes and Sons, Limited, London and Beccles

Contents

Introduction

In recent years, numerous circumstances have contributed to a
great upsurge of interest in the teaching of English; and one is
struck, particularly in connection with English as a second language,
not only by the scale of current activity, but by the very varied
needs which a knowledge of English is increasingly required to
meet. A good deal will be said about these things in the latter part
of this book. During the same recent period, though for reasons
which are in part different, much time and energy have been
devoted to the study of questions which have to do with the way
language 'works', as distinct from the way a given language might
best be taught.

These two broadly contrasting approaches interconnect, and it is
the main business of this book to show how they do so. Or perhaps
we should say, to show how they *should* do so, for though there is
no doubt of their interconnection, nor of their already having
interacted in many profitable ways, we must recognize at the outset
that such interaction as there has been has in general taken place
in a rather haphazard fashion. It is necessary to say something
about why this is so, and to consider the ways in which the two
kinds of approach may be more solidly integrated. This theme will
be found to run through most of the present volume.

The somewhat uncomfortable and maladjusted partnership
between these approaches is not surprising. For one thing, many of
those interested more in the theoretical side of the linguistic
sciences have had, and reasonably so, little or no direct concern with
the teaching of particular languages. They have been more occupied
with such matters as studying this or that aspect of one or more

languages simply for the sake of finding out more about the nature of language. Or they may have been interested in preserving for posterity some knowledge of a dying language which there was little or no question of anyone wishing to learn to speak. Moreover, much work has gone into languages of the past, such as Latin, where the problems of learning are of course very different from those which confront us when we consider the teaching of contemporary English.

On the other side, the long-established tradition of teaching people a living language, whether it be their mother tongue or not, has proceeded all over the world. It is important to recognize that this tradition, in its various forms, has usually succeeded in attaining at least its main objectives. And whether we like it or not, this has sometimes, indeed often, been so even when the tradition has been grounded only in the most rudimentary and sketchy way in any of the principles which would now have the approval of students of the linguistic sciences. In recent times, language teaching, particularly the teaching of English as a second language, has become what we might describe as big business. But this has not removed by any means all the imperfections of its foundations. For in the rapid expansion of the subject there has, almost necessarily, been no very carefully thought out plan of operations. Both in basic theory and in immediate practice the whole evolution of the subject has been rather unsystematic. The result is that many kinds of method (not all deserving of this label) co-exist, and their merits differ enormously. As we shall try to show, and wish to emphasize at the outset, this has had a bearing not only on the teaching of English as a second language but on the way such teaching has been handled in English-speaking countries.

The Second World War gave a special impetus to certain kinds of crash-programme teaching of a large number of languages, because for example German or Russian or Japanese (see p. 174) had to be acquired, for various purposes, in a hurry. A great deal was learnt from these emergency activities. Meanwhile, however, the war for the most part, at least in many places, impeded rather than furthered progress in the more normal and conventional programmes of language teaching. Even in the intervening period it is only here and there that most of the discoveries which resulted from the emergency projects have had any marked effect on these normal programmes. Indeed we must face the fact that in many places the teaching of modern languages, including English, at various levels, still goes on in a way which could scarcely be distinguished from that which was current forty or fifty years ago.

It has already been noted—and this is an important and complicating aspect of the whole approach to the improvement of language-teaching methods—that there is not in operation, except in the vaguest sense, any generally current and accepted body of theory, or system of practice. Instead we have numerous different kinds of approach, varying greatly in degree of sophistication, some of them long-established and conservative, some of them quite recent. Those of the more antiquated (which does not necessarily mean the same thing as 'long-established') kind die hard, and for very good reasons. Traditional methods of approach (as in almost any subject) are notoriously difficult to eradicate or seriously modify. Apart from anything else it is frequently argued, and often with some justification, that the alleged antiquated approaches at least produce positive results, and that there is no guarantee that anything more 'modern' or 'scientific', especially in the hands of those trained in and accustomed to some earlier way of setting about things, would produce anything better. Furthermore, it is often maintained that many of the latest and allegedly most up-to-date kinds of approach are in fact half-baked and therefore distinctly inferior to others they purport to supersede. Or that, though theoretically admirable, they are wildly impractical. The fact that such contentions are often justified does not lighten the task of those who try to make some real contribution to the development of the subject. We should note as an additional relevant factor that linguists are often unwilling to devote the time and effort necessary to explain fully why they believe their science can be useful and to take the trouble to discuss in detail just how it can be so.

The argument that new approaches are, for such reasons, dangerous or undesirable or unnecessary is naturally not accepted in the present volume. However, it is recognized that the mere unsupported recommendation of new theoretical or practical approaches is only a small part of the battle which must be fought to bring about real progress. It is necessary to show at some considerable length—and this is part of what will be attempted in succeeding chapters—*how* and *why* such new approaches are calculated to be helpful and useful. And to do this at all adequately it is necessary to face squarely the very complicated issues which confront us when we really go into the matters that are involved in the business of

*a**

teaching a language, whether native or foreign. In other words, we must first show how ramified are the problems, both theoretical and practical, which are bound to arise if the subject is taken with due seriousness. Something of this sort is attempted at many points in this book. In all this we certainly do not overlook a matter which is often allowed to obscure the issue: how much a gifted teacher may achieve even without a very adequate basis of reference. This is not at any point in question. Our contention is simply that with a better framework he can almost certainly achieve even more in a given time; a serious attempt is therefore made to show why it is that some frameworks are better than others.

It is not the purpose of this volume to supply a series of neat answers to all questions relating to theory or practice. The main intention is rather to raise the kind of questions which must be properly apprehended as a first and necessary move towards finding solutions to problems. But it also tries to present certain up-to-date views about the nature of language and about English in particular. In the early chapters a good deal is said about the fundamental disciplines of linguistics and phonetics and about how, using them, it is possible to describe how a language 'works'. There is a problem here which is frequently raised: how far does the practical teacher of English need to be a master of these disciplines? Here we must distinguish between various kinds of knowledge. Certainly an understanding of the aims and objectives of these approaches is greatly to be desired; this is something quite different from an ability to handle by oneself totally new problems of a linguistic or phonetic kind. Given some such perception of the general aims and objectives of these disciplines, it should thereafter become apparent that certain of them have a special relevance to problems of language teaching. All one can usefully say about these is that the more knowledge and understanding a practising teacher has of them the better. For it is the techniques associated with these which either are, or can be 'converted' into, valuable procedural and expository tools, and will thus provide the teacher with a new perception of the resources available to him for dealing with some of his difficulties.

In all this we are particularly concerned with certain special applications of linguistic and phonetic knowledge and insights. We may regard these applications as having three somewhat different targets or 'customers'. We have spoken so far of the teacher and his special needs. But, secondly, perhaps even more broadly and critically important is that these applications should be clearly perceived and understood by writers of textbooks of various kinds. For, as we shall suggest, the nature and quality of textbooks exerts a very powerful influence on the way the subject as a whole can develop. Finally, an attempt has been made to keep in mind those other readers whose administrative business it is to encourage and develop the disciplines relevant to English language teaching; in putting some of the major problems in perspective, we have therefore tried to do so in a way which may provide ammunition for those who are striving to put the subject on a proper footing. With these three kinds of reader in mind, a fairly systematic attempt is made to show the kinds of relevance which linguistic and phonetic theory have to a wide range of language-teaching problems.

There is gradually accumulating a large body of 'applied theory' to which reference is made in the Bibliography. Since such works exist, it may be asked why there is any need for a book like the present one, which places a good deal of emphasis on the underlying theory that lies behind such applications. The reasons should be fairly clear. First of all, the validity of such applications can scarcely be understood without such a background: the reliability of a book, say on the phonetics of English, cannot be assessed merely on the basis of its degree of fidelity to 'the facts' about English sounds. For the theoretical grounds for selecting, isolating and ordering these so-called facts in a certain way are also of the greatest importance, and for us to assess them we must have some knowledge of what phonetics and related studies are attempting to achieve and how they are setting about this. Secondly, and rather differently, when (as so frequently happens) some perfectly reputable piece of 'applied theory' is presented baldly, without preamble or explanation, it is often rather mystifying to the reader who wishes to make practical use of it. He will tend to wonder what are the reasons for it being what it is, and not something different, e.g. such as he himself may have been more accustomed to hitherto. It may well not be mere new terminology which bothers him, but the very system or method which the terminology partly embodies. Hence the attention which is devoted in this book to the theoretical justifications of certain approaches as against others, and to some explanation of their practical relevance.

One might say that these justifications divide themselves into two kinds. In the first place we have the kind which consists, at least to begin with, of calling attention to the complexity of language in order to show that a body of theory which is itself of considerable complexity and sophistication is required to enable us, for any serious purpose, to marshal in due order the great number of relevant items of information about the language we are seeking to teach. In other words it must be shown that language is not simple, and therefore that language teaching not only deserves but needs the best equipment with which linguistic theory can provide it. Not that this is all that it deserves or needs; the reader will discover that it is *not* claimed that such equipment is in itself sufficient, for nothing of this kind will replace good teaching or wholly make up for bad. Secondly, having said something about the complexity of language, it is necessary to go on to say something in detail about the different kinds of theory, or different parts of some general theory, and just how applications thereof can enable us to handle the various problems which crop up in a comprehensive language-teaching course.

Much could be said here about the numerous features of a language which many conventional grammars, even the larger ones, tend to ignore or slide hastily over. And one cannot but feel that in many cases this is not so much because the author considers them to be unimportant as that he simply lacks any adequate means of expounding them. In other instances, of course, one gets grave distortions of linguistic phenomena; here, as often as not, the author will be unaware that there is anything at all wrong with his techniques. For reasons of this kind it thus often comes about that what is 'conveyed' in grammars, dictionaries and kindred works is but a dim emasculated version of the language itself; more is said on this question in Chapter 6. It must be emphasized that this is much the more serious because it is rare for any modest hint of it to be conveyed anywhere in such works.

With such books in classroom use, it can be no more than a matter of chance whether a given teacher will have the experience and knowledge to make up for the graver of their deficiencies. Besides, even the best teacher will often have nothing more satisfactory to which he himself can go for enlightenment or guidance. In any case a good teacher should have better things to do than spend his valuable time trying to make up for any such inadequacies of textbooks; where these can be averted, they certainly should be. We have already suggested that it must inevitably be the case, broadly speaking, that the nature of the textbooks which are available to the teacher and to the class will have a profound effect on the way instruction is carried out. The writers of textbooks carry therefore a heavy weight of responsibility. The present volume might in part be described as a reminder to them, as well as to those who select and prescribe textbooks, of the seriousness of their tasks. Nor should we forget that these tasks are never-ending; as theories develop so must applications thereof be re-expounded, and books continually re-evaluated.

From another point of view, it is hoped that what is said in this book will serve a useful purpose in making such readers of it as are users of textbooks more critically demanding of their rightful due, and unwilling to accept anything second-rate. Much could be learnt about the place of linguistics and phonetics in English language teaching simply by scrutinizing run-of-the-mill textbooks and trying to establish how far certain theoretical deficiencies are responsible for making them less satisfactory, for their particular practical purposes, than they might otherwise have been. This does not mean, of course, that they could not profitably be scrutinized for defects of other kinds as well.

Something on similar lines might be said here about examinations. For if, as we have suggested, teaching programmes are to a considerable extent controlled by textbooks, it is also true to say that they are in another way controlled by such examinations as they are designed to lead towards. The extent to which examinations are themselves controlled by textbooks is a difficult problem. But, later on (see especially p. 215), enough will be conveyed, directly and by implication, to suggest how often examinations are unrealistic and unsatisfactory in their demands, whatever the reasons. Sometimes the skills they purport to be testing are simply not those which they should be testing. Furthermore, there is sometimes only a faint resemblance between these skills they purport to be testing and the skills (if that is the proper word) which they really do test. Examination papers, like textbooks, could therefore well be examined from the point of view of basic theoretical (as well as practical) deficiencies. If good examination techniques are not achieved, then advances in teaching techniques and in textbooks will have only a small fraction of their desired effects. The further problem of devising and implementing satisfactory syllabuses is of course intimately linked with the problem of adequate examining.

It is not suggested that the shortcomings of certain textbooks or examinations will all turn out to be because of weak theoretical foundations, any more than it is suggested that adequate basic theory is the single and final solution to language-teaching problems as a whole. Later in this volume various other relevant matters of a more *methodological* kind are considered, and stress is laid on the difference between theory as such and the ways in which, for teaching purposes, we may choose to apply or expound it. The reader should perhaps be reminded here, concerning the advocacy both of particular theories and particular methods, that it is often not possible to establish or claim with any certainty that one is better than all possible others. He must also be prepared to face the fact that quite similar theories may sometimes, in different books, be disguised by discrepant or contrasting terminologies; and still worse that, in other cases, the use of similar terms in two different books conceals the fact that the theories are not in fact at all alike.

What is important in all this is the development of an open, critical and vigilant frame of mind; it is hoped that the following chapters will bring out much more, but they will not have entirely failed of their purpose if they achieve this alone. We can at least hope to convey the fact that, though one may not always be able to pronounce in favour of one theory, or one methodological approach, as against another, it is nevertheless usually possible to advance very good arguments indeed in favour of either as against some third, about which it is obvious, once we look into the matter, that it is inferior or worthless.

A good deal is said in the course of this book about the many respects in which we still have a somewhat inadequate analytical knowledge of the English language, despite its having been more intensively studied than most other languages. And stress is laid, at many points, on the way theoretical advances are continually being made. This may seem rather daunting to the reader who is interested in the specific and concrete problems of applying theory and imparting knowledge not about linguistics but about a language. How much more comfortable it would be if these things stayed still and did not have to be continually re-assessed and re-interpreted. But the very complexity of this situation has suggested its remedy. One of the most encouraging of recent developments has been that of what is now coming to be called applied linguistics. The specialist in this subject is a kind of middleman who exists to bridge the gap between theory and newly acquired knowledge on the one hand and the everyday problems of teaching a language on the other. One may hope that by this process of mediation there will be no possibility in the future of the two end points—linguistics and language teaching—not being fruitfully and harmoniously linked to their common advantage.

The authors wish to express their special thanks to Professor David Abercrombie, Mr. J. C. Catford, Mr. Robert M. W. Dixon, Dr. J. O. Ellis, Mr. Trevor Hill, Mr. Ronald Mackin, Mr. J. McH. Sinclair, and Mr. J. P. Thorne, from whom they have gained many valuable ideas which they have drawn on freely in the preparation of this book. They are grateful also to MM. G. Gougenheim, R. Michéa, P. Rivenc and A. Sauvageot for permission to summarize the work done on *Le Français Fondamental* published by the Ministère de l'Éducation Nationale, and to quote material from *L'Élaboration du français élémentaire* published by Didier.

Symbols

Part 1

The Linguistic Sciences

Chapter 1

Linguistics and phonetics

1

We get through about fifteen hundred clauses an hour, conversing steadily in English at a normal pace. It probably takes most of us less than two months to speak as many words as are contained in the whole of Shakespeare's plays. Since so much of our time and energy is spent talking, quite apart from that spent listening, reading and writing, it is not surprising that we become interested in language and in our own use of it. More than that, the linguistic behaviour of human beings provides clues not only to many other aspects of their own biological, social or individual nature but also to more abstract fields of inquiry such as philosophy and logic. This is why people engaged in a wide range of different subjects of study use language as part of the material of their research.

These subjects include some which are usually classified as 'sciences' and some which are usually not. This arbitrary dichotomy, however, is more and more being shown to be inappropriate, and nowhere does it break down so completely as in the study of language: this is one of the attractions of linguistic studies, that they bridge, or rather annul, the gap between 'the sciences' and 'the arts'. The subjects that pay some attention to language include physiology, psychology, logic, mathematics, communication engineering, sociology, anthropology and literary criticism. In the behavioural and social sciences, for example, language forms an important part of the evidence, and a great deal of language activity is observed and described. In communication engineering, language is what is to be transmitted; if efficient and economical techniques for transmission are to be devised, the properties of language, or some of them, have first to be understood. In philosophy and logic, it is in part, and for some scholars primarily, linguistic relations that provide a framework, or at least an analogy, for the concepts being investigated. In literary criticism the object of study is language used in particular ways with particular effects. All this quite apart from the platitude that all branches of learning, whether organized under 'science' or 'arts', take the form of language about something: they are 'just so much talk', and that is their great strength and unifying force.

It might be expected, then, that the sum total of what all these subjects had to say about language was all that there was to be said. But the relevant fact is not that those working in these various fields study different parts of language; it is that they study language for their own different purposes. The physiologist may draw conclusions, by observing language activity and classifying types of aphasia, about the operation of the brain and the nervous system; to do this he needs to know something about language, the more so if he wishes to apply his understanding to the treatment of brain disorders affecting the use of language. So too the speech therapist studies the working of the vocal organs, the better to treat and cure speech defects. Neither need be concerned with all aspects of the phenomenon of language and of the part it plays in our lives. The communication engineer is interested in the properties of the message only to the extent that this knowledge allows him to improve the transmission of it. The logician is concerned with systems of concepts and relations which, though they cannot be described without reference to language, extend beyond language into any field where they can be systematized. The literary critic operates with scales of value-judgment whose criteria are formulated in non-linguistic terms.

None of these, however, studies language for its own sake, to find out how it works. This on the other hand is precisely the task of the linguistic sciences. They have been built up to throw light on language; not to use language to throw light on something else. Their purpose is to find out how languages work and how language works.

For this purpose language is best regarded as a form of activity. Specifically, it is a form of activity of human beings in societies; and it has the property of being patterned. So studying how language works means studying the patterns, and the items which enter into them; how people operate these patterns and items; and how they persist (and, by reference to this, how they diverge) at different times, in different places and among different groups of people. All these matters could be considered the domain of the 'pure' linguistic sciences, though in fact the term is never used, since, except perhaps in mathematics, the distinction between 'pure' and 'applied' is difficult to draw and not very useful when drawn. But we can say that, over and above the study of how language works, there are certain clear applications of these studies where the purposes, whether or not 'practical' in the ordinary sense (some are and some are not), go beyond the study of language for its own sake. The teaching of native and foreign languages is perhaps the most important of these applications.

2

To stress the essential unity of the sciences and the arts is not to deny the difference between scientific and unscientific observations. There is a definable sense of 'scientific' according to which statements about language, as about any other object of study, can be said to be scientific or not. What matters—and this is the reason for insisting on the linguistic *sciences* as the means of finding out and describing how language works—is that it is the *scientific* study of language which turns out to be most revealing. This is true even in the study of literature: the more rigorous and objective linguistic methods have become, the more they have thrown light on the literary use of language and on the patterning and impact of particular literary texts.

To study language scientifically means to construct a unified theory of how language works, and to derive from it certain exact methods for describing languages. The theory is not of course conjured out of the air: it has its origins in countless observations of language events. As in all scientific work, these observations are the basis of any theory. Once a theory has been constructed its relation to the observations, which we refer to as 'abstraction' (to be understood as a relation not as a process), may take various forms; in one way or another the theory exercises control over the statements made within its range of operation. It becomes possible to demand that statements should be rigorous, consistent and objective; and above all—since this presupposes the other requirements—that they should conform to the theory: in other words, that they should be scientific.

Such statements prove much more useful than unscientific ones. They are more useful not only in what they reveal of the working of language, in 'pure' studies so to speak, but also in their capability of application. For this reason it is sad that what is said about language by those working on it from the standpoint of outside disciplines is often so unscientific as to be of practically no value at all. This lack of co-operation among different disciplines—which is what it amounts to—arises because no one person can make himself an expert in all the subjects which impinge on his own field of study. A psychologist, for example, cannot be expected to take up linguistics, which is only one of many subjects bordering on his own. He may not even know that there exists a science having a theory and methods for dealing with language which he could apply for his purposes. Even if he is aware of it, it is often difficult to organize effective collaboration: university teachers frequently have to struggle to find time for research in their own line of study, and are forced to turn down requests for collaboration in joint projects that promise to be very fruitful, simply through lack of time. All too often, where scientific statements about language have been needed, workers in other fields have gone on working with their own do-it-yourself pseudo-linguistics, being content, as they never would be in their own subjects, with inexact observations and *ad hoc* categories. This is like attempting to do any other job with half the tools missing, or replaced by home-made improvisations: the results are such as might be expected.

It is necessary of course that the tools should be known to exist. The idea that language can be the object of scientific study is not a new one; but it has only recently become widely known that there exist subjects whose sole purpose is to undertake such studies. As always happens, publicity and support for the linguistic sciences has come with the discovery that they have applications. As long as the study of language was a 'pure' science, in which it was not yet clear how the theory related to any particular application, it had, reasonably enough, little publicity value. Quite suddenly it became clear that there were certain specific fields for the application of linguistic theory to practical ends. From that moment, the linguistic sciences became 'respectable'; and money for teaching and research was made available.

There is no objection to this at all: it is quite natural that an academic subject should be judged by its results. But it is not always possible to predict just what the application of an area of research will be; and it is useful to remember that if the linguistic sciences have turned out to have applications—and this is why this book has been written—this is due to many years of work, not always with much encouragement or support, by people interested in the study of language for its own sake. Application in turn contributes to theory; but if the range of application is not to remain static the 'pure' research must go on.

3

Any discussion of linguistic science must make use of technical terminology; no apology need be made for this. Technical terms after all are not created for their own sake. They come into being for exactly the same reason as any other items in language: because there are things—events, objects, properties, concepts and so on— to be named. What distinguishes technical terminology is that the named things are specialized categories, and it is because the *categories* are found to be needed, for observation and action, that specialized terms arise. Such categories are not derived from 'common sense'. This does not mean that they are divorced from 'reality', but that they are set up to handle complicated regions of reality, which we want both to understand and to be able to apply our understanding of, but where direct and unsystematized observation is not enough. Language is one such region, and linguistic science can no more be 'just commonsense' than nuclear physics can. Neither can be expounded in everyday, non-technical categories. If they could, they would not be sciences: a subject which did not need technical terms would not need to exist as a subject of research.

But there is no magic in the terms themselves—or rather, no more magic than in the rest of language. It will not do to assume that mastering a subject means simply learning a set of technical terms, as if these had the status of passwords. We often meet the request, even from specialists in other fields, the very people who ought to know better: 'Can you help me?—it'll only take a couple of minutes —I just need a name for something—I'm doing a bit of work which involves talking about language and I don't know what to call things.' This form of words shows clearly that the questioner is deluding himself: what he needs is categories, not names: not two minutes' help but two months' hard work on theory. The only answer is: 'Just call them *a*, *b* and *c*, or red and yellow, or carrots, leeks and cabbages—if names are all you need, these will suffice—it is the categories that count.' If the category is invalid or wrongly defined no elegant technical term will save it from futility.

In fact it is sometimes said that linguists do not take the choice of technical terms for their subject seriously enough. It is true that they regard the categories—and this implies the correct and consistent *use* of terms—as more important than the *choice* of one term rather than another. Perhaps there is a danger that, in taking care to avoid the magical notion that by naming a thing one has gained control over it, one may go too far and underrate the importance of the naming of things. Certainly choice of terms is important: the structure of a terminology should reflect the structure of the categories concerned, as in the naming of classes of chemical compounds. At the same time, the linguistic sciences have a long history: they are among the oldest of the sciences, and it is right that something of their tradition should be perpetuated by the continued use of traditional terms. There are some linguists who say that, since the old terms have to be redefined as names of new categories, it is less confusing to coin new terms; but this view is not shared by most linguists in Britain, and we have not adopted it here. We would rather use a term like 'noun', even though the category which it names is defined in a way very different from the way in which it was defined in earlier periods of the subject, than a mere label like 'class 2 word' or a neologism such as 'nominoid'.

In this book, which is a discussion of the subject and not a textbook, we have restricted the technical terms to that minimum necessary to a consideration of what the linguistic sciences are about and how they are applicable to language teaching. Each of the principal technical terms, where it is explained, is printed in SMALL CAPITALS: this means that it is to be understood as defined within the framework of the linguistic sciences, and therefore it is no use whatever going to the dictionary to look it up, since the definition given there will not correspond to the specialized use of the term. Since many of the terms, quite apart from those that are traditional in linguistic studies, are everyday words like 'level', 'form' and 'unit', rather than Graeco-Romance neologisms, the small capitals are a warning that an old word is being used in a new way. Further-more no technical term can be adequately defined in a single sen-tence, since such 'definition' presupposes no less than a complete statement of the place of the category concerned in the framework of the theory. For this reason there is no glossary, as this could only be misleading; instead the principal technical terms used are included in the index, with page references to the passage or pass-ages most relevant to the understanding of each.

4

The term 'linguistic sciences' covers two closely related but distinct subjects: linguistics and phonetics. They are closely related because they look at the same material, language, with the same aim, that of finding out how it works. They are distinct because they look at different aspects of language and need different methods to describe these aspects.

Language does not exist: it happens. It is neither an organism, as many nineteenth-century linguists saw it, nor an edifice, as it was regarded in the early modern 'structuralist' period of linguistics. Language is activity, activity basically of four kinds: speaking, listening, writing and reading. These activities entail certain material processes which are observable. When we speak, the bodily movements we perform can be observed and measured; so can the disturbances in the air which result, specifically and directly, from these movements. In spoken language, we are interested in both stages of the activity, precisely because the properties of a sound wave are uniquely determined by the articulatory movements per-formed to produce it. In writing, however, the link between the movements and the resulting marks, on paper or blackboard, is fluid: you cannot tell what movements of what organs are responsible for producing certain letters written, still less typed, on a page. In written language therefore it is only the result we are interested in observing, since the study of the movements that produce marks on paper tells us nothing of the linguistic significance of such marks, nor even helps us to say whether they constitute language or not.

There are of course other material processes in language which we cannot yet observe. In particular the perceptual stages of language activity, the processes associated with listening and reading

1*

that take place in the sense-organs, the nervous system and the brain, are the least well understood. Recent work is beginning to cast light on the perception of speech sounds, but we are still a long way from being able to record this accurately. Meanwhile, the processes that can be observed, accurately and in detail, are so revealing for the present purposes of describing language in its material aspects that we confine ourselves to these, avoiding the trap of trying to explain the known by the unknown, the observable by the unobservable.

Such are the basic material processes of language activity: the production and perception, and in spoken language the transmission, of the two kinds of raw material of linguistic events, audible sound waves and visible marks. The material aspect is, however, only one aspect of language activity, and there are two others which must be taken into account: the structural and the environmental. Language events, that is, not only take place in a material medium: they also exhibit certain regularities in their internal relations which are not directly observable in the material event, so that 'sounding alike' is not the only way in which two linguistic events are capable of 'being alike'. Furthermore, they take place not in isolation but in orderly relation to other events. These three aspects of language activity, or three types of pattern in language, the material, the structural and the environmental, are the reason for the separation of LEVELS in the linguistic sciences.

From these three types of patterning are derived the three principal levels: SUBSTANCE, FORM and CONTEXT. The substance is the raw material of language: auditory (PHONIC substance) or visual (GRAPHIC substance). The form is the internal structure. The context is the relation of language, which is in fact a relation of its internal patterns, its 'form', to other features of the situations in which language operates. The linguistic sciences have to account for language at all these levels.

Since we distinguish three principal levels, with certain subdivisions and interrelations to be mentioned later, it needs to be explained why we recognize two linguistic sciences rather than either one or three. The reason is that theories and methods of two distinct *kinds* are involved. For describing the substance, these theories and methods derive from the general fields of physiology and physics, so that the study of the substance belongs primarily to the natural (physical and biological) sciences. Since the study of graphic substance, the purely material aspect of written language, does not require such distinct specialized techniques, it is *phonic* substance that is in fact singled out in this way; and the study of phonic substance is phonetics. The other aspects of language, the formal and the contextual, require theory and methods characteristic of the behavioural, or social, sciences: these aspects can be grouped together as one field of study, and this is linguistics. If spoken language is considered as organized noise, then phonetics studies the noise and linguistics the organization.

While linguistics and phonetics have their different specialized roles in the study of language, the difference between them is less important than that which they have in common and which distinguishes them from other disciplines, including those involving some consideration of language: namely the study of language in its own right and for its own sake. To stress this essential unity of purpose and scope, some people use the term 'linguistics' to cover both, subsuming phonetics as one part of linguistics. This is quite acceptable but raises the difficulty that there is then no single name for that part of 'linguistics' which is not phonetics, and such a term is quite often needed in practice. The alternative, which we have adopted here, is to use linguistics and phonetics as mutually exclusive terms and to group them together as 'the linguistic sciences'. There was a practical convenience in separating the two when phonetics became a laboratory subject in the 1920s: it became possible for instrumental phonetics to dissociate itself from other aspects of linguistic theory, and indeed it was necessary to its own development that for a time it should do so. Linguistics did not become a laboratory subject till the 1950s, with the coming of tape recorders and computers into general use; even now computers are only just beginning to be widely used in the study of language. But the period when phonetics can profitably be separated from linguistics is now past; instrumentation on the one hand and theoretical developments on the other have reintegrated the two in the light of new observation and experience.

As far as those working in the linguistic sciences are concerned, they tend to be specialists either in linguistics or in phonetics. In general a linguist needs to be a competent phonetician and a phonetician a competent linguist: especially so if he is a teacher of his subject. In research there is work for specialists distributed at all points along the scale, at the extremes as well as in the middle.

Some laboratory phoneticians, qualified in physics or physiology, may be very little involved with linguistics; while some linguists, especially if mathematically trained and oriented, may not be directly concerned with phonetics. Even then each must be aware of the results obtained by the other. In the middle of the scale, there are those who specialize precisely in the meeting-ground of linguistics and phonetics, namely in phonology. The real point is that neither subject flourishes if cut off from the other; this is perhaps worth stressing to anyone who may be discussing the introduction of such studies into a college or university.

5

We should here briefly examine the claim of the linguistic sciences to be sciences. 'Claim' is perhaps misleading, since the reason for using the term is not that science is an 'OK word' nowadays, but that the subjects have certain specific characteristics to which the term is appropriate. What we have to do is rather to state in what sense the linguistic sciences are scientific. With phonetics there is no problem; it is, as we have seen, closely related to established natural sciences, and is scientific in the same sense that they are. More specifically, articulatory phonetics is related to human physiology, while acoustic phonetics, the study of sound waves, is linked to physics: phonetics thus has a place in both the physical and biological sciences. In the study of the perception of speech, it is linked again with physiology and also with psychology.

Linguistics on the other hand is concerned with patterns of relationship between events. These events are pieces of socially determined human activity; the link here is with the social sciences, psychology, sociology and social anthropology. The patterning of these events is, as we have seen, both internal and external. The internal patterning is what is known as linguistic 'form'; the study of the form of language follows the general principles governing the study of systematically related properties and events, being in essence logical and potentially statistical. The external patterning is what we here call 'context'; this is the patterned relation between linguistic events and non-linguistic phenomena. The study of context, best known under the name 'semantics', is difficult to classify; 'semantics' has usually implied a specifically conceptual approach and one which has tended to be somewhat separate from other linguistic studies. The approach through language and 'situation', which owes much to anthropology, is still at an early stage of development.

There is a warning to be made here. If we say that linguistics is partly a 'logical' study, this is not to be taken to imply that there is any relation between logic and *language*, that propositional or predicate logic can be used to explain the relations between linguistic items. This assumption was held for many years, but it is not a fruitful one. What we do imply is a relation between logic and *linguistics*: that a symbolic or 'scientific logic' may be considered to underlie the *theoretical* validity of the categories used to describe language, and the consistency of their relations to each other within the total framework of categories.

So when we classify the linguistic sciences according to which other sciences they resemble, they turn out to be a mixture. The mixture includes components of natural science, social science, and logic and mathematics. That the mixture itself is unique hardly needs pointing out, since language is a unique phenomenon.

If, however, we talk about 'the linguistic sciences' it is not so much because they are like this or that other science in particular, but because they share something which is common to all sciences: their methods fall within what could be called general scientific method. What we understand by this is as follows. Behind any statements made about languages in linguistics and phonetics lies a chain of abstraction. First, certain events, linguistic events, are observed. They are found to display partial likenesses: so, second, generalizations are made about them. Third, on the basis of these generalizations hypotheses are formulated to account for the events. These are tested by further observations, and out of them, fourth, is constructed a theory of how language works. From this theory are derived methods for making statements about linguistic events. These statements link the theory to the events it is set up to account for, and they can now be evaluated by reference both to the theory and to the events: the best statements are those which make maximum use of the theory to account most fully for the facts.

The chain is thus 'observation—generalization—hypothesis—theory—descriptive statement'.This is not of course a process carried out by each linguist, or even carried out in successive steps at all. It is a model of the relation between observation, theory and description, a relation which results from developments taking place over many years. Any particular theory will be judged by its effectiveness; while in use it controls and gives meaning to the descriptive statements made. A theory of this kind can take the form of a set of categories of a high order of abstraction; the nature and status of each category is explicitly formulated, and so are the inter-relations among them. The categories and their interrelations can then be examined to see whether they are valid, consistent and complete.

We are not concerned with the label 'scientific' as a status symbol. If a subject which uses such methods is scientific, then linguistics and phonetics are sciences. If we require 'experiment' and 'prediction', as used in the natural sciences, as prerequisites of a scientific discipline, linguistics (though not phonetics) is, with other social sciences, largely excluded. There is a sense in which all theories predict, linguistic theory included: they predict that all events falling within their field of observation will be accounted for by the theory. The relation between this and the prediction of the natural sciences is complex and, since we are not trying to prove anything, irrelevant. What the linguistic sciences do is to use theory to account for language, how it works and how it persists. The reason for dis-cussing why they are called 'sciences' is to show in what respects they are like other subjects that are called 'sciences'.

Until recently linguists were more concerned to state the unique-ness of their subject than to claim for it relationships with other subjects. This attitude was understandable: linguistics had been able to advance only after the success of a long struggle to dis-entangle it from other subjects. It had to set up its own categories for talking about language, instead of adopting ready-made ones from elsewhere. Once linguists learnt to do this our understanding of language was immeasurably increased; and it is not surprising that for a time they were a little sensitive on this point and inclined vigorously to proclaim the autonomy of linguistic science. This claim can now be regarded as beyond dispute, and we can turn our atten-tion to the much more interesting question of the ways in which the linguistic sciences are *not* unique. They are not unique in the way they use theory. They are unique in what theory they use and in what they use it for.

6

The names covering this body of theory are 'General Linguistics' and 'General Phonetics'. The term 'general phonetics' is the less commonly used of the two because those who include phonetics under linguistics include general phonetics under general linguistics and therefore do not give it a name. Others deny that there is such a thing as phonetic theory, claiming that the categories of phonetics are in fact derived from linguistic theory—in other words that one does not talk about speech sounds except in relation to the way they work in language. The point of view adopted here is that it is useful to recognize a 'general phonetics' as a general theory for the description of speech sounds. This is taken up in Chapter 3, while in Chapter 2 we are concerned specifically with linguistic theory. Phonology, the level at which linguistics and phonetics meet, is discussed in both chapters.

General linguistic theory provides for both the dimensions which are common to all the strictly social sciences, the descriptive and the historical. The two main branches of linguistics are known as 'Descriptive Linguistics' and 'Historical Linguistics'. The first is the study of how language works, the second the study of how it persists and changes. Both arc equally important to the total understanding of language, but in application to language teaching it is descriptive linguistics that is relevant. Linguistics in its 'classical' form, in India and China, in the Arabic and Jewish traditions, and in Europe until nearly 1800, was entirely descriptive. In the nineteenth century the focus of attention shifted, as in so many subjects from zoology to literature, on to history. The detailed history of specific languages and of language families, as a study of change, was the massive achievement of nineteenth-century linguistics. The present-day view of linguistic history tends to emphasize what is constant rather than what changes, and insists that the history of an item cannot be separated from its place in the language as a whole at different periods; but the interest in the history of languages, and in the general theory of linguistic history, remains. The term 'scientific' in the sense defined applies to historical as well as to descriptive linguistics. Not that one cannot talk about the history of language in an unscientific way, as in folk etymologies, value judgments about 'corruption' and 'decay', speculations about the

origin of language and the like: but such observations are not part
of linguistics.

Since the purpose of our discussion here of linguistics and
phonetics is to examine their relevance to language teaching, we
shall ignore the study of the history of language, important though
it is in linguistics as a whole, and concentrate on description, the
study of how language works. There is one aspect to this, however,
which does not strictly fall within 'descriptive linguistics': the
study of language in relation to those who use it. This, since it is
really the study of language as an institution, is recognized as a
separate branch of the linguistic sciences and has come to be known
as 'institutional linguistics'. There is no sharp line dividing institutional from descriptive linguistics. The same piece of language
activity may be examined under both headings. But there is a difference of standpoint: different things will be said about it, and
different criteria used. Whereas in a descriptive statement we may
note for example that a speaker has used a transitive and not an
intransitive clause, or the category 'future tense' and not 'present
tense', or the item 'fling' and not 'throw', in an institutional
statement we may note that he has spoken English and not French,
British and not American English, and that he spoke conver-
sationally and not formally. The two studies meet when we consider
the relation of the forms he used to the type of situation in which he
was speaking. Institutional linguistics is discussed as a separate
subject in Chapter 4.

In general therefore when we use the terms 'linguistics' and
'phonetics' we shall be using them to refer specifically to the
descriptive, not the historical, study of language.

Again, not all observations describing language fall within
linguistics: coffee-time talk about the relative efficiency of languages,
or the influence of race or climate on language, is unscientific and
therefore not part of linguistics, just as discussions of the aesthetic
merits and demerits of the pronunciation of certain dialects and of
'slovenly accents' are unscientific and therefore not part of
phonetics. Let us stress once again that we are not using 'scientific'
as an emotive term, for polemic purposes. It is simply that unscientific statements about language are inadequate: they are misleading
in 'pure' description, in that they distort the picture of the working
of language, and they are worse than valueless when one seeks to
apply them, except perhaps for purposes of entertainment.

By contrast, what has been found to be of value, in application in certain fields, is the scientific description of language. This means, as we have said, the methods of descriptive linguistics together with that part of general linguistic theory from which these are derived— in other words the theory and practice of the linguistic description of language. It is this that we shall say more about in the next two chapters. There remains one thing to be added here: the complete framework of 'levels' for the description of language.

7

Language is, as is well known, too complicated for all its features to be described by any one method, within any one scheme of categories. The principle of splitting a language up into 'levels' in order to talk about it is long established and well founded. Any account of a foreign language which has different chapters for 'spelling', 'pronunciation', 'morphology', 'syntax' and 'vocabulary' is doing just that. There have been various ways of dividing, and various names for the divisions: whatever the division adopted, the *kind* of statement made in each section would be quite different. The reason for splitting is not just that there is too much to say to put into one chapter, but that there are too many different kinds of things to say. The nature of the abstractions involved in the statements differs from one level to another.

The exact nature of the demarcations among the different levels is a matter much discussed in linguistics; it is one of the things about which linguists tend to disagree most, and linguists disagree neither more nor less than scientists of any other kind. But in the matter of levels, as in other disputed regions of the subject, two things should be borne in mind. One is the wide area of solidly established common ground, the facts that are known and embodied in linguistic theory: what is commonly held is far more significant and fundamental than what is in dispute. The second is that what are put forward as different views are often not so much conflicting theories, of which one must be right and the others wrong, but rather what we might call different 'models' co-existing within, and relatable in terms of, the same general theory. It is not true that only one model can represent the nature of language; language is much too complex for any one model to highlight all its different aspects equally clearly. The problem in any instance is to select, or devise, the model that will be most suitable for the purpose in view. The subject advances, so that we can say that models in use today are more powerful in general than those of twenty-five years ago; but the choice among current models depends first of all on what one wants linguistics to do for one.

In this book we have presented the model which we think is most useful for language-teaching purposes. This does not mean that we think that every language teacher should become a linguistic theorist; it means that, in our view, if language is described according to the version of linguistic theory outlined, the task of the language learner, and of the language teacher, will be made easier. Other versions of the theory, other models, are discussed very briefly in the Appendix; and in places we have referred to these and assessed them from our own standpoint. But it should be emphasized that a description of a language based on another version of linguistic theory, though we may think it less useful for the teacher, will be much more like a description based on the version put forward here, and much more effective, than will an account which is not based on linguistic theory at all.

The complete framework of levels for linguistic description as we are representing it can best be shown in tabular form:

Subject concerned:	Phonetics		Linguistics		
Level (general):	SUBSTANCE (phonic or graphic)	relation of form and substance	FORM	CONTEXT (relation of form and situation)	situation (non-linguistic phenomena)
Level (specific):	PHONETICS	PHONOLOGY	GRAMMAR & LEXIS (vocabulary)	SEMANTICS	
	SCRIPT	'GRAPHOLOGY' (writing system)			

These show the different aspects of linguistic patterning that have to be accounted for. The question may be asked: how far are these 'levels' levels of language and how far are they levels of linguistic analysis? That is, are they different kinds of patterning *in language*, properties of the linguistic events themselves, or are they put in by the linguist to make the description of language simpler?

The answer here is that the general levels are properties of language; when we call them 'different aspects of linguistic patterning', 'linguistic' here means 'of language'. But, since they are properties of language events, they will also be reflected in the description of language; so that 'linguistic' also implies 'of linguistics'. There is, however, a difference. Language does display the different types of pattern—primarily, as we have seen, those of form and those of substance; but it displays them, not in clear contradistinction to each other, but in interaction in one and the same event and with no sharp boundaries between them. Like the patterns associated with many other forms of social activity, the patterns of language are superimposed on one another: they do not follow each other in time. A handshake, for example, could be described in substance: as a physical and physiological activity. Precisely the same event can be described from the point of view of its form (its place in the total framework of meaningful gestures and actions—both what it might have been but was not, say a salute or a kiss, and what went before and after it) and of its context (who were the participants, what was their relation to each other, under what conditions did they meet?). Both form and context are aspects of the meaning of the activity. So with language. The same event has substance and also form and context; both the substance (the medium of the activity) and the form and context (its internal and external meaning) have their patterns.

With substance, form and context it is clear, on the whole, which patterns belong to which; the problem is to find suitable theories to account for, and state, these patterns, and then to describe them accurately and consistently. With the total set of levels, however, there arises the further problem of drawing the boundaries. Phonic and graphic substance are clearly differentiated: this is a matter of the medium—speech or writing. The distinction here is not between different kinds of pattern in the same event but between different kinds of event. But two events differing in the nature of their substance, one spoken and the other written, can be alike in meaning (form and context), so that even here there is a problem— where do they meet, and how alike can they be? The least obvious distinction perhaps is that between grammar and lexis, since these are two aspects of linguistic form; yet we gain by separating them, because they represent two different ways in which language is organized, internally, into meaningful patterns, and there are different things to be said about each. The next chapter examines in more detail the different types of patterning recognized at the various levels that are ranged under 'linguistics'.

BIBLIOGRAPHY:

For further reading in connection with the subject matter of this chapter, see especially items 3, 7, 9, 13, 46, 53, 86, 87 *in the Bibliography.*

Chapter 2

Linguistics in the description of language

1

When we describe linguistic *form*, that is the two levels of grammar and lexis, we are describing the meaningful internal patterns of language: the way in which a language is internally structured to carry contrasts in meaning. The problem is to recognize and account for all those places in the language where there is a possibility of meaningful choice; and to state the range of possibilities at each place. What causes us to draw a distinction between grammar and lexis is the variable *range* of the possibilities that arise at different places in the language.

In some instances we face a choice among a very small number of possibilities. This happens for instance when we have to choose between 'this' and 'that'; or between singular and plural; or between past, present and future; or between positive and negative. There are some places in every language where we have to make such choices; we cannot avoid them or remain neutral, and there is a limited number of possibilities to choose from. Moreover the range of choice is exhaustive: where 'positive' can be chosen, 'negative' is the only possible alternative. There are other places, however, where we are choosing from a very large number of possibilities; we cannot count them, or draw a clear line round them such as will separate what is possible from what is impossible. In a clause which begins 'he was sitting there on the . . .', certain items—chair, settee, bench, stool and so on—are quite likely to follow, but very many others are perfectly possible, and probably no two people would agree on the hundred most likely items.

This is the basis of the difference between grammar and lexis. Grammar is concerned with choices of the first kind, where there is a small fixed number of possibilities and a clear line between what is possible and what is not. The second kind of choice is the domain of lexis. These two types of choice are known respectively as 'closed' and 'open'; the range of possibilities in a closed choice is called technically a SYSTEM, that in an open choice a SET. As a reminder of this distinction we often talk of 'closed system' and 'open set'. The closed system is thus characteristic of grammar, the open set of lexis.

It is not the case, however, that all choices in language are clearly of one type or the other, closed or open. What we find is really a gradient, or 'cline': that is, there is a continuous gradation in the patterns of formal choice in language. At one end we have a large number of systems interacting with each other in highly complex ways, but with a small number of fixed possibilities in each: here we are clearly in grammar. At the other end, we have open sets, in very simple interrelations with each other but with a much wider range of choice in each, whose limits are hard to define: here we are equally clearly in lexis. But every language has choices which are round about the middle of this cline, where the number of possibilities is limited but large and the interaction of one choice with others is still fairly complex. Instances of items entering into choices of this intermediate type in English are 'in, at, on, under', 'if, seeing that, provided that, in case', 'often, never, sometimes, always'.

Language, therefore, does not draw a clear distinction between grammar and lexis. In the formal patterns of language, closed systems in complex interrelations, at one end of the scale, shade gradually into open sets in simple interrelations at the other. Linguistics, however, has to draw a line, because these two types of phenomenon need different theories to account for them: that is to say, we cannot account for both patterns of the grammatical type and patterns of the lexical type with the same categories and relations. This has been recognized since the earliest days of linguistics; we take it for granted that we need both a grammar and a dictionary to describe the form of a language, though we may seldom ask exactly how they differ.

There is in fact some confusion about the difference between the grammar and the dictionary, including three familiar notions all of which are misleading. One is that a dictionary deals with words and a grammar with everything else, including smaller things that words are made up out of and larger things that words are made up into. Another is that a dictionary deals with the items of a language and a grammar with its abstract relations; this is the 'meat and bones' or 'bricks and mortar' view of language. The third is that a dictionary deals with meaning and a grammar with form.

The last of these observations is wholly false: form is part of meaning, not opposed to it (see Section 4 of this chapter), and both grammar and dictionary are concerned with meaning. There is, however, some truth in the first two, though both are misleading. The thing called a 'word', at least in English, belongs in fact *both* in the grammar *and* in the dictionary; but it is not quite the same thing in the two cases. Similarly, *both* grammar *and* dictionary deal *both* with items *and* with the abstract relations into which they enter, though it is true that more abstraction is possible in grammar than in lexis. A better short statement of the difference would be this: grammar deals with closed system choices, which may be between items ('this/that', 'I/you/he/she/we/they') or between categories (singular/plural, past/present/future); lexis with open set choices, which are always between items ('chair/settee/bench/stool' etc.).

Closed systems lend themselves to more abstraction and generalization than do open sets. That is to say, the natures of grammar and lexis are such that any statement made in grammar can account for a larger number of events than a statement made in lexis. Since the purpose of the theory is to account for the largest number of events as simply as possible, this means that the theory of grammar is more powerful than the theory of lexis. So in making a description of any language we try to bring as much as we can within the framework of the grammar. If we can account for the prepositions of English by grammatical statements, we shall have said a great deal more about them, and about the way they work, than we can do by entering them in the dictionary. But it is of course precisely these middle range choices that are the hardest to account for in grammar.

2

In grammar and lexis we are accounting for the FORMAL ITEMS of a language. A 'formal item' is any meaningful stretch of language, of any extent, like 'the' or 'chair' or 'in case' or 'I've thrown it away' or the '-s' in a plural like 'chairs'. The reason for calling this a 'formal item' instead of simply 'item' is that it is defined within linguistic form and is thus itself the product of a process of abstraction: 'the formal item "the"' is an abstraction from countless actual and potential events that make up the English language. Although in one sense no two events are ever identical, all science rests on generalizations; we need to assume that two or more events, or parts of two or more events, can be *treated as* identical—in fact they must be so treated if we want to account for them. The concept of a formal item rests on a generalization of this kind: a large number of, though not necessarily all, occurrences of 'the' must be treated as occurrences of a single formal item if we want to understand how the English language works.

Out of the total mass of formal items recognizable in a language we seek to recognize the grammatical items and the lexical items. In English, for example, 'chair' is a lexical item: it operates as an item in open set choices. 'the', 'chair', the '-s' in 'chairs', 'in case' and 'I've thrown it away' are grammatical items. But in grammar there is a further distinction to be made. 'the', '-s' and 'in case' are '*fully* grammatical items': they operate only in closed system choices and can be fully explained by reference to these. A property of a closed system is that its terms can be defined just as well negatively as positively: the meaning of the '-s' can be stated as 'plural' or as 'not singular' and it comes to exactly the same thing—whereas we could not explain the meaning of 'chair' as 'not settee'.

The items 'chair' and 'I've thrown it away' on the other hand, although they both have to be accounted for in English grammar, yet enter into closed system choices not as items but as instances of CATEGORIES. 'chair' is an *instance* of the choice of, for example, noun as opposed to adverb and other classes of the word; 'I've thrown it away' is an *instance* of the choice of, for example, the transitive as opposed to the intransitive class of the clause. In these cases it is the *classes*, not the items, which are the terms in the closed system, the possibilities among which the choice is being made; the items which are instances (or, to use the technical term, EXPONENTS) of these classes are thus grammatical but not fully grammatical items.

The CLASS is one of the four fundamental categories of this model of grammar. These are the four theoretical categories that are required if we want to account fully for the kind of patterning in language that we recognize as the level of grammar. Two of these have already been mentioned: class and system. The other two are UNIT and STRUCTURE. With the concept of the formal item, and with these four categories as theoretical abstractions, we can describe the grammatical patterns of all languages.

Notice that these general *theoretical* categories are not things like 'sentence' and 'clause' or 'verb' and 'noun' or 'subject' and 'complement'. Such terms as these are *descriptive* categories: that is to say they belong to the descriptions of particular languages. They are therefore *instances* of the underlying theoretical categories. Thus 'sentence' and 'clause' are instances of the category of *unit*, 'verb' and 'noun' of the category of *class*, and 'subject' and 'complement' of the category of *structure* (more accurately, of 'elements of structure'). This amounts to saying that *all* languages have units, structures, classes and systems; whereas not all languages have anything that could be called 'clauses' or 'verbs' or 'subjects'. The former are thus categories of the *theory* of grammar; the latter are *descriptive* categories, particular instances, that is, of the theoretical categories such as may happen to be appropriate in the description of a given language.

The unit is the stretch of language that carries grammatical patterns. Wherever a grammatical choice is made, there is a unit that carries that choice. It is a property of all languages that one can recognize units in their grammar, and that these units are built up one inside the other. However many units we recognize in the grammar of any given language, there is always a fixed relation among them: an occurrence of any unit is said to consist of one, or more than one, complete occurrence of the unit *next below it*. English, like many other languages (but by no means all), has, if we start with the sentence, five units carrying its grammatical patterns: (in descending order) sentence, clause, group, word and morpheme. 'Morpheme' is the term used to name the smallest unit in the grammar of any language. The fixed relation among the units means that every sentence consists of one or more than one complete clause, every clause of one or more than one complete group, every group of one or more than one complete word, and every word of one or more than one complete morpheme. The formal item 'yes', if it is a whole utterance, 'Yes!', is one sentence which is one clause which is one group which is one word which is one morpheme. Here, by contrast, are two more complex sentences that show, as far as possible in orthographic notation, the breakdown into all the smaller units:

||| I | was+ go+ing+to say || they | were+ | probably+ |
all | in [tent+s] | then |||
||| oh | that character [last night] || was+ nt | he |
wonder+ful |||

The key to the notation is given in the table of symbols at the beginning of the book. Each unit boundary of course implies all those below it: a clause boundary, for example, must be also a group, word and morpheme boundary. When the morpheme boundary symbol + *follows* a word (e.g. 'was+'), this indicates fusion (see below): 'was' consists of two fused morphemes but not two segments. Square brackets indicate 'rankshift' (see below). If the sentences seem odd, this is because they are genuine, taken from actual conversation recorded on tape. It often happens that when linguists make up their examples, these are readily accepted, whereas when they cite examples from actual speech they are told: 'But no one would ever *say* that!'

The sentence is not the largest pattern-carrying unit in English: some patterns clearly extend above it. A great deal of current work in English grammar is directed towards the recognition and description of patterns above the sentence, towards a unit something like the paragraph but which is valid, though with differences, for speech as well as for writing. These studies, however, require very large samples, for obvious reasons, and take a long time. At the moment only a very partial account can be given of grammar above the sentence, whereas from the sentence downwards the patterns can be filled in in considerable detail. It may turn out that only a part of the relations above the sentence can be brought within the framework of any grammatical theory.

The sentence is in any case somewhat distinct from the smaller units, in the sense that, in general, if the order of sentences in a text is changed the text loses its meaning, whereas the re-ordering of units below the sentence either yields impossible structures or results in change rather than loss of meaning. The sequence of sentences, that is, is not determined by structure, as is the sequence of the lower units: this can be shown in translation, which often entails a change in the sequence of units up to the clause, but rarely entails or even permits a change in the sequence of sentences. Even granted that this is in the last resort a matter of degree, the sentence is still significantly the lowest 'non-disorderable' unit; it is the unit with which, as it were, language operates in situations. Whereas traditionally in linguistics the main interest was often focused on the word, and in early 'structural' linguistics on the morpheme, the tendency in more recent studies is to pay much more attention to the sentence as the unit showing language in use.

The successive occurrences of the various units are not always clearly delimited for us. Often they follow one another in simple sequence, with one, for example one clause, ending where the next one begins; exponents of this type are called SEGMENTAL. But there are other possibilities. Sometimes they overlay one another; sometimes they occur one inside the other. Exponents of these two types, one which overlaps with another and one which 'includes' another, are called respectively FUSED and DISCONTINUOUS. 'was', for example, is a fusion of two morphemes 'be' and '(past tense)', as is 'feet' of 'foot' and '(plural)'; there is no question of saying where one ends and the other begins. Fusion is more common among the smaller units, discontinuity among the larger ones.

The term used to name the hierarchical relation among the units is RANK; they can be considered as arranged on a scale, and this is known as the 'rank scale'. For each language we recognize a particular set of units ranged in a fixed order on the rank scale. It is this order that is being referred to when we speak of one unit as being 'next below' another in rank.

In addition to the usual relation among the units, by which each operates in the structure of the one above it, languages display a phenomenon known as RANKSHIFT. This happens when a given unit is as it were 'shifted' *down* the rank scale to operate as part of the pattern of one further down or of equal rank to itself. For instance a clause, by definition, normally operates in a sentence: it contributes to the pattern of the sentence of which it is a part. But in English some clauses are rankshifted and work inside the pattern of a group. If I say 'where I live it always rains', this sentence consists of two clauses, which together make up the structure of the sentence. But if I say 'the house where I live is very damp', the sentence consists, *in its structure*, of only one clause; the clause 'where I live' is rankshifted and operates in the structure of the *group* 'the house where I live'.

It is important to distinguish rankshift clearly from discontinuity.

If I say 'you'll find me, if you want me, in the library', this is one sentence consisting of two clauses of which one, 'you'll find me in the library', is discontinuous; the other, 'if you want me', is inside ('included in') the first but is still operating in the structure of the sentence. But if I say 'you'll find the person you want in the library', 'you want' is rankshifted and operates in the structure of the nominal group 'the person you want'; there is thus only one clause in the structure of this sentence, and no discontinuity.

The category of 'structure', which has now been introduced, is the category that accounts for the various ways in which an occurrence of one unit may be made up out of occurrences of the unit next below it (including, sometimes, rankshifted occurrences of a unit higher than the one next below it). In English, sentences are made up of clauses, clauses are made up of groups, and so on. But not *all* combinations of groups can make up clauses. Each unit exhibits a range of possible structures.

It is the structure that determines the value that a particular clause has in a sentence, a particular group in a clause, and so on. The different values are accounted for by ELEMENTS of structure, such as 'subject' and 'complement' in the structure of the clause. The value may be, but is not necessarily, shown by the sequence in which the items are arranged; this is one of the features in which languages vary considerably. So that one of the tasks of description is to say what it is that shows the value of an occurrence of one unit in the structure of the unit above it. For example, if we say that a certain group is the subject in a clause, has it this value because it comes in a certain place or because of some other feature? If the first, then it is SEQUENCE that expounds the structure; if the second, then it is something else, namely the 'class' of the item itself, as in a language where the subject of the clause is that nominal group belonging to the class 'nominative'. The relation among elements of structure is not the same thing as their arrangement in sequence; sequence is one possible exponent of structure, but not the only one. By contrast with some European languages, English makes considerable use of sequence as an exponent of structure.

The category of 'structure' applies to all units in the grammar of a language except the smallest, which by definition has no structure, since it is not made up of anything smaller that can be identified *at the level of grammar*. So English has sentence structures, clause structures, group structures and word structures, whose elements have as their exponents respectively clauses, groups, words and morphemes. The morpheme itself has no structure since there is nothing below it in the grammar. Thus the word 'gladness' has a structure consisting of two elements whose exponents are the morphemes 'glad' and 'ness', but these morphemes cannot be further analysed *grammatically*. At another level, the level of phonology, we can abstract smaller segments, such as the '*g*-sound' in 'glad', segments having no formal meaning. But phonology must not be thought of as a kind of continuation of grammar down to the smaller units. Phonology is abstraction of a quite different type. In phonology we account for a range of different units, just as we do in grammar. But these are not *smaller* than the grammatical units: indeed, exponents of some phonological units, such as the 'tone group' in English, may be as long as a grammatical clause or sentence. They are units of a different *kind*. A phonological statement may be about the same bit of text as a grammatical statement; it will say different things about it because it is describing a different aspect of linguistic patterning.

Besides recognizing the different structures for each unit, and the elements that make up these structures, we have to account for the fact that each element of structure implies a kind of choice. There are two sides to any choice situation; restriction and freedom— what we cannot choose from and what we can choose from. Each element of structure implies a choice, with these two aspects to it. For example, for the element 'subject' in the structure of a clause, we are free to choose singular nominal group or plural nominal group but we cannot choose verbal group. To handle these we need the remaining two basic categories of grammar, the CLASS and the SYSTEM. A 'class' is any set of items having the same possibilities of operation in structure; it follows from what was said earlier that this always means, except in cases of rankshift, 'in the structure of the unit next above'. The items making up a class must, of course, all belong to the same unit, since otherwise they could not have the same structural possibilities. Thus the class 'verbal group', a class of the unit 'group', is that set of items that can operate as 'predicator' in clause structure; the class 'noun', of the unit 'word', is that class of word operating as 'head' of a nominal group. Such classes may have any number of items in them, and represent the

total set from which a choice can be made; the class thus simply
distinguishes what may be chosen from what may not be chosen.

To make sense of the word 'choice', however, we must show that
there is more than one possibility and that it makes a difference
which we choose. This is where the 'system' comes in. Wherever
we can show that, at a given place in structure, the language allows
for a choice among a *small fixed* set of possibilities, we have a
system. Such sets of possibilities are called the TERMS in the system.
For example, we can identify a place in a particular structure in
English where the choice is among 'who', 'whose', 'what' and
'which', and nothing else. These four items form a system, tied to
the particular place in structure where they, and they alone, can
occur. (Notice that, e.g. in ' . . . have we left behind?', 'who'
and 'whom' do *not* constitute different terms in a system since,
although we can choose between them, it makes no difference: they
represent variant forms of the same term.)

Very often the terms among which we are choosing are not themselves items in the language but *classes* of items recognized at a more
detailed stage of the analysis (more DELICATE classes). So for the
subject in clause structure we can choose singular or plural nominal
group; for the predicator we can choose positive or negative verbal
group. There are in each case hundreds of thousands of possible
items that we could choose from; but one choice we must face is
that between the *classes* of positive and negative whenever we come
to a verbal group. This shows the characteristics of the 'system' in
language. It is a choice that *must* be faced at a certain place in
structure; there may be two, three, four, perhaps up to seven or
eight possibilities (where there *appear* to be more these usually seem
to turn out, when one analyses them more thoroughly, to be combinations of different smaller systems, from each of which a choice
is made at the same time), but the range of choice is fixed and there
is no doubt what lies inside and what outside it. The only variable,
apart from the total *number* of terms, is that some systems have a
'neutral' term by which one can choose not to choose. For example,
both Russian and Chinese have a system of 'aspect' in the verbal
group, with terms 'perfective' and 'imperfective'; but Chinese also
has a third term, 'neutral in aspect', which Russian lacks. So whereas in Russian you must choose between perfective and imperfective,
in Chinese you first choose whether to choose or not. European
languages tend not to have neutral terms in their systems, whereas

East Asian languages often do; this is one of the sources of difficulty to language learners in both directions.

With these four basic categories of unit, structure, system and class it is possible to describe the grammar of all languages. What is significant here is that in order to find anything 'universal' in grammar—common, that is, to the grammar of all languages—we have to go to the very high level of abstraction represented by these categories. Only such *theoretical* categories can be treated as universal. The *descriptive* categories, those used to talk about the grammar of any particular language, which as we have said are instances of these theoretical categories, are *not* universal and cannot be assumed to be found in all languages. Indeed, they must be redefined for each language.

It is quite likely, though by no means certain, that we might recognize the units 'sentence' and 'word', and the word classes 'verb' and 'noun', in the description of all languages; but probably no more than these, and even these would mean something a little different in each language. Obviously, we do not erect a completely new terminology for each language—this would be absurd; we use the same terms over and over again wherever we can find a reasonable degree of equivalence. But complete identity must never be assumed, even in languages as similar in their grammar as English and French; what 'noun' means for French is defined by the total description of French grammar, not by what 'noun' means for English, even though the two categories have a very great deal in common.

The purpose of a grammatical theory is to enable us to make useful and powerful statements about how each language works. 'Powerful' here means 'having a high degree of generality'. The nature of grammar is that it lends itself to precisely such powerful statements. Provided the theory is valid, comprehensive and consistently applied, *but not otherwise*, we can make statements about the grammar of a language which apply to vast numbers of different actual speech events, and are therefore of great value to the learner of the language: they provide source material for what the textbook and the teacher have to tell him.

This fundamental point needs to be laboured, so often is it misunderstood. It seems to have been misunderstood, for example, by the authors of the British Council 'Annual Report' for 1960–61, who say on p. 7: 'no theoretical explanation of language merely in terms of system or structure can be a substitute for a full description of the contemporary English language based on careful observation of its use'. This is like saying no blueprint for a jet airliner can be a substitute for the metals it is made of. Of course a theory cannot be a substitute for observations; nobody has ever suggested it could. It is precisely the theoretical linguists who have insisted, not always with much support, on the need for 'a full description of the contemporary English (and any other) language based on careful observation of its use'. But we do not want to see all this work weakened by the lack of an adequate theory. It is impossible to begin to make such a description without *some* theory; as soon as a single statement is made about the grammar of a language, a theory is implied. For the sake of the millions of people who have to make use of other people's statements about language, it is desirable that it should be sound theory.

3

The grammatical analysis of a language can account for all formal patterns involving 'system'-type choices: those where there is a restricted set of contrastive possibilities. It is, as we have said, a characteristic of such patterns that as much information is given by a negative statement as by a positive one. That is to say, in English 'not singular' means exactly the same thing as 'plural'; 'not present or past' is the same as 'future'; 'not passive' equals 'active'. Wherever we can recognize a formal pattern of this sort, we are in grammar.

There is, however, another type of pattern in linguistic form, which can be approached through the grammatical category of 'class'. In grammar, we can always fully describe the distinctions between *classes* of items: for example, grammar can account for the whole of the contrast between 'active' and 'passive' as terms in the English 'voice' system. But we cannot always, in grammar, describe fully the distinctions between *items*, because, while some items operate as terms in systems, being reducible as it were to one-member classes, others do not.

'this/that' and 'who/whose/what/which' each form a grammatical system in which the items themselves are terms; these are 'fully grammatical' items and we can account for the whole of the contrast between them in grammar. 'this', for example, can be defined as 'not "that"', or better as 'not "that" and not "(plural)"', 'that' and '(plural)' being the other terms in the two systems in which 'this' operates. But we cannot, in grammar, distinguish between the items 'table', 'desk' and 'bench'. 'table' does not equal 'not desk' or 'not desk or bench'. There is *no* set of items (x) such that 'table' can be identified as 'not (x)'; in other words there is no system in which 'table' is a term.

Here then we leave grammar, and move over to the other formal level, that of lexis. 'table', 'desk' and 'bench' are LEXICAL ITEMS. Contrary to what is often assumed, it is *not* because an item is grammatically a *word* that it operates in the language as a lexical item. Many lexical items are also words, but some of them are not. For example, 'turn off', in 'turn off the light', is one lexical item though two words. Similarly many items, such as 'this' and 'the', though grammatically words, are not lexical items, if we think of a lexical item as that which enters into a certain kind of choice that is different from a grammatical choice. It operates, not in a closed system, but in an open set. Since closed systems are characteristic of grammar and open sets of lexis we often speak of a 'grammatical system' and a 'lexical set'. 'table', 'desk' and 'bench' are not terms in a grammatical system but they are members of a lexical set.

Lexical sets are not bounded in the way that grammatical systems are. Whereas in grammar we can say: 'at this place in structure, these terms are possible, and all others are impossible', in lexis we can never say: 'only these items are possible'. Lexical sets in fact are bounded only by probabilities. Given the item 'chair', we are more likely to find in the same utterance the items 'sit' or 'comfortable' or 'high' than, say, 'haddock' or 'reap', though no one could maintain that the latter are impossible.

This tendency to co-occurrence is the basic formal pattern into which lexical items enter. It is known as COLLOCATION, and an item is said to 'collocate with' another item or items. A lexical set is simply a grouping of items which have a similar range of collocation. 'chair', 'seat' and 'settee' belong to the same lexical set because they have a number of highly probable collocations in common: they collocate readily, for example, with 'comfortable' and 'sit'. This is not the same thing as saying that they refer to similar objects. Clearly members of the same lexical set often do: 'chair' and 'seat' have similar, or at least overlapping, shapes and functions. But the

2＋L.S.L.T.

criteria are different, and do not always yield the same groupings. 'shop' and 'emporium', for example, refer to very much alike objects but have very different ranges of collocation. The formal criterion of collocation is taken as crucial because it is more objective, accurate and susceptible to observation than the contextual criterion of referential or conceptual similarity.

Lexical choice, therefore, is different from grammatical choice. In lexis, not only are there more items to choose from at any given point, compared with the items or classes one is choosing from in grammar; also there is no line to be drawn between those that can and those that cannot be chosen. There are only 'more probable' and 'less probable' items. This type of choice is more complex than the systematic choice of grammar. Language, however, compensates for this complexity, if we may put it that way, by making the overall patterns of lexis much simpler than those of grammar.

In the first place there is no rank scale in lexis: no 'Chinese box' arrangement of pattern-carrying units. Lexical items are not organized by rank. In the second place, there is no complex interaction of lexical sets comparable to the interaction of grammatical systems. In grammar, while the number of terms in each system is small, we sometimes have to choose, especially in spoken language, from up to a dozen different systems at one and the same time. For example, each time we use a verbal group in spoken English we select for finiteness, modality, contrastiveness, polarity and voice, and up to five times for tense; but only one of those systems, that of modality, has more than three terms in it. In lexis we make one choice at a time. We can thus think of grammar as few items in complex patterns, lexis as many items in simple patterns.

The consequence of this difference is that less abstraction is possible in lexical theory. We cannot make such powerful generalizations about lexis as we can about grammar. Every statement in lexis has to be based on more observations and yet accounts for fewer events. In other words, we have to take larger samples in order to describe the lexis of a language. Recently linguists have begun using computers to study collocations in large samples of text, and this work should yield much new information about the lexical level of language.

In drawing a distinction between grammar and lexis we should stress that the distinction is itself an abstraction from the language events. The speaker is not aware that he is making choices of two different types. In the first place the relation between the two levels is, as we have emphasized, a 'cline': formal patterns in all languages shade gradually from the grammatical to the lexical. In the second place language is a unified activity in which all patterning is subject to succession in time: there are thus analogies between the categories of lexis and those of grammar, analogies based on the two fundamental dimensions of any patterned activity, chain (one thing after another) and choice (one thing as opposed to another). The chain relations are 'structure', in grammar, and 'collocation', in lexis; the choice relations are 'system', in grammar, and 'set', in lexis. Lexis has no category analogous to the grammatical 'unit', since there is no interrelated set of units (no rank scale) in lexis, but only the lexical item; 'class', on the other hand, provides the bridge between grammar and lexis, in the sense that many grammatical classes are, as we have seen, made up of items which cannot be fully described in the grammar and must therefore be handled as lexical items.

In such cases we cannot tell from grammar exactly *what* the lexical item is; we can merely tell that here is something the grammar cannot fully describe. The lexical item must be identified within lexis, on the basis of collocation. In grammar, 'put' is a different item from 'putting'; but the 'put' in 'put on' ('put on the light') is the same item as the 'put' in 'put up' ('put up a guest'). In lexis, we are not interested in the difference between 'put' and 'putting', which is purely grammatical and does not affect collocation; but we are interested in the fact that 'put up' collocates with different items from those that 'put on' collocates with, and both differ in this respect from 'put'. We could show this in tabular form, using a different example such as that on page 36; lexical items are indicated by a line above and grammatical items by a line below. In grammar we distinguish four items: (1) a word 'took', (2) a word 'taking', (3) a morpheme 'take' and (4) a word 'take'; but these are the same items whether followed by 'off' or by 'over'. In lexis on the other hand we distinguish two items: (1) 'take off' and (2) 'take over'; but 'take off', 'taking off', 'takeoff' and 'took off' are all the same item. In any given utterance a lexical item may not be co-extensive with any grammatical item at all: for instance in 'will be taking off' we still have to abstract the lexical item 'take off' even though it consists, grammatically speaking, of a bit of one word plus the whole of another.

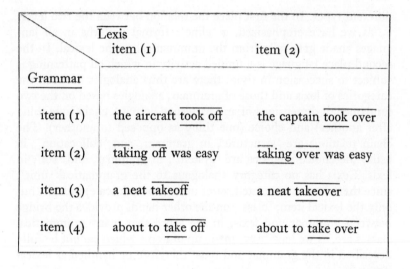

Lexis Grammar	item (1)	item (2)
item (1)	the aircraft took off	the captain took over
item (2)	taking off was easy	taking over was easy
item (3)	a neat takeoff	a neat takeover
item (4)	about to take off	about to take over

The term 'word', in fact, causes a great deal of confusion in discussion about language. It tends to be used in three different ways: orthographically, grammatically and lexically; as if the items identified at these three levels were always the same. But they are not necessarily so. The orthographic word, in English, is what is written between two spaces. This is not bound to be coextensive with the grammatical word; obviously not in languages whose scripts are of certain types very different from English (in Chinese for example the grammatical unit most clearly delimited by the script is the morpheme), but not necessarily even in English, where for example 'teatime', 'tea-break' and 'tea interval' can all be regarded grammatically as single words. The situation is further complicated if it is assumed that this 'word' is also invariably the unit we identify as the lexical item. There is of course a high degree of coextensiveness: many formal items, like 'table', may be at one and the same time orthographic word, grammatical word and lexical item. Even in these cases, however, it is important to recognize the three different processes of identification that are involved.

Dictionaries, whose purpose is to describe lexical items, remain in general subservient to the tyranny of grammar. They tend to conflate the categories of 'lexical item' and '(grammatical) word', and this determines their view of what is and what is not one lexical item; the decision is based on *word class* distinctions, which are purely grammatical and irrelevant to lexis. Thus on the one hand, 'turn off' (in 'turn off the light') is entered under 'turn', simply because both are verbs; so also 'put up with' under 'put'; although in each case the two are, as Roget's *Thesaurus* recognized a hundred years ago, quite distinct lexical items. On the other hand, to cite the *Shorter Oxford Dictionary*, *cut* 'to penetrate so as to sever the continuity of with an edged instrument' is presented as a different item from *cut* 'the act of cutting', simply because one is a verb and the other a noun. Moreover the relation between them is shown as no different from that between *bear* 'to support and remove' and *bear* 'a heavily-built, thick-furred, plantigrade quadruped of the genus *Ursus*', though it is quite clear that the two *cuts* are one and the same lexical item whereas the two *bears* are not.

When as a result of current large-scale research projects we have more information about the nature and operation of lexical items, it will be possible to identify these with much greater accuracy and objectivity. There will probably no longer be any need to invoke grammatical criteria for identifying the item to be entered in the dictionary. It will be profitable then to blend the two traditional vehicles of lexical statement, the dictionary and the thesaurus, into one. Roget's *Thesaurus*, with its brilliant intuitive identification of lexical items and their grouping into lexical sets, shows the advantages of the thesaurus as a method of arrangement: the order of items is itself significant, instead of being a mere indexing device as in a dictionary. In many cases it makes *definition* entirely unnecessary. At the same time the dictionary *citation* gives essential information about formal patterns in lexis: the citation is a statement of high probability collocation. A lexical description combining the best features of thesaurus and dictionary would be an invaluable aid to the language student, whether he was studying his native language, a foreign language, or linguistics.

4

In the study of linguistic form, and especially of grammar, linguistics is much more advanced than in the study of context. 'Context' is the name, perhaps a rather awkward one, used by some linguists for the relation of the forms of language to non-linguistic objects and events. It thus corresponds roughly to 'meaning' in the general, non-specialized sense of the term. But 'meaning' in linguistics has to be used in a broader way, to cover not only CONTEXTUAL MEANING but also FORMAL MEANING. The reason is that if we want to understand how language works we must realize that form, the purely internal patterning of language, is itself also meaningful.

Let us consider a grammatical system like that of 'number' in English, its terms being 'singular' and 'plural'. Contextually, the meaning of this system is easy enough to state in general terms: it has something to do with choice of reference to one object or more than one object, though of course there is much to be added to this in a more delicate description. But we have not fully explained the *meaning* of number until we have also described it formally. Where does the language make this selection, and what are the terms to choose from? We need to know the unit which carries the distinction, and the class or classes with which it is associated; the fact that the choice is between two terms and not among three, as in languages having a dual number, and that there is no neutral term; whether or not concord is involved, and if so where.

All this is just as much part of the meaning of 'number' in English as are the external, situational features that are reflected by it. Each time the contextual statement is made more delicate, to deal with problems raised by such examples as 'these kids are a nuisance' or 'the committee were divided' or 'two pound(s) ten', so also the formal statement must be made equally delicate, to recognize the necessary sub-classes and sub-sub-classes with which the language is actually operating. Since the aim of linguistics is to describe languages, to explain the operation of linguistic items and patterns, it is not surprising that the method which has proved most successful and useful is that which starts by describing linguistic *form*. We first state the patterns of internal relations, with the items that enter into them; and in doing so we use formal criteria as crucial in recognizing grammatical and lexical categories. In other words, it is more fruitful to *identify* for example the unit 'clause' and the element of structure 'subject', or the unit 'word' and the class 'noun', from *within* the language itself, on the basis of formal features, rather than by reference to external contextual meaning.

This does not mean that we do not then try to go on to say something about the contextual meaning of these categories: what 'clause' and 'subject' and 'noun' reflect in the situations in which language is playing a part. It is important to know that the clause is, among other things, the vehicle for making the distinction between statements and questions, and that the nominal group is, among other things, a class of items referring to objects that can be distinguished according to whether there is one or more than one of them. But we cannot use such statements to define or identify our linguistic categories. For one thing, they are not accurate enough, because there is no one-to-one correspondence between the categories of language and the categories of external events and objects; and it is language we are describing, not these external features. In the second place a great deal of what is 'reflected' in language is not itself observable: abstract concepts, for example. We cannot observe anything outside language that is common to all situations in which, say, the grammatical item 'in case' occurs, or the lexical item 'hope'. Indeed the language provides the only evidence that there *is* something in common: and therefore to attempt to use that 'something' to define and classify the linguistic items would simply be to go round in a circle.

It is for these reasons that it is an axiom of modern linguistics that criteria for description must be formal. We first define, for example, the word class 'noun' *inside* the language, and then, after stating all its formal properties, say what we can about the contextual meaning of this class. Linguistics has not yet progressed very far with methods for this second stage. There are three probable reasons for this. First, formal theories had to be worked out in order for there to be any further progress in description at all. Second, the contextual level of language, though easy to describe in a speculative and imprecise way, is more difficult to describe rigorously and usefully than the formal levels. Third, there was a time when, in reaction against the use of contextual statements as defining criteria, which failed to produce good descriptions, some linguists refused to consider contextual meaning at all. Today they have turned their attention back to this level of patterning, but are looking at it in a rather different way from before.

The emphasis is now on the description of language activity as part of the whole complex of events which, together with the participants and relevant objects, make up actual situations. In this way we can make maximum use of what is observable, in the attempt to understand exactly what the language activity is doing. This is why the term 'context' is sometimes used as the name of the study of this aspect of language in preference to the term 'semantics'. 'Semantics' implied an approach to contextual meaning from outside language, with consequent emphasis on thought and thought processes. The important work that has been done in conceptual semantics has not been integrated with the rest of descriptive linguistics, because it operates with categories which have not so far been shown to be clearly relatable to what can be described at the formal levels.

Meanwhile the development of the theory and methods of contextual description is perhaps the most important task of general linguistics for the next decade. If we are optimistic about solving these problems it is partly because of the recent advances in other aspects of linguistic theory, but even more because of the greatly enlarged scope of linguistic observations. The more events we can record and the more we can compare and correlate different events, the sooner it becomes possible to make valid generalizations about them. For the description of a language to be of the greatest use, it must account for contextual as well as formal patterns. But it is essential to realize that the formal patterns of language are themselves meaningful. The view that somehow 'form' and 'meaning' were distinct entities was far too long allowed to obstruct our understanding of the nature of language.

5

Because of its insistence on formal criteria as crucial in the description of language, descriptive linguistics has sometimes been referred to as 'formal linguistics'. This is perhaps a pity, since it suggests two false dichotomies: that between form and meaning referred to above, about which more is said in Chapter 6, and another one between form and function.

Form and function are no more opposed to one another than are form and meaning. If we take these terms in the sense in which they are usually used, a linguistic description is both formal and functional at the same time. An example will show this. It might be said that, since we recognize a 'class' on the basis of the way in which items at one rank operate in the structure of the unit above (for example the class 'verbal group' being the set of items of *group* rank operating as 'predicator' in the structure of the clause), the 'class' is a functional category. But when we describe the unit above, the same set of items is now regarded as an element of structure in relation with other elements: for example, the element 'predicator' in the *clause* is related to other categories having different values in clause structure such as 'subject' and 'complement'. In the clause 'I met him', which has structure: Subject—Predicator—Complement, 'met' is a *group* belonging to the *class* 'verbal'; so is 'haven't met' in 'I haven't met him'. The verbal group is what operates as predicator in the clause, so 'met' and 'haven't met' are, seen from a different angle, instances of the 'predicator' as *element* of *clause* structure. What is from one point of view a 'functional' relation becomes a 'formal' relation when viewed from another: 'verbal group', being a class, is definable by the function of the group, whereas 'predicator', being an element of structure, is definable by the form of the clause. There is not a choice between two ways of describing grammar, a formal way and a functional way; the whole framework of unit, structure, system and class is both 'formal' and 'functional' at once.

Another label for descriptive linguistics is 'structural linguistics'. This is understandable, though there is no reason for picking out structure as more important than any other category of linguistic theory; it might just as well be called, for instance, 'systematic (or systemic) linguistics'. The label 'structural' has never been much used in Britain. Linguists feel it to be unnecessary, since the sense of it is fully implied in the term 'descriptive linguistics'. Furthermore it came into use first in reference to a trend in linguistics which, although for positive reasons, tended to neglect the meaningful aspect of language activity; which in fact accepted the form/meaning dichotomy and applied it by excluding the study of meaning from linguistic science. But perhaps the label 'structural' is useful, in that it emphasizes the formal and relational character of twentieth-century linguistics by contrast to the conceptual and mechanical account of language implicit in non-structural, 'traditional' descriptions.

Both these labels, 'formal' and 'structural', have perhaps the disadvantage of suggesting that descriptive linguistics treats language as somehow dehydrated or deep-frozen, without regard for its place in life as an essential, defining activity of human beings. Both 'form' and 'structure' carry unfortunate overtones of being opposed to vitality, purpose or meaning. As we have tried to show, the linguistic view of language is in fact very different from this. Linguistics emphasizes the vital and meaningful qualities of

2*

language. But in order to explain how language works the linguist has to devise theories which involve abstract categories like 'form' and 'structure', in the same way as in any other science: a biologist who talks of the 'structure' of the cell does so in order to understand, not to deny, its role as a fundamental unit of living matter. It need be no cause for surprise that, in the application of linguistics to the study of literature, it is modern 'structural' linguistics that proves to be really illuminating.

Equally in the field of language teaching, it is 'structural' linguistics that has the significant contribution to make. The reason is the same: that as a result of the 'structural' study of language very much more is understood about language now than was known fifty or a hundred years ago. It perhaps needs emphasizing that there is no magic in the *word* 'structure'. It has come to be rather fashionable in textbooks of English; but often, unfortunately, without any clear and consistent manner of use. A structure is *not* just a string of items with one or more variable in it, like 'there ... two ...s here, ...n't ...?' A structure is a highly generalized statement of the meaningful relations between elements; it is the basic pattern of relationship between the parts of a clause, of a sentence or of any other unit, and thereby determines their value. It is much more powerful than a substitution frame, which is what the above example is. This is not of course to deny the usefulness of substitution frames in foreign language drills.

6

When we describe the formal features of a language, its grammar and lexis, we are trying to account for all the possible meaningful contrasts that the language makes. We have not yet, however, said how it makes them. Clearly the language makes these contrasts by exploiting the 'raw material' resources at its disposal: the sounds used in speaking the language and the symbols used in writing it. We need some statement to show how the language uses these resources to carry its formal patterns. This requires analysis and abstraction at another level which, if we restrict ourselves for the moment to spoken language, is the level of phonology.

It would be helpful for everyone, especially foreign-language learners, if languages used the contrastive possibilities of their phonic substance, their total range of *distinct* sound patterns, in a consistent way: if, that is, one sound pattern always carried the same formal meaning. An example of this in grammar would be if *every time* we used a rising tone it meant 'present tense', or if *every time* we used an item beginning with a certain type of consonant it meant 'item collocated with "sit"'; contextually, something people sit on'.

Unfortunately this is impossible, since the number of formal contrasts is so great that a language cannot afford to waste its phonic resources by allowing any one sound feature to do only one formal job. We might be able to construct an artificial language which organized its *grammar* along these lines, since although the number of grammatical systems is bound to be very large the number of choices to be provided for with each would be closely limited. But in fact no natural language ever shows such regularity, or anything like it.

English, for example, has the sounds [s] and [z]. Sometimes these enter into lexical items, in which case if you replace [s] by [z] you get a different item: 'bus', 'sip', 'muscle' become 'buzz', 'zip', 'muzzle'. But the change has no consistent formal significance: there is no lexical sense in which 'buzz' is to 'bus' as 'muzzle' is to 'muscle'. [s] and [z] also do considerable grammatical work, making 3rd person singular simple present tense in the verbal group, and plural and possessive in the nominal group. Here, however, they are not in contrast at all: we have [s] in 'cats', 'sleeps' and 'Jack's' but [z] in 'dogs', 'dreams' and 'Jill's', and the 'choice' of one or the other is determined entirely by the preceding *sound*.

The same point, the lack of correspondence between contrasts in form and contrasts in substance, could equally well be made the other way round. A given set of formal contrasts, say a grammatical system or complex of systems, may be carried by any possible selection and combination of the phonetic features that the language makes use of. In English, for example, the grammatical contrasts in the verbal group, the systems of tense, voice, finiteness and so on, are carried by any and all of the following devices: addition of a phoneme ('walk/walked'), replacement of one phoneme by another ('ring/rang'), addition of a syllable, change in rhythm and change in intonation.

This means that we cannot describe a language by just writing a grammar and a dictionary and stating, for each formal feature, the sounds and sound patterns that carry it. Theoretically, perhaps, we could; but it would be intolerably complex. Equally, we cannot just describe the phonology and state, for each feature of sound, what formal meanings it carries. This would be far worse, because it would fail to take account of the systematic, meaningful relations of linguistic form: we should find present tense turning up in one place and past tense in three different places, with no indication of the relation between the two. This is why phonology has to be treated as a separate level in the description of a language.

By recognizing a distinct level of phonology, we can describe in an orderly way *all* the contrasts of sound which are used, somewhere and somehow in the language, to make distinctions of meaning, grammatical or lexical. The description of the grammar is then linked to the description of the phonology by cross reference, and if necessary by the use of a phonological transcription (see p. 66).

Sometimes the formal contrasts can be related directly to the phonological features, as in the case of those grammatical systems in English which are carried by intonation: for example, 'where are you going?' may be falling, with tonic on 'going', or rising, with tonic on 'where'. At other times we do not relate grammatical statements directly to phonology, since we can account for the facts more simply by referring to other features within the grammar: for example, the sequence in which the items occur in 'he was coming' as against 'was he coming?'. A generalized statement of this contrast in phonological terms would be enormously complex. In most instances there is the implication that the contrast *could* have been so described, since after all it is recognizable in speech. There are, however, many instances of grammatical or lexical ambiguity, where no phonological distinction is made between different utterances: for example 'she called him a doctor' has two different grammatical descriptions (represents two different clauses) although phonologically the two are identical.

Languages organize their phonology, like their grammar, into a number of different units. That is to say, in each language we can recognize a small number of stretches of speech sound, such as the 'syllable', of varying extent, at each of which the speaker selects from among a limited number of contrasting possibilities. It might be, for example, in a given language, that the syllable was the unit which carried contrasts of duration: all syllables were either long or

short. The name given to the smallest phonological unit in any
language is the 'phoneme'.

In grammar, the fact that a given contrast is assigned to a given
unit can often be related to the context. We may reasonably expect,
for example, that the choice between 'question' and 'statement'
will be made at a higher rank than the choice between 'singular'
and 'plural', as is the case in English. In phonology, which is the
organization of phonic resources, the assignment of a given choice
to a given unit is to be related rather to features of the phonic
substance. It takes more time to change from one pitch to another,
say high to low, or from one pitch movement to another, such as
rising to falling, than from one position of the tongue, or of the
vocal cords, to another. Contrasts of intonation therefore are likely
to be associated with higher units than are contrasts of articulation.
But these are only general tendencies, and languages differ in the
total number of units, and in the unit to which they assign a given
contrast, in phonology, just as they do in grammar.

English has four phonological units: tone group, foot, syllable
and phoneme. These are related to each other on a 'rank scale' in
the same way as the grammatical units: each tone group consists of
one or more than one foot, each foot of one or more than one
syllable and each syllable of one or more than one phoneme. The
tone group carries, as its name implies, contrasts of intonation. In
English, intonation is used grammatically: that is, the distinctions
made by intonation carry grammatical meaning. There are five basic
tones, and all utterances are spoken on (sequences of) one or other
of these five tones. In a more delicate analysis, each of these five can
be subdivided into 'sub-tones' and 'sub-sub-tones' carrying always
finer shades of meaning: the contrasts that speakers make in this
way, however delicate, are still part of English grammar. Tone 2,
for example, which ends with a steeply rising pitch movement, has
two varieties of 'tonic', straight rise and fall-rise. The tonic may
further be preceded by a 'pre-tonic' which may, in either case, be
either high or low. This already gives four possible varieties,
schematically ‾/, ‾∨, __/ and __∨, each grammatically distinct. The utterance written as 'haven't you seen him?', with tonic
starting at 'seen', can be spoken in all four ways, and it is grammatically a different utterance in each case.

There is, however, no *one* grammatical system carried by the
English tones. The change from, say, Tone 1 to Tone 4 may mean

different things according to the grammatical structure involved. We select different sets of two, three, four or, occasionally, all five tones to make various meaningful contrasts at different places in the grammar. Moreover, the tone group does not correspond, in extent, to any *one* of the grammatical units. Usually one tone group extends over either one clause or one group in the grammar, but it may be as much as a sentence or as little as a single word or even morpheme.

Below the tone group is the foot, which is the unit of rhythm, the 'bar' of spoken English. English has a roughly regular beat, produced by the succession of strong syllables which occur at roughly equal intervals of time, with or without weak syllables in between. Since the contrast between strong and weak syllables is exploited in both the grammar and the lexis of English, this beat is also meaningful. Moreover, it is possible to make contrasts in meaning by varying the beat of an utterance and leaving everything else constant. More often, however, it is the combination of intonation and rhythm that is grammatically significant.

The rest of the work is done by syllables and phonemes; strong syllables having certain features, in the way that they are made up out of phonemes, that distinguish them from weak ones. All four units thus contribute to the totality of patterns that make up English phonology. Moreover all present problems to the foreign student. One cannot say that any one unit is more important than any other; but it is certainly true that intelligibility is affected by wrong rhythm and intonation just as it is by faulty articulation. The foreign visitor who wants a ticket to 'Oxford Street' or 'Tottenham Court Road' must get the tonic in the right place; otherwise he should not blame the bus conductor for not understanding him.

The phonological units are related to each other by structures and systems just as are the units in grammar, but with two differences. One is that in the last resort all phonological distinctions are systematic: they can be reduced finally to closed systems. We still recognize classes, since at any given place the set of possibilities may be treated as open: for example the class of strong syllables in English, defined as having a certain value in the foot. The phonemes that make up these syllables, however, themselves enter into closed choices. The other difference is that, whereas in grammar it is possible, and therefore in the interests of clarity desirable, to assign each distinction to one (or more) specific unit, in phonology this may not always be the case. Phonology is more closely tied to phonetic observations than is grammar, since it is precisely the use of phonetic resources that phonology is required to describe.

A phonetic feature which, whether or not assignable to a specific phonological unit, occurs distinctively with any stretch other than a phoneme is called a PROSODIC feature, or simply a 'prosody'. Prosodic features may be, and often are, associated clearly with a syllable or some higher unit; but they may also be associated with a less easily definable segment. In this case they have to be accounted for as a property of, for example, a consonant cluster at the beginning of a syllable. One feature of this kind is exemplified by pairs of English syllables like 'rise' and 'rice'; these are distinguished by two features, [z] and a longer vowel in the first as against [s] and a shorter vowel in the second. These could be described as distinct features and assigned to different phonemes; but this is unrealistic, since they always go together. On the other hand they do not strictly speaking affect the whole syllable, but only the vowel and final consonant.

In the description of a language, it is in phonology that linguistics and phonetics meet. The role of phonology is precisely to relate the substance of language to its form; this is the purpose of making abstractions at the phonological level. By treating the sound system of a language as an independent set of patterns and describing these patterns in their own right, we construct a bridge linking the two main components of the study of language: its social aspect, as systematic and meaningful activity, and its material aspect, as physiological or physical events. Having made the approach through linguistics, we have now, so to speak, in coming to phonology, reached the point where phonetics takes over.

It should not be forgotten that the description of a language forms a unified whole. We have to separate the different levels, in order to say anything useful at all; not only in the analysis, but also in the presentation, when the description is 'written up' as it were. But this separation is never rigid or opaque. In analysis, the linguist, or the phonetician, casts his eye over all levels all the time. The linguist needs therefore to be a phonetician, and the phonetician also a linguist, so that each may understand in full how the language works. In presentation, the levels, first separated, are brought into relation with each other, either in special sections or by constant cross-referencing. We are describing language as used by human beings, and they do not use just one level of it at a time.

7

So far we have restricted ourselves to spoken language to avoid extra complication. For written language, all that has been said about grammar and lexis still applies. There are usually differences of grammar and lexis between the written and spoken forms of the same language, but these do not affect the theories and methods used to describe these levels. The substance, however, is quite different, and so therefore is the relation of substance to form. We can talk about 'graphic substance' instead of phonic substance and 'graphology' instead of phonology; but graphic substance has distinct properties and stands in a different relation to the formal levels. This can best be explained by reference to the nature of a script.

Historically, writing evolved not as the representation of speech but as a means of visual communication independent of language. Messages in pictures or knotted cords carried no implication of utterance and could not be read aloud. Gradually this visual method of communication became linked to language; the symbols came to be attached to items in the language, which now replaced their original non-linguistic referents. Once this had happened, the symbols had become a SCRIPT. A 'script' is a system of visual communication whose symbols stand for items in a language. All scripts can therefore be read aloud, and anything that cannot be read aloud is not a script.

There are, however, two ways in which a script can represent the items of a language; or, better, there are two different levels of language whose items can be represented by the symbols of a script. One is form, the other phonology. The symbols either stand for the *formal* items, grammatical and lexical, of the language, or they stand for *phonological* items. The Chinese script is of the first type; all other scripts used in the world today are of the second, except Japanese and Korean which are mixed.

The number of formal items in a language is very large, even if these are identified at the lowest rank in the grammar, that of the morpheme. A formal script thus has the disadvantage of needing a large inventory of symbols. It takes some 3,500 to write the whole of Modern Chinese, and two or three thousand more to cover the classics. For various reasons Chinese is less unsuited to this type of script than most other languages. One of the few other major languages for which it would work quite well is English; and in fact English orthography does display one of the features of a formal script, the tendency to distinguish between different formal items that happen to be homophonous, like 'deer' and 'dear'. But the number of symbols does make such a script difficult to learn; and the Chinese are now, very slowly and by deliberate steps, changing over to a phonological script using the roman alphabet.

This is perhaps the place to correct two misconceptions. The Chinese script is not ideographic: the symbols do not represent ideas, they represent formal items of the language. If they did represent ideas, then items with similar contextual meaning would be written alike, which they are not, and it would not be possible to read the script aloud. Strictly speaking an ideographic script is a contradiction in terms. The confusion here arises through the failure to distinguish graphology from graphic substance: as substance, namely as regards their actual shape, the symbols of the Chinese script were in origin pictorial. So were the letters of the roman alphabet and, indeed, the symbols of most other scripts.

The second misconception, which follows from this, is that the Chinese script is a unifying factor in a country of widely divergent dialects. This is true only in the sense that, in learning to read and write, the Chinese learn a standard written variety of the language; but it is precisely the script which makes it difficult for them to learn a standard spoken variety. The reader knows exactly which item in the language is indicated by each symbol, but it is abstracted for him at the wrong level; the script has no phonetic implications at all other than those put into it by each speaker from his own dialect.

In a phonological script the symbols represent phonological items, in practice always syllables or phonemes, or something in between the two. Historically, syllabic scripts, or 'syllabaries', preceded phonemic ones, or 'alphabets'. The number of distinct syllables in a language varies enormously from language to language: it may be anything from about fifty to about five thousand. The number of phonemes, however, can be relied on not to exceed a hundred, and will often be under fifty. The alphabetic script is thus the most economical in terms of the number of distinct symbols. It therefore takes less time to learn, though, since obviously each symbol has to be written more often, it takes about the same amount of time as any other script to write.

Almost all phonological scripts in existence are to some degree 'imperfect', in the sense that they rest on an intuitive analysis of the phonology of the language, an analysis which is generally not as simple and accurate as it could be, though it is remarkable what good phonologists our ancestors were. This imperfection is aggravated by the linguistic conservatism of literate communities, who generally refuse to allow the script to keep up with the changes in the phonology of the language that take place in the course of time.

When we talk of 'graphic substance' we refer to the raw material of scripts: the signs themselves, their shapes in isolation and in combination. There is no special branch of linguistics to cover the study of graphic substance, but it is often of linguistic interest: the linguist interested in literary studies ignores typography at his peril, and the mechanical recognition of printed characters is now a major research problem. Some linguists have proposed the term 'graphetics' for such studies, to draw attention to the analogy with phonetics. In China, graphic substance is an art medium; calligraphy is to graphic substance as is literature to linguistic form.

Graphology, however, is an essential part of the description of any written language. The use of the word may be unfamiliar. It has been chosen to parallel 'phonology', and the term includes orthography, punctuation, and anything else that is concerned with showing how a language uses its graphic resources to carry its grammatical and lexical patterns. Here, however, the parallel to phonology breaks down. Whereas the formal features of a language are always linked to its phonic substance directly by phonology, the direct link of form to graphic substance via graphology holds good only for a formal script: for Chinese, in fact, including the Chinese elements in the Japanese and Korean scripts. With the other type of script, the link goes through phonology: that is to say, the symbols represent not formal items of the language but phonological ones. We can only show how the English script works by relating it to the phonology of English, whereas we can relate the Chinese script directly to the grammar and lexis of the language. Of course we could also describe written English by relating the grammar and lexis directly to written items, but this would not account for how the script itself works.

The 'graphological' level of language, whatever the nature of the script, is characterized by its own distinctive patterns, just as is the level of phonology. Although 'graphology' refers to the way a language uses its graphic resources to represent, directly or via phonology, its meaningful contrasts, there is again no regular correspondence between items at different levels. English graphology has its own units: paragraph, orthographic sentence (capital letter to full stop), sub-sentence (separated by colon, semicolon or comma—or we could treat this as two units, with the colons subsuming the comma but not vice versa), orthographic word (between spaces) and letter. The letter corresponds roughly to the phonological unit 'phoneme'. The orthographic word corresponds more to the lexical item and to the grammatical unit above the morpheme (hence also called 'word') than to anything in the phonology; the sub-sentence corresponds roughly to a tone group, surprisingly accurately with some writers, but with a great deal of possible variation. The syllable can be identified roughly as being represented by certain combinations of letters, while the foot is not marked in the script at all.

The following table shows the most probable equivalences between the units of English at different levels: those most frequently co-extensive are placed opposite each other.

GRAPHOLOGY	PHONOLOGY	FORM (Grammar)	FORM (Lexis)
Paragraph Orthographic sentence Sub-sentence	Tone group	Sentence Clause Group	
	Foot		
Orthographic word		Word	Lexical item
	Syllable	Morpheme	
Letter	Phoneme		

In the way it represents the terms in the phonological systems English graphology is similarly uneven. At the lowest rank, just as each *occurrence* of a letter does not necessarily represent one *occurrence* of a phoneme, so each *item* in the letter inventory (each different letter of the alphabet) does not necessarily represent one *item* phoneme (one and the same distinct phoneme). In this respect English and French contrast with, for example, Russian and Italian, which have a much closer letter-to-phoneme correspondence. This is what is meant by the observation that these languages are 'written phonetically'. This is an inaccuracy, perhaps harmless, for 'written phonemically', which is itself a harmless inaccuracy for 'written with a phonemic script and with a close correspondence of letters to phonemes'. (The expression 'Russian is a phonetic language', however, is *not* harmless; it involves so many mutually incompatible errors that it should not be tolerated.)

Above the phoneme, the English script is even less informative. It shows no distinction between strong and weak syllables; this does not worry the native speaker but is a source of great inconvenience to the foreign student. Intonation is virtually ignored. There is no indication whatever in the English script either of 'tone' or of 'tonicity': that is, it shows neither which tone is selected nor on which foot the tonic falls. The question mark is of little help, since questions can select four out of the five basic tones.

This absence of intonation marking is perhaps the one serious defect of the English script, and it bothers natives and foreigners alike. Many of us, in private correspondence, try and plug this hole in the script by the use of underlining, dashes, exclamation marks and various more or less idiosyncratic devices: at least one of the present writers sometimes marks the complete intonation of a passage in a letter if the recipient is someone who knows the system of marking. Here is a specimen of English, written in ordinary script but showing tone group boundary, foot boundary, tone and tonicity. It is taken from a passage of recorded 'live' conversation.

A.   //4ˏ I / think / teachers of / **Rus**sian are //1 quite / **wor**ried about / this //1ˏ because there / are quite a / **lot** of / children of . . . of . . . //4 **Slav** / parentage //13 in Great / **Brit**ain / **now** //4ˏ who / know their / **own** / language it mi . . . //4 not / **Russian** / necessarily but //4 **Polish** //4 **Slovene** //4 something of / **this** sort //53ˏ and it / **helps** / **them** //1 +ˏ a / great / **deal** //

B.   //13 Yes . . . / I I it / **seems** to / **me** that . . . that //

A.   //1 −ˏ The res /ˏ the re/sults are quite . . . / **different** //

B.   //1 +ˏ I mean /ˏ all / **right** //1ˏ th this sh / this is just . . . / their good / **luck** //

C.   //4 Yes . . . I / don't think you can / do much a/**bout** it //

A.   //1 + ˌ On the / **other** hand this //1 + 3 **does**n't level / up
er . . . you / **see** because //1 + 3ˌ when it / comes to the /
English a/**gain** they //1 + know that / equally / **well**
because they've //1 + lived / most of their / **lives** here
and //1 + ˌ perhaps / **all** their / lives here //

C.   //1 – **Yes** //4ˌ but I / don't see / why they should lose /
marks for / this //

B.   //1 **No** //5 **I** don't //

C.   //1ˌ I / mean it's . . . I / th . . . I / think this

B.   //4ˌ I / think I / don't see / why you / shouldn't er . . .
I mean / if you're / **lucky** e/nough to / be a bi/lingual
well //1 + O / **K** //4ˌ I / think th this is / still to your /
credit / even if you //

C.   //1 + **Yes** it //1 + **should** //1 + ˌ I / mean you / should
be . . . /marked / **up** for this //

B.   //4ˌ After / all if you / happened to be / born with a /
knowledge of / mathe/**mat**ics you this //4 wouldn't count
a/gainst you when you / did your / **maths** paper //

C.   //1 + **No** or //1 if you could

A.   //1 + ˌ You / **can't** be though //

We are not putting this forward as a suggestion for reforming the
English script. But in order to understand how English works, it is
important to realize that spoken English makes extensive use of
intonation to carry grammatical meaning; while at the same time
contrasts of intonation, like some other major contrasts in the
phonology of the language, are almost entirely unrepresented in the
script.

The fact that rhythm and intonation are not shown in English
graphology probably helps to maintain the gap between the written
and the spoken language. There are certain grammatical systems,
such as those carried by intonation, that the written language
cannot display. This failure of the script to match all the phonological resources is not limited to English: probably no script has
ever represented the phonology of a language in full. A written
language, in other words, never has at its disposal all the resources

of its spoken counterpart. It may, on the other hand, add some more of its own.

But the role of the script in keeping spoken and written language apart should not be exaggerated. However well the graphology mirrors the phonology, written language will always differ to a certain extent from spoken. One reason is that very few people can write as they or others speak. Dramatic dialogue is no disproof of this; it is very little like actual conversation, and it would be much less effective as dramatic dialogue if it was, since the two are not doing the same job. Some dramatists, like Arthur Miller and Arnold Wesker, have achieved a specific purpose by coming closer to conversation; while others, like Ionesco, have effectively parodied certain features of it. But dramatic dialogue remains a distinct type of language; it is not spoken language written down.

Equally it is very difficult to simulate conversation either in reciting (speaking what is memorized) or in reading aloud, even if the text is a transcript of a genuine 'live' conversation. Anyone who has recorded, in his native language, textbook material for foreign students will confirm this. The skill of the actor is again different here; he is not, except on rare occasions, trying to mimic conversation. Recently a new course of spoken French was recorded by a group of actors; the result was unsuccessful and the recording was done again, this time by phoneticians. Part of the difficulty is simply that actors do not usually learn any phonological transcription or notation, though they might find this quite helpful. It would be perfectly easy, for example, to give a complete indication of intonation, as in the passage above, in the acting edition of a play; anyone can be taught to interpret the symbols unambiguously in a very short time. The actor, or producer, could still disregard the author's intention when he wished; but it should be noted that there is no more justification for replacing an occurrence of his 'tone 1' by a 'tone 4' than for changing one of his 'present' tenses into a 'past'.

But we have still not considered what is really the central difference between spoken and written language. This is that, whereas speech takes place against the background of a situation which includes other, non-linguistic activity, writing has to compensate for the absence of a situation of this kind by supplying equivalent information linguistically. More accurately, since in the last resort the difference is one of degree only, in written language the language usually accounts for the whole of the relevant *activity* in the situation, and even, in the case of literature, for the whole of the *situation*; whereas with spoken language, the proportion of linguistic activity to the total activity in any situation may vary almost from a hundred per cent to zero.

In a game of football, for example, the language activity may play only a small and highly specific part. In an academic discussion, on the other hand, it may play almost the whole part, with only very occasional interaction between language and situation. Of the two, the academic discussion will be more like written English. Broadcast talks are closest of all to the written language, since speaker and hearer share no common situation; they are related to each other more as are writer and reader.

While therefore there is obviously a great deal in common between both written and spoken English, and it is possible to make a description that is valid for both, for some purposes it is necessary to treat them one at a time. It cannot be assumed that a statement made about the grammar of written English is valid for spoken English, or the other way round.

Although we have referred to 'spoken English' and 'written English', we do not imply that either a spoken language or a written language comprises in itself one homogeneous body of activity. Even if one makes abstraction from time, ignoring the history of the language, and considers simply a corpus of texts from the year 1964, these will display a vast range of variety: between different genres of written language, different spoken dialects, different types of situation and different individuals. All these have to be taken into account in our total picture of the language. In considering varieties of language such as these, we move over, though with no sharp line of demarcation, into institutional linguistics, which is the subject of Chapter 4. Before moving over, however, we must complete the sketch of what descriptive linguistics has to say about language. We have examined the form of language: we must now look a little more closely at its phonic substance.

BIBLIOGRAPHY

See items 13, 14, 16, 18, 25, 26, 27, 41, 47, 63, 71, 73, 77, 80, 81, 84.

Chapter 3

Phonetics in the description of language

1

Like many words which have a popular use in addition to a technical one, the term 'phonetics' means different things to different people. In discussing the place of phonetics within the linguistic sciences, we are of course using the term in a precise technical sense, and this differs from the senses in which many people understand it in everyday speech. Phonetics, in the way in which we use the term here, is not another name for elocution, nor for instruction in 'beautiful speech'. It is not a campaign in favour of, or against, the abolition of local dialects or accents. It is not a means for teaching foreigners to speak like Englishmen, nor a system for teaching 'pure vowels'. It is not a set of exercises in the sounds of a particular language. It is not a system of, or campaign for, reformed spelling. Nor is it, finally, an alphabet of oddly shaped letters.

Beliefs such as these about the nature of phonetics have been current for many years, and some of them die hard. They tend to be periodically revived through a process in which a section of public opinion misunderstands campaigns designed to educate it. An interesting example is Bernard Shaw's play, *Pygmalion*. Here Shaw portrayed an academic phonetician, Professor Higgins, and explored some of the relations between the speech-habits of the individual and his place in society. Those who read the Preface to *Pygmalion* discover that Shaw (who was a friend and admirer of Henry Sweet, perhaps the greatest of British phoneticians) knows what he is talking about. His attitudes may be those of phonetics in an early form, but those which motivate the sciences of phonetics and linguistics today are basically similar. On the other hand, those who read only the play itself and ignore the existence of the preface can be forgiven for reading into the play a confirmation of one of the

popular ideas about what a phonetician does. Now, however, scores
of millions of people know only the Professor Higgins of *My Fair
Lady*; this may be a splendid piece of entertainment but it is even
more widely separated from Shaw's Preface than was the original
play. Thus the very success and popularity of the musical play may
have made yet more widespread a misunderstanding of the nature
and purpose of one of the fundamental branches of linguistic study.

What, then, *is* phonetics? To begin with, it is one of the two
linguistic sciences. It is by nature analytical, descriptive and
classificatory. It deals with the observation, measurement and
description of a special kind of data, namely the sounds of human
speech. It has the monopoly of such operations: no other discipline
carries out these functions. These are the fundamentals of phonetics
as a science, and all the many and widespread activities to which the
techniques and theories of phonetics contribute are applications or
derivations of these.

The raw data of phonetics are, as we have said, the sounds of
human speech. Speech events are real events of vital importance to
society, to letters, to education, to science. The teacher, the communication engineer, the psychologist, the speech therapist and the
dentist, to say nothing of the descriptive linguist and many others,
all need to be able to understand, for their own purposes, how
human speech works. The theory and the techniques for analysing
and describing the sounds of speech are provided by phonetics.

Since the full range of phonetic studies is perhaps not widely
realized, we shall mention some of the sub-divisions of the subject
in its present form, and describe some recent applications of phonetic
theory and techniques apart from those which will be dealt with as
part of the principal theme of this book.

2

A simple way of considering the main branches of phonetics is to
label each of them according to the discipline with which it most
nearly coincides. Hence we have 'acoustic phonetics', 'physiological
phonetics' and 'psychological phonetics'.

Acoustic phonetics has revolutionized the whole subject by providing a new way of describing sounds, a way which complements
and supports the kinds of description previously available, but of a
different order. This revolution came about through the application

of techniques of acoustic measurement, using the physical concepts of frequency, intensity, phase and bandwidth, to the sounds produced by human beings. In return, phonetics has assimilated these concepts and now provides for communication engineers, for the first time, adequate ways of describing those acoustic by-products of human activity which it is their task to transmit by radio or by wire from place to place.

Research has reached a state of great sophistication in a short time and many projects are being pursued with great vigour. In the first half of the twentieth century communication between individuals and nations changed profoundly because of radio and television. In the second half of the century, a second and greater revolution may be expected if we learn to carry out three different operations upon human language. In the first, speech will be automatically converted into writing; progress towards this goal is taking place with increasing speed. In the second, written language will be automatically converted into speech; this is technically more difficult to achieve. For both these operations, the techniques of acoustic phonetics are vital. When, thirdly, the devices that carry out these procedures are perfected and can be linked with machine translation devices that convert written forms of language A into written forms of language B, the revolution will be complete. We shall then, for example, be able to speak into a microphone in one language and have our speech translated into the written or spoken form of another language, automatically. And acoustic phonetics will have contributed to the design and development of these systems.

Physiological phonetics has a long history: much of our knowledge about the production of human speech sounds dates from physiological research in the nineteenth century. It is clear that the sounds of human speech are caused by muscular activity in the human body, and techniques for studying some of that activity, though not all of it, have been available for a long time. It is obvious, for instance, that speech occurs in conjunction with a stream of air generated by the lungs, which are made to contract or expand by various sets of muscles disposed around the chest.

For a long time it seemed equally obvious that normal speech took place only when the air-stream was issuing out from the mouth. But this assumption was shown to be false when speakers of a number of languages from South America, Africa and Asia were studied in detail. It was found that speakers of these languages make use from time to time of inward-flowing air and of temporary closure of the air passage. Air-stream mechanisms for speech are more complex than they seemed to be at first when only the evidence from speakers of one particular group of languages had been taken into account.

Movements of the jaw and the lips are easily observed from the exterior. Movements of the tongue and the soft palate can be in part seen, in part subjectively described with fair accuracy by a person trained to do so, and in part studied by means of probes and levers attached to measuring instruments. The combination of all these techniques led to the descriptions of the articulations of speech-sounds, and these descriptions have remained largely unchanged for over fifty years, because they reflect with reasonable accuracy the physiological facts of sound production.

But descriptions of sounds in terms of tongue-position and the posture of the lips have generally been accompanied by statements about *what kind of noise* was being produced. To take an example, in the English word 'sea', there is a 'hiss' sound at the beginning of the word which is evidently different in type from the sound at the end of the word; and although a physiological description, or more specifically an articulatory description, describes the posture and movements of the organs of speech, it does not account for the different kinds of sounds produced. To do this it is necessary to use auditory description, to give labels to our judgments of what the sounds are like in quality. A typical example of conventional phonetic description is the following, which describes the first sound in a word like 'zoo': 'The formation of the sound may . . . be expressed shortly by defining it as a *voiced blade-alveolar fricative* consonant' (Daniel Jones, *Outline of English Phonetics*, pp. 188–9). In this definition the terms 'voiced' and 'fricative' refer to the *kind* of sound produced and are thus auditory criteria. The term 'blade-alveolar', and also in part the term 'voiced', refer to the mechanism by which the organs of speech produced the sound; they are there-fore articulatory criteria. The term 'consonant' (like 'voiced') is mixed in its usage; it is, like the classification system as a whole, an auditory-articulatory label.

These labels have worked very well, in practice, for a great many years, but there is no doubt that they have not been very precise or absolute. Particular sounds can be made with a number of different tongue positions or lip positions, while conversely one posture of the major organs of speech seems capable of accompanying several different qualities of sound. What is more, the tongue is such a mobile organ, and is set so deeply in the vocal tract, that close observation of its main body was extremely difficult until techniques of X-ray cinematography made some of the details visible. At the same time, however, our knowledge of radiation dangers has made it clear that this window into the workings of the speech mechanism can be opened only with the greatest care.

Recent advances in electronics have led to a new wave of investigations in this field, in particular into the functioning of the muscles that control breathing in speech respiration, the measurement of pressure and air-flow in speech, and the ways in which the vocal cords perform their task. The results of this work have been of immediate benefit to medicine and dentistry.

Psychological phonetics is recent in origin. It has arisen out of modern developments in perception psychology. The processes of vision have been the subject of study for a long time, but those of hearing have been relatively neglected. Now we are beginning to understand the ways in which sounds in general and speech-sounds in particular are perceived by human beings.

All the branches of phonetics described briefly above share the common aim of phonetic studies: the observation, measurement and description of the sounds of human speech. It is in the techniques and procedures adopted that they differ. At the same time there are certain techniques which have a place in all branches of phonetics, and with which every phonetician must be equipped. Central to all phonetic analysis is the technique known as PHONETIC TRANSCRIPTION. This is the technique for unambiguously representing the sounds of speech in written form. Although it may seem on first acquaintance to be simply a special version of ordinary, orthographic writing, in fact it serves a quite distinct purpose, which is discussed in more detail below (Section 4 of this chapter).

In addition, every phonetician must be able to identify sounds accurately by ear and himself to produce them. 'Ear training' and 'performance' classes make up a large part of the training of a phonetician, who should be able to discriminate and produce every kind of sound known to occur in human speech. All the rigorous practical training that a phonetician receives is directed towards enabling him to identify sounds, to perform them, and to transcribe them in written form.

3

There is one further misconception about phonetics which is relevant to our description of the place of phonetics in linguistic studies. Many people recall from their school-days, or from their time as university undergraduates, certain forms of instruction in speaking foreign languages which were, and still are, labelled 'phonetics'. It is true to say that the major justification for phonetics in Britain in the past has been its application to the teaching and learning of an acceptable pronunciation of some language other than English.

This is an important application which, if the theoretical basis is sound, can be widely effective and successful. It must be admitted that, at its worst, such instruction can be a travesty of the branch of phonetics concerned, and may misrepresent the nature of language without materially helping the language student. At its best, however, it can serve as a major training-ground for phoneticians and linguists. Probably the most famous example of phonetics serving this latter purpose is the course in the Phonetics of French which was given by the late Dr. Hélène Coustenoble at University College London over the past thirty years. During this time, in carrying out the workmanlike job of replacing in thousands of students the typical 'Englishman's accent' with a Parisian accent of surprising competence and acceptability, Dr. Coustenoble was in practice also giving the first training in certain basic phonetic techniques to a great number of present-day British phoneticians and linguists.

Having paid tribute to the way in which this kind of phonetics course can operate at its best, we must point out that relatively few of those who recall courses in the phonetics (so-called) of French, or German, or Spanish ever in fact had the good fortune to experience such courses at their best. Instruction by those who are perhaps only the second- or third-generation products of a good course, and are themselves untrained as phoneticians, has left thousands of pupils with a justifiable dislike and distrust for what they knew as 'phonetics'. It is not the elementary nature of such instruction that is objected to; there are many subjects in which the results of quite simple observations, provided they are accurate and well organized, can be very powerfully applied. What has happened unfortunately is that much classroom 'phonetics' has consisted of statements that are invalid and irrelevant, based on observations that are inaccurate.

In the years since 1950 a change has taken place in British phonetics which has linked it more firmly than before with the science of descriptive linguistics. This change further widens the gap between what phonetics actually is and what it is often thought to be. What has happened, roughly speaking, is that the growth of instrumental and experimental work, allied to the rigorous concepts borrowed from the physical and biological sciences, has led to a greater preoccupation with the general principles underlying phonetics as a whole. As a result of this, in addition to 'English phonetics' and 'French phonetics' and 'Russian phonetics' we now study, to a much greater extent than was formerly possible, 'general phonetics'; that is to say, those principles relating to the nature of human speech which are true for all languages and for every language.

There have been various stages in the development of phonetic theory to its present position. At first, when relatively few languages had been observed, it was assumed that the categories of articulation that had been devised to describe the sounds of European languages were universally adequate. As observations were extended to cover more and more languages, it became clear that there were considerably more variables than had been supposed; and moreover that within those already recognized, such as tongue position, there was continuous variation rather than a limited set of discrete values. The result was a move away from universal phonetic categories towards the detailed observation and description of the largest possible number of languages and their varieties.

Most recently, however, it has been possible to synthesize the knowledge gained from a study of very many languages, and work out a general theory of the nature and properties of speech sounds. The categories of phonetic theory are of a different kind of abstraction from those of linguistic theory such as 'system' and 'unit'. Since their purpose is to account for phonic substance, they represent physiological and physical properties, such as 'voice' and 'frequency', rather than scientific-logical abstractions. They have, however, the same theoretical status as the categories of linguistics. Both sets of categories are abstractions based on extensive observation and are designed to make possible the effective and useful description of all languages.

It is not enough of course that phonetic theory and method and linguistic theory and method should simply co-exist. The effective description of language requires that the two should be fully integrated into an overall theory of language, in which the relation among the different levels of linguistic patterning is clearly set out. Within this integrated theory, phonetics provides the means, not only for studying the sounds of spoken language, but also the organization of these sounds into recurrent patterns. In terms of the levels of descriptive linguistics, the description of phonic substance falls wholly within phonetics, while in phonology, phonetics and linguistics meet.

Here, therefore, we come back to the point made earlier, that phonology provides the bridge between form and substance, in the sense that it is in phonology that the sounds of a language are organized into patterns; these sound-patterns are then exploited as exponents of the formal items of the language. Seen from the standpoint of phonetics, the phonological patterns represent a wide range of resources which are exploited only partially and selectively in grammar and lexis. Many phonologically possible utterances do not in fact occur: for example, the syllable written 'plin' is possible in English phonology, but does not in fact represent any formal item.

We can relate this to everyday experience if we think of the kind of impersonation of speakers of foreign languages with which comedians often amuse us. In these impersonations, the speaker produces noises which are indistinguishable from French, or Russian, or Japanese, or whatever language it may purport to be, to the ear of a non-speaker of the language. The comedian has reproduced phonetic features with surprising accuracy; he may even have organized them into phonological patterns, but not in such a way as to produce meaningful speech. The substance is there, but formal patterning is absent.

We have now used three terms which are obviously related to each other and yet which correspond to important distinctions in our ways of talking about the sounds of speech. These terms are PHONIC, PHONETIC and PHONOLOGICAL. The most restricted of these three terms is 'phonic'; when we use it, we refer solely to the fact that the language substance we are talking about is not graphic. It is a simple term of polarity. The term 'phonetic' is used to describe details of speech using the categories of phonetic theory but without reference to the organization of sounds into potentially meaningful patterns in the given language. For example, it is easy to learn to

identify different accents of a language, and the different speakers of
a given accent, purely by the phonetic details: details such as voice
quality, or vowel quality, or lengthening of certain sounds, or
regional or individual varieties of intonation. These are phonetic
details and may be described in terms of articulation, auditory
judgment or acoustics. To talk of phonology one must take the
process of analysis a stage further towards language, and describe
the 'families of sounds' which constitute phonological items and the
units, structures and systems into which they are organized. It is
to the phonological items and categories that we refer in stating
how the formal properties of a language are realized in speech
sounds; the descriptive categories of phonology, like those of
grammar, are thus recognized and defined afresh for each language.

To put the distinction differently, when we talk of phonic substance we make no statement about what sounds or patterns of sounds
are occurring, but simply assert that that particular piece of language occurs as speech and not as writing. When we talk of phonetic
data we have so organized our observations as to recognize every
different kind of sound that is made in that piece of language; but
we have said nothing about the patterns in which these sounds occur.
We have not analysed their occurrences or grouped them into
phonemes, syllables or other units. The phonology of a language,
however, is a descriptive statement which is based precisely on such
an analysis. (There is another use of the term 'phonology', sometimes qualified as 'historical phonology', referring to the study of
the historical development of the sounds of a language. This special
use of the term in historical linguistics is distinct from the use of
the term in descriptive linguistics as adopted here; neither use of
course invalidates the other.)

It is important to notice that phonetic statements are about how
people *do* speak, not opinions about how they *should* speak. Phonetics, like linguistics, is descriptive in its nature. The speech
described may be of any language, of any individual from any social
or educational group, at any moment of time for which evidence
exists. But in every case the statements describe what the events
are, not what someone thinks they should be. We return later
(Chapter 4) to the consideration of prescription and standards of
speech; at this stage we are concerned to make it clear that whatever
use may be made of phonetic statements, the statements themselves are purely descriptions of speech events.

Such descriptions may be, as we have seen, of different kinds: one and the same speech event may be described in articulatory, in auditory or in acoustic terms. In the first case we are describing how the sound is produced; in the second, what it sounds like; and in the third, we are stating the measurements of the sounds in terms of physics. Any sound or sequence of sounds in any language spoken by man can be exhaustively described in all three ways, and observations made on any one plane support and reinforce those made on the other two.

4

We said earlier that the techniques of phonetics enable the sounds to be *identified*, *performed* and *transcribed* in written form. It now remains to discuss in more detail the technique of TRANSCRIPTION.

Of itself, transcription has nothing to do with spelling. A common confusion has arisen here, no doubt because we have all seen attempts to reform the inconsistencies of English spelling by means of some new alphabet, using either unfamiliar shapes or merely unfamiliar conventions, but operating on a more consistent basis than that of normal spelling. Most of these schemes use symbols taken directly from the alphabet of the International Phonetic Association; that does not mean or imply that phonetic symbols need necessarily have anything whatever to do with spelling reform. Spelling reform is an entirely separate issue, for which the principles and techniques of phonetics may or may not be invoked. Transcription, on the other hand, as we have suggested already, is a technique for unambiguously and consistently representing phonetic data in graphic form. It is a form of shorthand, in the sense that a very great quantity of detail about sounds and sound qualities can be conveyed in a rapid and economical fashion. In addition, it is a means of making speech open to inspection and imitation at whatever stage of analysis may have been reached.

There will always be more than one way of transcribing any given utterance, and different transcriptions are often required at different stages in a particular study. They may differ in one or two ways: either corresponding to different levels of analysis, or corresponding to different degrees of delicacy at one and the same level.

As regards the different levels, the need for graphic symbolization does not stop when we move from phonetics to phonology, and we regularly make use of both phonetic and phonological transcriptions. An example of a partial use of phonological transcription, in a passage of English, has already been given above (p. 52). Here now is one of the sentences from the same passage, first in complete phonological transcription (see table of 'symbols') and then in phonetic transcription, representing 'Standard English' speech:

(*Orthography*)

'Yes, but I don't see why they should lose marks for this.'

(*Phonological transcription*)

//ɪ – **jes** //4̰ bᵊt aⁱ /dᵊᵘnt siⁱ/ waⁱ ðeⁱ ʃᵊd luᵘz /**maᵊks fᵊ**/ ðis //

(*Phonetic transcription*)

ˈjɛs, bət aɪ ˈdoɷnt sɪɪ ˈwaɪ ðeɪ ʃɷd lɷuz ˈmaːks fə ˈðɪs

Strictly speaking, a transcription is a special type of NOTATION: a notation in which the symbols represent categories of *sound*. The other type of notation frequently used in descriptive linguistics is grammatical notation. Here the symbols do not of course refer directly to phonic data; such a notation is therefore not a transcription. Grammatical notation can be extremely complex if a detailed representation of grammatical categories is desired. A relatively simple linear representation of the same sentence in a form of grammatical notation would be as follows:

||| α– Aa ||&α||. A⁺a |Sh |Pfpø |||||β A²a |Sh |Pfmø
|Ch |Ap[c↓h] |||

In addition to the distinction between phonological and phonetic transcription, within phonetic transcription there may be variation in delicacy. A very delicate transcription is known as a NARROW transcription; this is one in which an extremely fine classification is used to mark the exact quality of each sound. Narrow transcriptions are especially used in dialectology, where the purpose is to note regional variations in pronunciation, however slight. A less delicate transcription is a BROAD transcription. A broad transcription uses far fewer symbols and diacritical marks; it is thus much simpler and better suited to such purposes as, for example, general accounts of human articulation and non-technical references to particular languages.

In practice, however, for many purposes a broad phonetic transcription can be replaced by a phonological transcription. A phonological transcription records all and only such sounds as are contrastive in the language concerned. If for example speakers of a given language use a vowel sound [a] which they pronounce sometimes long and sometimes short, a narrow phonetic transcription would recognize this, representing the short version as [a] and the long one as [aː]. This distinction might or might not be phonological in the given language: that is, it might or might not be used to carry formal contrasts, to make differences of meaning, grammatical or lexical. If it was never used to make contrasts of meaning, it would not be a phonological distinction and would not be noted in a phonological transcription: the vowel, whether long or short, would be represented simply /a/. If, however, the distinction was significant for the language, the two would have to be differently transcribed; since in a phonological transcription diacritics are avoided where possible, the symbols used would be /a/ and /aa/.

A phonological transcription is therefore not the same thing as a broad phonetic transcription: the latter still represents sounds considered and analysed purely as sounds, whereas the former is representing sounds systematized according to the job they do in the particular language.

A phonological transcription thus presupposes a thorough analysis of the language concerned, which a phonetic transcription does not. But the phonological transcription can serve most of the purposes served by a broad phonetic transcription, and has the added advantage of giving information relevant to other levels of the language; so that, once it has been devised, it is generally preferred for descriptive purposes. For foreign language teaching the ideal combination is probably a phonological transcription and a fairly narrow phonetic transcription; the two between them give all the information a student requires about the sounds of the language.

The phonetic transcription of the sentence given above was fairly broad. Naturally the narrower the transcription, the less general its application: while a broad transcription could be taken to represent the utterance in question as it might be spoken by any member of at least that dialect community, a very narrow transcription will represent the utterance as recorded on a particular occasion by a particular speaker. Here finally is the same sentence, as it was spoken in the conversation from which the passage was taken, represented in a rather broad and then in a very narrow transcription:

> (*Orthography*)
> 'Yes, but I don't see why they should lose marks for this.'
> (*Broad phonetic transcription*)
> ⟍ǀjes bət ai ǀdount sii ǀwai ðei ʃud luuz ⟎ ǀmaaks fə ǀðis
> (*Narrow phonetic transcription*)

―――――――――――――――――――――――――――――――――――――――

> ǀjị̆ę̧s bə̣r aɛ ǀdəent sị̇ ǀɦiwaˑɛ ðeị̣ ʃu̞d lu̞ˑz ǀmã̊ˌks fÿ̈ ǀðë̯ə̧s

5

Just as a grammatical notation may indicate the succession and wherever segmentation is possible, the boundaries of grammatical units, so also the phonological transcription shows the succession and boundaries of phonological units. (Such boundaries, incidentally, are *not* shown by pauses; pauses do not mark phonological or grammatical unit boundaries, but tend rather to occur before items of relatively low probability, or high 'information content'.) For each language, we have to recognize certain phonological units, those which will enable us to describe most economically and consistently all the significant sound patterns of that language.

These units are not universals; they are not the same for all languages. English, as we have seen, requires tone group, foot, syllable and phoneme, the last sometimes also called 'phonematic unit'. In the transcription, each alphabetic symbol on the line represents one phoneme; raised [i], [ə] and [u] represent 'prosodic' vowel markers. A prosodic feature in phonology, as mentioned above (p. 47), is any feature operating contrastively over a stretch other than a phoneme; it may be a property of a syllable or tone group, for example, or of a consonant cluster at the beginning of a syllable, or of a transition at the end of a consonant or vowel phoneme.

The terms 'phoneme' and 'syllable' are likely to recur in the description of the phonology of every language. This does not, however, mean that these categories are 'universals'. 'Phoneme' means simply 'the smallest segmental unit in the phonology of any language'; but the status and role of this unit varies considerably from language to language. There is little in common between the 'phoneme' of Chinese, that of Japanese, that of Arabic, and that of English, except the property of being the smallest phonological unit.

Similarly the syllable, though there does tend to be some phonetic property in common to what is called the syllable in every language, plays a very different part in the phonology of different languages. It is quite meaningless, for example, to count the syllables in a Russian text and in its English translation and draw conclusions therefrom about the relative compactness of the two languages: the English syllable carries quite a different kind of load from that carried by the syllable in Russian.

For each phonological unit in each language, we can recognize structures and systems in the same sense as in grammar. Some indication of what this implies, and of the steps taken to analyse these categories, can be given by illustration from English. Let us consider this set of English words:

leaf   feel   beetle   been   tea   eaten

If we think of their pronunciation, it is clear that these words exhibit permutations of a rather small number of sounds. We can identify these as phonemes, assign a symbol to each, and list them as follows:

$$/l \quad i^1 \quad f \quad b \quad t \quad n/$$

One of them, the vowel phoneme $/i^1/$, is prosodically marked: it is characterized by the movement of the tongue towards a certain position, rather than by its attainment of a fixed position for a fixed segment of time. If we continue the process of identification until, whatever new items are considered, no further distinctions are revealed, we shall have some idea of the total range of phonemes of the particular variety of the language we are describing.

At this point it is necessary to issue two warnings. First, the above is merely a simplified model of some of the complex procedures that might be employed. Nevertheless, for English, at least, word-pairs can be used to demonstrate most of the phonemic contrasts in the language. Secondly, we have begged a large question in assigning the same symbol to the last sound of the word 'feel' as we gave to the first sound of 'leaf'. We have implied that 'they are the same sound'; but in fact if we were to examine in close detail a tape recording of these words we should find many differences between them, and most of us can feel a difference in ARTICULATION, the posturing of the vocal organs, when we make these two different *l*-sounds. We are also, of course, aware of the similarities in the way in which the sounds are pronounced; but it is important to realize that there may be quite considerable phonetic variation among the sounds that are grouped together as one phoneme.

There is a wide range of variety in the way in which phonemes may be organized into syllables; different languages exhibit characteristic patterns and restrictions on phoneme combinations. One can sometimes give instances showing by direct contrast how two languages may differ in the structure of their syllables. Spanish speakers learning English often have difficulty with syllables beginning with /s/ followed by another consonant: for example, their pronunciation of the word 'spade' would be such as an English speaker would want to write as 'espade'. Their difficulty is caused by the differences in English and Spanish syllable structure. In English, a syllable may begin with the phoneme sequence /sp/, whereas in Spanish these sounds only occur together following a vowel. To take another example, the last two sounds in the word 'ink' occur in English only in syllable-final position, or across a syllable boundary. But Nzima, one of the languages of Ghana, may have [ŋk] at the beginning of a syllable, as in the name of President Nkrumah.

Syllables are units of sound, not of writing. Typically, a syllable consists of a vowel phoneme, with possibly one or more consonants before it, and possibly one or more consonants after it. Below are some examples of English syllables of different structures, the elements of structure being indicated as V (vowel) and C (consonant):

/eⁱ/	V	(name of the letter 'A')
/en/	VC	(name of the letter 'N')
/reⁱ/	CV	ray
/ren/	CVC	wren
/renz/	CVCC	wrens, wren's, wrens'
/reⁱn/	CVC	rain, rein, reign

/treˡn/	CCVC	train
/treˡnd/	CCVCC	trained
/streˡnd/	CCCVCC	strained

Syllables in turn combine to make up larger phonological units. In so doing, they exhibit another contrasting feature, one which we all learn to manipulate in our own native tongue, but which few people learn to handle really well in a foreign language. This feature is extremely complex, and is found in such enormous variety in different languages that it is doubtful whether any single component is common to all the phenomena grouped under the one heading. For the present discussion, however, we will accept the over-simplified classification that is in general use, and recognize a single category under the name of STRESS.

English has many examples of pairs of words written alike but differently pronounced, usually with one member of the pair a verb and the other a noun; for example, 'import', or 'discount'. If the two words 'discount' are spoken one after the other on the same monotone, and at the same tempo, the remaining difference between them is one of stress: one syllable is STRONG, the other WEAK. It is rare in English for this distinction to be made with all other features remaining constant. Strong syllables tend to be not only louder but also longer, and often to be accompanied by pitch movement: falling pitch, for example. But it is at least theoretically possible to isolate stress as an independent variable, to be correlated with what is perceived as variation in loudness.

In some languages, such as French, stress variation is minimal: there is not much variation in loudness between different syllables within one utterance. Other languages, of which English is one, make use of stress to provide a rhythmic unit greater than the syllable, somewhat analogous to the bar in music. This unit is called the 'foot'. In English phonology each foot consists of one strong syllable, either alone or followed by one or more weak syllables; rarely more than six. Since the strong syllables tend to occur at roughly regular intervals of time, whatever the number, including zero, of weak syllables occurring in between, the language has a definite 'beat'. This is one of the characteristic features of English, and one in which foreign students, especially those whose native language is of a very different type, need to be specifically drilled: incorrect rhythm is as often responsible for unintelligibility

as are incorrect vowels and consonants. The English type of rhythm
is known as 'stress-timing', by contrast with the 'syllable-timing'
of French.

A useful illustration of stress-timing in English can be taken from
the practice of counting aloud. The series of numbers '28, 29, 30,
31, 32' is normally spoken as follows: / ˌ twenty/EIGHT twenty/NINE
/THIRty thirty/ONE thirty/TWO/ with the strong (first) syllable of
each foot, shown here in capitals, occurring at an extremely regular
interval of time. The beat represents the normal rhythm of the
language and is not determined by the fact that the numerals form
an ordered series. Nor is it determined by the number of syllables:
in this example one foot consists of one syllable only, /NINE/, while
one foot, /THIRty thirty/, has one strong and three weak syllables.

In verse, the rhythm of the language is one of the basic resources
out of which patterns are constructed. Verse rhythm is, as it were,
the product of the natural rhythm of English speech in interaction
with 'metre', the rhythmic framework of a given poetic form. This
often involves the occurrence of 'silent beats', as in the following
familiar example:

	THREE	BLIND	MICE	(silent beat)
	THREE	BLIND	MICE	(silent beat)
	SEE	HOW they	RUN	(silent beat)
	SEE	HOW they	RUN	(silent beat)
they	ALL ran	AFter the	FARmer's	WIFE
who	CUT off their	TAILS with a	CARving	KNIFE
did	Ever you	SEE such a	THING in your	LIFE
as	THREE	BLIND	MICE	(silent beat)

If the rhythm is made to fit exactly, and without variation, into
the metrical structure of the verse form, the result is a jingle. The
rhythm of poetry is characterized by complex and highly varied
interaction of the metre with the natural patterns of English phonology.

The phoneme, the syllable and the foot account among them for
all the phonological patterning of English other than the meaningful variations in pitch. Probably all languages exploit the possibilities
of pitch movement in some way or other; in English, as we have
seen, intonation plays an important part in carrying grammatical
patterns. In some languages, pitch contrasts may be associated with
a unit as small as the syllable; in English, however, the melodic

unit, the 'tone group', is a distinct unit above the foot, a unit whose sole function is precisely to carry such melodic patterns.

What is known as INTONATION in English in fact covers three distinct choices, choices involving both the tone group and the foot. First there is the location of the tone group boundaries, the splitting up of an utterance into tone groups, one for each major 'information unit'. Second there is the selection of one foot within the tone group to carry the 'tonic', or main pitch movement; this choice, known as 'tonicity', assigns the 'information point' to a particular item in the tone group. Third there is the selection of one out of the various possible 'tones'; the basic system is one of five tones, but these can be sub-divided to show more delicate distinctions. Each tone is characterized by a specific rising or falling, or complex, pitch movement, the major part of which falls on the tonic foot. All these three phonological choices are used to carry differences of meaning in English, differences which, as we have stressed above, must be accounted for in any comprehensive grammar of spoken English.

6

It is not surprising that there is a great deal in common to the phonological patterning of all languages, since human beings the world over possess the same range of vocal apparatus. On the other hand, the phonic resources that this apparatus is capable of generating are so infinitely variable that no two languages are alike in their selection and distribution of phonetic features. French and English provide many familiar examples. Both languages have vowel and consonant phonemes, but the inventory of items is different in each language: for instance, French has nasal vowels but lacks diphthongs, English has the dental fricative consonants [ð] and [θ]. Both languages arrange their phonemes in syllables, but with different patterns of arrangement: for instance, in English, the sound [j], as at the beginning of the syllable 'yes', cannot occur at the end of a syllable as it does in French 'fille' and other words. Both languages have their characteristic rhythm; but in French the unit of rhythm is the syllable, and there is no distinct unit 'foot' in which syllables of different length are organized into rhythmic groupings. Both languages display variations in pitch over the

3*

highest unit of all, the tone group; not only do the melodies differ, however, but also the role of intonation in the two languages is very far from parallel.

Although, therefore, the basic concepts and categories of phonological theory are constant to all languages, a separate and independent description must be made for the phonology of each language. Where the same terms are used, as in the names of units such as 'phoneme' or 'syllable', there is certainly an implication of phonetic properties in common; but in the last resort these terms can only be defined in relation to the total description of each particular language that they are used to describe. Phonetic categories, on the other hand, whether articulatory, like 'dental' and 'plosive', or acoustic, like the measurements of fundamental frequency of sound waves, are truly general, in that they refer to properties of sounds irrespective of the language in which they occur or of their function in that language.

Phonetics is thus a classificatory science, whose techniques overlap with those of several other disciplines, and especially with physiology, acoustics and psychology; as applied phonetics, it is widely used in teaching an acceptable pronunciation in a foreign language. Its importance for linguistic science is that it provides the only body of theory and method for analysing and describing the phonic data of language. This analysis can be carried through to the level of phonology, where it links up with the description of the other levels of language. It is possible to study phonetics without studying linguistics, just as it is possible to study linguistics without studying phonetics; but neither subject without the other can suffice to give an accurate and meaningful picture of how language works.

BIBLIOGRAPHY:

See items 17, 20, 29, 30, 31, 32, 33, 34, 37, 43, 48, 52, 55, 70, 76.

Chapter 4

The users and uses of language

1

In Chapters 2 and 3 we discussed some theories and methods that have been developed in linguistics and phonetics for the description of how language works. As said in Chapter 1, description is not the only approach to the study of language. There are other branches of linguistics: one may for example treat language historically, showing how it persists and modifies through time. In application to language teaching, it is descriptive linguistics that is the most important. Even for this purpose, however, description is not the only type of linguistic study which is relevant.

In this section we are concerned with the branch of linguistics which deals, to put it in the most general terms, with the relation between a language and the people who use it. This includes the study of language communities, singly and in contact, of varieties of language and of attitudes to language. The various special subjects involved here are grouped together under the name of 'institutional linguistics'.

There is no clear line dividing institutional from descriptive linguistics; the two, though distinct enough as a whole, merge into one another. The study of context leads on to the analysis of situation types and of the uses of language. The descriptive distinction into spoken and written language naturally involves us in a consideration of the different varieties of language they represent. In institutional linguistics we are looking at the same data, language events, but from a different standpoint. The attention is now on the users of language, and the uses they make of it.

There are many ways of finding patterns among people. Some patterns are obvious: everyone is either male or female, with a fairly clear line between the two. Some, equally obvious, are less clearly demarcated: people are either children or adults, but we may not be sure of the assignment of a particular individual. Humorously, we may recognize all sorts of *ad hoc* patterns, like W. S. Gilbert's classification of babies into 'little liberals' and 'little conservatives'. The human sciences all introduce their own patterning: people are introverts or extroverts; negriform, mongoliform, caucasiform or australiform; employed, self-employed, non-employed or unemployed. No clear boundaries here, though the categories, statistically defined and, sometimes, arbitrarily delimited, are useful enough. Other patterns, such as national citizenship, are thrust upon us, often with conflicting criteria: each state tends to have its own definition of its citizens.

In linguistics, people are grouped according to the language or languages they use. This dimension of patterning is sometimes applied outside linguistics: a nation, in one view, is defined by language as well as by other factors. On the other hand, the category of 'nation' defined politically has sometimes been used in linguistics to give an institutional definition of 'a language': in this view 'a language' is a continuum of dialects spoken within the borders of one state. On such a criterion, British English and American English are two languages, though mutually intelligible; Chinese is one language, though Pekingese and Cantonese are not mutually intelligible; and Flemish, Dutch, German, Austrian German and Swiss German are five languages, though the pairing of mutually intelligible and mutually unintelligible dialects does not by any means follow the various national boundaries.

This is not the only way of defining 'a language'; there are as many definitions as there are possible criteria. Even within institutional linguistics various criteria are involved, each yielding a definition that is useful for some specific purpose. The concept of 'a language' is too important just to be taken for granted; nor is it made any less powerful by the existence of multiple criteria for defining it. But we have to be careful to specify the nature of this category when we use it.

In institutional linguistics it is useful to start with the notion of a LANGUAGE COMMUNITY, and then to ask certain questions about it. The language community is a group of people who regard themselves as using the same language. In this sense there is a language community 'the Chinese', since they consider themselves as speaking 'Chinese', and not Pekingese, Cantonese and so on. There is no language community 'the Scandinavians'; Norwegians speak Norwegian, Danes Danish and Swedes Swedish, and these are not regarded as 'dialects of the Scandinavian language', even though they are by and large all mutually intelligible. The British, Americans, Canadians, Australians and others all call their language 'English'; they form a single language community.

This method of recognizing a language community has the advantage that it reflects the speakers' attitude toward their language, and thus the way they use it. All speakers of English, for example, agree more or less on the way it should be written. At the same time, like all institutional linguistic categories and most of the basic categories of the human sciences, it is not clearcut, because people do not fall into clearcut patterns. There is a minor tendency for Americans to regard themselves as using a different language from the British, and this is again reflected in minor variations in orthography. But it is a mistake to exaggerate this distinction, or to conclude therefrom that there is no unified English-speaking language community.

Some of the questions that can be asked about a language community and its language are these. First, what happens when it impinges on other language communities? Second, what varieties of its language are there? Under the second question come these subdivisions: varieties according to users (that is, varieties in the sense that each speaker uses one variety and uses it all the time) and varieties according to use (that is, in the sense that each speaker has a range of varieties and chooses between them at different times). The variety according to user is a DIALECT; the variety according to use is a REGISTER. Third, what attitudes do the speakers display towards their language and any or all of its varieties?

2

Situations in which one language community impinges on another have been called 'language contact' situations. Such situations are characterized by varying degrees of bilingualism. Bilingualism is recognized wherever a native speaker of one language makes use of a second language, however partially or imperfectly. It is thus a cline, ranging, in terms of the individual speaker, from the completely monolingual person at one end, who never uses anything but his own native language or 'L1', through bilingual speakers, who make use in varying degree of a second language or 'L2', to the endpoint where a speaker has complete mastery of two languages and makes use of both in all uses to which he puts either. Such a speaker is an 'ambilingual'.

True ambilingual speakers are rare. Most people whom we think of as bilingual restrict at least one of their languages to certain uses: and in any given use, one or the other language tends to predominate. There are probably millions of L2 English speakers throughout the world with a high degree of bilingualism, but who could neither make love or do the washing up in English nor discuss medicine or space travel in their L1. Even those who have learnt two languages from birth rarely perform all language activities in both; more often than not a certain amount of specialization takes place.

This distinction, between an L1 and an L2, a native and a non-native or learnt language, is of course not clearcut. Moreover it cuts across the degree of bilingualism. Some bilingual speakers, including some who are ambilingual, can be said to have two (occasionally more) native languages. There is no exact criterion for this; but one could say arbitrarily that any language learnt by the child before the age of instruction, from parents, from others, such as a nurse, looking after it, or from other children, is an L1. It is clear, however, that only a small proportion of those who learn two or more languages in this way become ambilingual speakers; and conversely, not all ambilinguals have two L1s.

A point that has often been observed about native bilingual, including ambilingual, speakers is that they are unable to translate between their L1s. This does not mean of course that they cannot learn to translate between them. But translation has to be learnt by them as a distinct operation; it does not follow automatically from the possession of two sets of native language habits. This has been linked with the fact that those with two L1s are usually not true ambilinguals: that they have usually specialized their two or more native languages into different uses. But this cannot be the only reason, since even those who approach or attain true ambilingualism are still usually unable to translate without instruction. It appears that it is a characteristic of an L1, defined in the way suggested above, to operate as a distinct set of self-sufficient patterns in those situations in which language activity is involved. However ambilingual the speaker is, in the sense that there is no recognizable class of situation in which he could not use either of his languages, there is always some difference between the actual situations in which he uses the one and those in which he uses the other, namely that each of the two is associated with a different group of participants.

This raises the question: how unique is or are the native language or languages in the life of the speaker? No sure answer can yet be given to this question. It is clear that for the great majority of bilingual speakers the L2 never replaces the L1 as a way of living; nor is it intended to do so. We may want to attain a high degree of competence in one or more foreign languages, but we usually do not expect thereby to disturb the part played in our lives by the native one. On the other hand those who move permanently to a new language community may, if they move as individuals and not as whole families, abandon at least the active use of their native language and replace it throughout by an L2.

This in itself is not enough to guarantee a particular degree of attainment in the L2. Some speakers are more easily content: they may, for example, not try to adopt the phonetic patterns of the L2 beyond the point where they become comprehensible to its native speakers. Others may simply fail to achieve the standard of performance that they themselves regard as desirable. In this way they cut down the role played by language in their lives. On the other hand there is clearly no upper limit to attainment in an L2. The L2 speaker may live a normal, full life in his adopted language community, absorb its literature and even use the language for his own creative writing, as Conrad and Nabokov have done so successfully with English. Whether the learnt language will ever be so 'infinitely docile', in Nabokov's words, as the native language, it is hard to say. Certainly the user of an L2 may learn to exploit its resources as widely as do its native speakers; and though he is more conscious of these resources than the majority of native speakers, in this he merely resembles that minority who have learnt to be conscious of how their native language works: principally the creative writers, literary analysts and linguists. But while one can set no limit to the possible degree of mastery of an L2, it remains true that such a level of attainment is rarely aimed at and still more rarely achieved.

The individual speaker, in contact with a new language

community, may react by developing any degree and kind of bilingualism within this very wide range. Over language communities as
a whole, in contact-situations certain patterns tend to emerge.
Sometimes the solution adopted, at least in the long term, is not
one of bilingualism. What happens in these instances is either that
one language community abandons its own language and adopts
that of the other—here there will be a transitional period of
bilingualism, but it may be very short; or that a mixed language
develops which incorporates some features of both.

Such mixed languages have usually had either English or French
as one of their components; less frequently Dutch or Portuguese.
Those that remain restricted to certain uses, as many have done,
without ever attaining the full resources of a language, are called
PIDGINS. Some mixtures, however, have developed into full
languages; these are known as CREOLES. In some areas, for example
in language communities in Sierra Leone, Haiti, Mauritius and
Melanesia, creoles are acquired by children as their L1. Here they
have full status as community languages, and there is not necessarily
any bilingualism at all. The fact that in most of these areas children
are expected to acquire a second language as L2 at school reflects
the social status of the mixed languages, but is entirely without
prejudice to their linguistic status as full community languages.

In other instances the long term solution has been one of as it
were institutionalized bilingualism. This frequently takes the form
of a LINGUA FRANCA. One language comes to be adopted as the
medium of some activity or activities which the different language
communities perform in common. It may be a common language
for commerce, learning, administration, religion or any or all of a
variety of purposes: the use determines which members of each
language community are the ones who learn it.

Latin was such a lingua franca for a long period in the history of
Europe; in certain countries it retains this status to the present day,
though to a much restricted extent, as the lingua franca of religion.
Among other languages which have been linguae francae at certain
times, over certain areas and for certain uses, are Arabic, Malay,
Hausa, Classical and Mandarin (Pekingese) Chinese, Swahili,
Sanskrit, French, Russian and English. Since the lingua franca
normally operates for certain specific purposes, it is often a more or
less clearly definable part of the language that is learnt as L2.
There may even develop a special variety for use as a lingua franca,

as with Hindustani and 'bazaar Malay'. These are distinct in practice from the mixed pidgins and creoles, in that each has clearly remained a variety of its original language; but it is difficult to draw an exact theoretical distinction.

Languages such as English and Russian, which are widely learnt as second languages in the world today, are a type of lingua franca. They are a special case only in the sense that they are being learnt by unprecedentedly large numbers of people and for a very wide range of purposes, some of which are new. In any serious study of the problems and methods of teaching English as a second language it is important to find out what these purposes are, and how they differ in different areas and according to the needs of different individuals. Possibly the major aim that is common to all areas where English is taught as L2 is that of its use in the study of science and technology. But there are numerous other aims, educational, administrative, legal, commercial and so on, variously weighted and pursued in different countries.

The task of becoming a bilingual with English as L2 is not the same in all these different circumstances; and it is unfair to those who are struggling with the language, whether struggling to learn it or to teach it, to pretend that it is. English is 'a language' in the sense that it is not Russian or Hindi; any two events in English are events in 'the same' language. But if we want to teach what we call 'a language', whether English or any other, as a second or indeed also as a first language, we must look a little more closely at the nature of the varieties within it.

3

In one dimension, which variety of a language you use is determined by who you are. Each speaker has learnt, as his L1, a particular variety of the language of his language community, and this variety may differ at any or all levels from other varieties of the same language learnt by other speakers as their L1. Such a variety, identified along this dimension, is called a 'dialect'.

In general, 'who you are' for this purpose means 'where you come from'. In most language communities in the world it is the region of origin which determines which dialectal variety of the language a speaker uses. In China, you speak Cantonese if you come

from Canton, Pekingese if you come from Peking and Yunnanese
if you come from Yunnan.

Regional dialects are usually grouped by the community into
major dialect areas; there may, of course, be considerable differentiation within each area. The dialects spoken in Canton, Toishan,
Chungshan and Seiyap, all in Kwangtung province, are clearly
distinct from one another; but they are all grouped together under
the general name of 'Cantonese'.

Within Cantonese, the local varieties form a continuum: each
will resemble its neighbours on either side more closely than it
resembles those further away. Among major dialect areas, there is
usually also a continuum. There may be a more or less clear dialect
boundary, where the occurrence of a bundle of ISOGLOSSES (lines
separating a region displaying one grammatical, lexical, phonological or phonetic feature from a region having a different feature
at the same place in the language) shows that there are a number of
features in which the dialects on either side differ from each other:
but the continuum is not entirely broken. Thus there is a fairly
clear distinction between Cantonese and Mandarin in the area
where the two meet in Kwangsi, and there is indeed a strip of
country where the two coexist, many villages having some families
speaking Cantonese and some speaking Mandarin. Nevertheless
the variety of Cantonese spoken in this dialect border region is
closer to Mandarin than are other varieties of Cantonese, and the
Mandarin is closer to Cantonese than are other varieties of Mandarin.

This situation represents a kind of median between two extremes:
an unbroken continuum on the one hand, as between Mandarin
and the 'Wu' or lower Yangtsze dialect region, and a sharp break
on the other, as between Cantonese and Hakka in Kwangtung. In
this case the reason for the break is that the Hakka speakers arrived
by migration from the north roughly a thousand years after the
original settlement of Kwangtung by the ancestors of the modern
Cantonese speakers.

This general dialect pattern turns up in one form or another all
over the world. An instance of wide dialectal variety in modern
Europe is provided by German. Here we have to recognize three,
and possibly four, different language communities. The Flemings,
in Belgium, speak Flemish, though this is now officially regarded
as a variety of Dutch; the Dutch speak Dutch; Germanic speakers
in Switzerland regard themselves, in general, as speaking a distinct

'Swiss-German'. The Germans and the Austrians, and the Swiss in certain circumstances, regard themselves as speaking German. But over the whole of this area there is one unbroken dialect continuum, with very few instances of a clear dialect boundary; ranging from the High German of Switzerland, Austria and Bavaria to the Low German of Northwest Germany, Holland and Belgium.

The normal condition of language is to change, and at times and in places where there is little mobility between dialect communities there is nothing to cause the various dialects of a language to change in the same direction. Under these conditions dialects tend to diverge from each other at all levels, perhaps most of all in phonology and phonetics. It may happen that mutual intelligibility is lost; that the language community is as it were broken up into dialect regions such that there are many pairs of regions whose speakers cannot understand one another. This happened in China. There are six major dialects in modern China: Mandarin, Cantonese, Wu, North Min, South Min and Hakka; each of which is mutually unintelligible with all the others.

This situation tends to be resolved by the emergence of one dialect as a lingua franca. In China, the spoken lingua franca has traditionally been the Pekingese form of the Mandarin dialect. But under the empire very few people from outside the Mandarin-speaking area ever learnt Mandarin unless they were government officials. Mandarin was the language of administration and some literature; but classical Chinese remained the lingua franca for most written purposes, being supplemented as an educational medium, since it could no longer function as a spoken language, by the regional dialects. In nationalist China some progress was made towards introducing Mandarin as a 'second language' in schools, and the process has continued in communist China, where with the expansion of educational facilities, Mandarin is now regularly taught at some stage in the school career. It is in fact becoming a 'standard' or 'national' language.

A similar process took place in Germany. 'Standard German' of course is 'standard' only for the language community that considers itself as speaking German (not, however, limited to Germany itself). The concept of a standard is defined in relation to the language community: to a Dutchman 'standard' could only mean standard Dutch, not standard German.

In Germany, and similarly in China, there is no suggestion that the dialect chosen as the 'standard' language is any better than any other dialect. A modern state needs a lingua franca for its citizens, and there are historical reasons leading to the choice of one dialect rather than another. It may have been the one first written down, or the language of the capital; or it may, as in Germany, include a somewhat artificial mixture of features from different dialects. Nor is there any suggestion that those who learn the standard language should speak it exactly alike. The aim is intelligibility for all purposes of communication, and if a Cantonese speaks Mandarin, as most do, with a Cantonese accent, provided this does not affect his intelligibility nobody will try to stop him or suggest that his performance is inferior or that he himself is a less worthy person.

In the history of the English language, dialects followed the familiar pattern. In the fifteenth century England was a continuum of regional dialects with, almost certainly, some mutual unintelligibility. With the rise of urbanism and the modern state, a standard language emerged; this was basically the London form of the South-east Midland dialect, but with some features from neighbouring areas, especially from the South-central Midlands. The orthography, which in Middle English had varied region by region, became more and more standardized according to the conventions associated with this dialect. As in other countries, for ease of communication, the notion of a 'correct' orthography grew up: by the late seventeenth century educated people were expected to spell alike, although in earlier times individuality had been tolerated in spelling just as it had been (and still was) in pronunciation.

The emergence of a standard language gives rise to the phenomenon of 'accent', which is quite distinct from 'dialect'. When we learn a foreign language, we normally transfer patterns from our native language on to the language we are learning. These may be patterns at any level. Those of form, however, and most of those of phonology and orthography, tend to be progressively eliminated. This is because they may seriously impair intelligibility; they are less directly interrelated, thus reinforcing each other less; and they are easier to correct once observed, because they are not patterns of muscular activity. With phonetic patterns, on the other hand, there is greater intelligibility tolerance, more reinforcement and much greater difficulty in correction even when they are observed. Transference of phonetic habits, in other words, is easier to tolerate and harder to avoid than transference at other levels. So we usually speak with a 'foreign accent', even when our grammar and lexis are in general conformity with the native patterns of the learnt language.

So also when a speaker learns a second dialect. He generally speaks it with 'an accent': that is, with phonetic features of his native dialect. The learning of a standard language is simply the learning of a second dialect, the dialect that happens to have been 'standardized'. Most speakers, learning the standard language of their community, continue to speak with the phonetics of their native dialect, and there is usually no loss in intelligibility.

It is quite normal for members of a language community which has a standard language to continue to use both the native and the learnt (standard) dialect in different situations throughout their lives. This happens regularly in China and even in Germany. But while in a rural community, where there is less movement of people, the native dialect is appropriate to most situations, in an urban community the relative demands on native and standard dialect are reversed. The population is probably made up of speakers of various different dialects, so that the standard language becomes a lingua franca amongst them; in addition there is greater mobility within and between towns.

As a consequence, many speakers drop their native dialect altogether, having very few situations in which to use it, and replace it with the standard language. In so doing, they transfer to the standard language the phonetics of the native dialect, speaking it with a regional 'accent'. In time, this form of the standard language with regional accent comes to be regarded itself as a dialect. Today, for example, people use the term 'Yorkshire dialect' equally to refer both to the speech of Leeds, which is standard English with generalized West Riding phonetics, and to the speech of Upper Wharfedale, which is an 'original' West Riding dialect. Since urban speech forms expand outwards at the expense of rural ones, the longer established dialects of England are disappearing and being replaced by the standard language spoken with the various regional accents.

This process is liable to happen anywhere where there is a high degree of industrialization and consequent growth of cities. What is peculiar to England, however, is the extent to which, concurrently with this process, a new dimension of dialect differentiation has come into operation. In most countries, even those highly industrialized like Germany, the way a person speaks is determined by the place he comes from: he speaks either the regional dialect or the standard language with regional accent. In England, however, and to a lesser extent in France, Scotland, Australia and the United States, a person's speech is determined not only by the region he comes from but also by the class he comes from, or the class he is trying to move into. Our dialects and accents are no longer simply regional: they are regional and social, or 'socio-regional'. Nowhere else in the world is this feature found in the extreme form it has reached in England. It is a feature of English life which constantly amazes the Germans and others into whose national mythology the facts, or some version of them, have penetrated.

The dialect structure of England today can be represented by a pyramid. The vertical plane represents class, the horizontal one region. At the base, there is wide regional differentiation, widest among the agricultural workers and the lower-paid industrial workers. As one moves along the socio-economic scale, dialectal variety according to region diminishes. Finally at the apex there is no regional differentiation at all, except perhaps for the delicate shades which separate Cambridge and Oxford from each other and from the rest.

This regionally neutral variety of English, often known as 'RP', standing for 'received (that is, generally accepted) pronunciation', carries prestige and may be acquired at any stage in life. It tends to be taught by example rather than by instruction. Certain institutions, notably the preparatory and public schools, create, as part of their function, conditions in which it can be learnt. The speaker of this form of English has, as is well known, many social and economic advantages. There are, for example, many posts for which he will automatically be preferred over a candidate who does not speak it. If there are any posts for which the opposite is true, as is sometimes claimed, these are posts which are not likely to arouse serious competition.

When a speaker states what language he regards himself as speaking, he is defining a language community. By implication a language community may be delimited regionally, although national frontiers may enter into the definition of the region. When he states what dialect he speaks, he is defining a dialect community. Here again the delimitation that is implied is normally regional; but there are some countries, notably England, in which it is socio-regional.

If the community has a standard language, there may be not only dialects but also accents: in other words 'new dialects', varieties of the standard language having regional or socio-regional phonetic patterns. [The distinction between] dialect and accent is often not clearcut, and the speaker may well conflate the two. All his observations, but especially those on dialect and accent, may be coloured by value-judgements; but the discussion of these we leave to the final section of this chapter.

4

A dialect is a variety of a language distinguished according to the user: different groups of people within the language community speak different dialects. It is possible also to recognize varieties of a language along another dimension, distinguished according to use. Language varies as its function varies; it differs in different situations. The name given to a variety of a language distinguished according to use is 'register'.

The category of 'register' is needed when we want to account for what people do with their language. When we observe language activity in the various contexts in which it takes place, we find differences in the type of language selected as appropriate to different types of situation. There is no need to labour the point that a sports commentary, a church service and a school lesson are linguistically quite distinct. One sentence from any of these and many more such situation types would enable us to identify it correctly. We know, for example, where 'an early announcement is expected' comes from and 'apologies for absence were received'; these are not simply free variants of 'we ought to hear soon' and 'was sorry he couldn't make it'.

It is not the event or state of affairs being talked about that determines the choice, but the convention that a certain kind of language is appropriate to a certain use. We should be surprised, for example, if it was announced on the carton of our toothpaste that the product was 'just right for cleaning false teeth' instead of 'ideal for cleansing artificial dentures'. We can often guess the source of a piece of English from familiarity with its use: 'mix well' probably comes from a recipe, although the action of mixing is by no means limited to cookery—and 'mixes well' is more likely to be found in a testimonial.

The choice of items from the wrong register, and the mixing of items from different registers, are among the most frequent mistakes made by non-native speakers of a language. If an L2 English speaker uses, in conversation, a dependent clause with modal 'should', such as 'should you like another pint of beer, ...', where a native speaker would use a dependent clause with 'if', he is selecting from the wrong register. Transference of this kind is not limited to foreigners; the native schoolboy may transfer in the opposite direction, writing in his Shakespeare essay 'it was all up with Lear, who couldn't take any more of it'.

Linguistic humour often depends on the inappropriate choice and the mixing of registers: P. G. Wodehouse exploits this device very effectively. Fifty years ago the late George Robey used to recite a version of 'The house that Jack built' which ended as follows: '... that disturbed the equanimity of the domesticated feline mammal that exterminated the noxious rodent that masticated the farinaceous produce deposited in the domiciliary edifice erected by Master John'.

Dialects tend to differ primarily, and always to some extent, in substance. Registers, on the other hand, differ primarily in form. Some registers, it is true, have distinctive features at other levels, such as the voice quality associated with the register of church services. But the crucial criteria of any given register are to be found in its grammar and its lexis. Probably lexical features are the most obvious. Some lexical items suffice almost by themselves to identify a certain register: 'cleanse' puts us in the language of advertising, 'probe' of newspapers, especially headlines, 'tablespoonful' of recipes or prescriptions, 'neckline' of fashion reporting or dressmaking instructions. The clearest signals of a particular register are scientific technical terms, except those that belong to more than one science, like 'morphology' in biology and linguistics.

Often it is not the lexical item alone but the collocation of two or more lexical items that is specific to one register. 'Kick' is presumably neutral, but 'free kick' is from the language of football. Compare the disc jockey's 'top twenty'; 'thinned right down' at the hairdresser's (but 'thinned out' in the garden); and the collocation of 'heart' and 'bid' by contrast with 'heart' and 'beat'.

Purely grammatical distinctions between the different registers are less striking, yet there can be considerable variation in grammar also. Extreme cases are newspaper headlines and church services; but many other registers, such as sports commentaries and popular songs, exhibit specific grammatical characteristics. Sometimes, for example, in the language of advertising, it is the combination of grammatical and lexical features that is distinctive. 'Pioneers in self-drive car hire' is an instance of a fairly restricted grammatical structure. The collocation of the last four lexical items is normal enough in other structures, as in 'why don't you hire a car and drive yourself?'; but their occurrence in this structure, and in collocation with an item like 'pioneer' or 'specialist', is readily identifiable as an advertising slogan.

Registers are not marginal or special varieties of language. Between them they cover the total range of our language activity. It is only by reference to the various situations, and situation types, in which language is used that we can understand its functioning and its effectiveness. Language is not realized in the abstract: it is realized as the activity of people in situations, as linguistic events which are manifested in a particular dialect and register.

No one suggests, of course, that the various registers characteristic of different types of situation have nothing in common. On the contrary, a great deal of grammatical and lexical material is common to many of the registers of a given language, and some perhaps to all. If this was not so we could not speak of 'a language' in this sense at all, just as we should not be able to speak of 'a language' in the sense of a dialect continuum if there was not a great deal in common among the different dialects.

But there tends to be more difference between events in different registers than between different events in one register. If we failed to note these differences of register, we should be ignoring an important aspect of the nature and functioning of language. Our descriptions of languages would be inaccurate and our attempts to teach them to foreigners made vastly more difficult.

It is by their formal properties that registers are defined. If two samples of language activity from what, on non-linguistic grounds, could be considered different situation-types show no differences in grammar or lexis, they are assigned to one and the same register: for the purposes of the description of the language there is only one situation-type here, not two. For this reason a large amount of linguistic analysis is required before registers can be identified and described. It is one thing to make a general description of English accounting, to a given degree of delicacy, for all the features fo some or other variety of the language. Most native speak agree on what is and what is not possible, and the areas agreement are marginal. It is quite another thing to find special characteristics of a given register: to describe for e the language of consultations between doctor and patient surgery.

For such a purpose very large samples of textual materi needed. Moreover much of the language activity that needs to be studied takes place in situations where it is practically impossible to make tape recordings. It is not surprising, therefore, that up to now we know very little about the various registers of spoken English. Even studies of the written language have only recently begun to be made from this point of view. For this reason we are not yet in a position to talk accurately about registers; there is much work to be done before the concept is capable of detailed application.

While we still lack a detailed description of the registers of a language on the basis of their formal properties, it is nevertheless useful to refer to this type of language variety from the point of view of institutional linguistics. There is enough evidence for us to be able to recognize the major situation types to which formally distinct registers correspond; others can be predicted and defined from outside language. A number of different lines of demarcation have been suggested for this purpose. It seems most useful to introduce a classification along three dimensions, each representing an aspect of the situations in which language operates and the part played by language in them. Registers, in this view, may be distinguished according to field of discourse, mode of discourse and style of discourse.

'Field of discourse' refers to what is going on: to the area of operation of the language activity. Under this heading, registers are classified according to the nature of the whole event of which the language activity forms a part. In the type of situation in which the language activity accounts for practically the whole of the relevant activity, such as an essay, a discussion or an academic seminar, the field of discourse is the subject-matter. On this dimension of classification, we can recognize registers such as politics and personal relations, and technical registers like biology and mathematics.

There are on the other hand situations in which the language activity rarely plays more than a minor part; here the field of discourse refers to the whole event. In this sense there is, for example, a register of domestic chores: 'hoovering the carpets' may involve language activity which, though marginal, is contributory to the total event. At the same time the language activity in a situation may be unrelated to the other activities. It may even delay rather than advance them, if two people discuss politics while doing the washing up. Here the language activity does not form part of the washing up event, and the field of discourse is that of politics.

Registers classified according to field of discourse thus include both the technical and the non-technical: shopping and games-playing as well as medicine and linguistics. Neither is confined to one type of situation. It may be that the more technical registers lend themselves especially to language activity of the discussion type, where there are few, if any, related non-language events; and the non-technical registers to functional or operational language activity, in which we can observe language in use as a means of achievement. But in the last resort there is no field of activity which cannot be discussed; and equally there is none in which language cannot play some part in getting things done. Perhaps our most purely operational language activity is 'phatic communion', the language of the establishment and maintenance of social relations. This includes utterances like 'How do you do!' and 'See you!', and is certainly non-technical, except perhaps in British English where it overlaps with the register of meteorology. But the language activity of the instructor in the dance studio, of the electrician and his assistant, of the patient consulting the doctor in the surgery, or of research scientists in the performance of a laboratory experiment, however technical it may be, is very clearly functioning as a means of operation and control.

This leads to 'mode of discourse', since this refers to the medium or mode of the language activity, and it is this that determines, or rather correlates with, the role played by the language activity in the situation. The primary distinction on this dimension is that into spoken and written language, the two having, by and large, different situational roles. In this connection, reading aloud is a special case of written rather than of spoken language.

The extent of formal differentiation between spoken and written language has varied very greatly among different language communities and at different periods. It reached its widest when, as in medieval Europe, the normal written medium of a community was a classical language which was unintelligible unless learnt by instruction. Latin, Classical Arabic, Sanskrit and Classical Chinese have all been used in this way. By comparison, spoken and written varieties of most modern languages are extremely close. The two varieties of French probably differ more than those of English; even popular fiction in French uses the simple past (preterite) tense in narrative. But spoken and written English are by no means formally identical. They differ both in grammar and in lexis, as anyone by recording and transcribing conversation can find out.

Within these primary modes, and cutting across them to a certain extent, we can recognize further registers such as the language of newspapers, of advertising, of conversation and of sports commentary. Like other dimensions of classification in linguistics, both descriptive and institutional, the classification of modes of discourse is variable in delicacy. We may first identify 'the language of literature' as a single register; but at the next step we would separate the various genres, such as prose fiction and light verse, as distinct registers within it. What is first recognized as the register of journalism is then subclassified into reportage, editorial comment, feature writing and so on.

Some modes of discourse are such that the language activity tends to be self-sufficient, in the sense that it accounts for most or all of the activity relevant to the situation. This is particularly true of the various forms of the written mode, but applies also to radio talks, academic discussions and sermons. In literature particularly the language activity is as it were self-sufficient. On the other hand, in the various spoken modes, and in some of the written, the utterances often integrate with other non-language activity into a single event. Clear instances of this are instructions and sets of commands. The grammatical and lexical distinctions between the various modes of discourse can often be related to the variable situational role assigned to language by the medium.

Third and last of the dimensions of register classification is 'style of discourse', which refers to the relations among the participants. To the extent that these affect and determine features of the language, they suggest a primary distinction into colloquial and polite ('formal', which is sometimes used for the latter, is here avoided because of its technical sense in description). This dimension is unlikely ever to yield clearly defined, discrete registers. It is best treated as a cline, and various more delicate cuts have been suggested, with categories such as 'casual', 'intimate' and 'deferential'. But until we know more about how the formal properties of language vary with style, such categories are arbitrary and provisional.

The participant relations that determine the style of discourse range through varying degrees of permanence. Most temporary are those which are a feature of the immediate situations, as when the participants are at a party or have met on the train. At the opposite extreme are relations such as that between parents and children. Various socially defined relations, as between teacher and pupil or labour and management, lie somewhere intermediately. Some such registers may show more specific formal properties than others: it is probably easier to identify on linguistic evidence a situation in which one participant is serving the others in a shop than one involving lecturer and students in a university classroom.

Which participant relations are linguistically relevant, and how far these are distinctively reflected in the grammar and lexis, depends on the language concerned. Japanese, for example, tends to vary along this dimension very much more than English or Chinese. There is even some formal difference in Japanese between the speech of men and the speech of women, nor is this merely a difference in the probabilities of occurrence. In most languages, some lexical items tend to be used more by one sex than the other; but in Japanese there are grammatical features which are restricted to the speech of one sex only.

It is as the product of these three dimensions of classification that we can best define and identify register. The criteria are not absolute or independent; they are all variable in delicacy, and the more delicate the classification the more the three overlap. The formal properties of any given language event will be those associated with the intersection of the appropriate field, mode and style. A lecture on biology in a technical college, for example, will be in the scientific field, lecturing mode and polite style; more delicately, in the biological field, academic lecturing mode and teacher to student style.

The same lecturer, five minutes later in the staff common room, may switch to the field of cinema, conversational mode, in the style of a man among colleagues. As each situation is replaced by another, so the speaker readily shifts from one register to the next. The linguistic differences may be slight; but they may be considerable, if the *use* of language in the new situation differs sharply from that in the old. We cannot list the total range of uses. Institutional categories, unlike descriptive ones, do not resolve into closed systems of discrete terms. Every speaker has at his disposal a continuous scale of patterns and items, from which he selects for each situation type the appropriate stock of available harmonies in the appropriate key. He speaks, in other words, in many registers.

He does not, normally, speak in many dialects, since the dialect represents the total range of patterns used by his section of the language community. But he may, as a citizen of a nation, learn a second dialect for certain uses, and even a third and a fourth. In Britain, choice of dialect is bound up with choice of register in a way that is unique among the language communities of the world: it is a linguistic error to give a radio commentary on cricket in cockney or sing popular songs in the Queen's English. Many of the languages of older nations show some such mutual dependence between dialect and register.

In the newer nations, this is less apparent; instead there is often a tendency for the register to determine, not the choice of dialect, but the choice of language. Machine translation will in time make it possible for each community to use its own language for all purposes. Meanwhile, in many parts of the world, it is necessary to learn a second language in order to be equipped with a full range of registers; and foreign language teaching has become one of the world's major industries. By the time when it is no longer necessary for anyone to learn a foreign language in order to be a full citizen of his own community, it may well be recognized as desirable for everyone to do so in order to be a citizen of the world.

5

It is the individual who speaks and writes; and in his language activity dialect and register combine. In the dialect range, the finer the distinctions that are recognized, the smaller, in terms of number of speakers, the unit which we postulate as the dialect community becomes. Eventually we reach the individual. The individual is, so to speak, the smallest dialect unit: each speaker has his own IDIOLECT.

Even the homogeneity of the idiolect is a fiction, tenable only so long as we continue to treat language SYNCHRONICALLY, in abstraction from time. As soon as we consider DIACHRONIC varieties of language, taking in the dimension of persistence and change in time, we have to recognize that changes take place not only in the transmission of language from one generation to the next but also in the speech habits of the individual in the course of his life.

Literacy retards linguistic change. But even in a community with a high literacy rate we can usually observe some differences in speech between successive generations. The individual member of the dialect community may retain his own idiolect unchanged; or he may adopt some features of the dialect of the next generation, even consciously adjusting his language performance to incorporate the neologisms of the young. At the least these will enter into his receptive use of language. In this sense the smallest dialectal unit is not the individual but the individual at a certain period in his life. Here we are approaching the theoretical limit of delicacy on the dialect dimension.

In the register range, the countless situations in which language activity takes place can be grouped into situation types, to which correspond the various uses of language. A corpus of language text in a given use is marked off by its formal properties as a register. Registers, like dialects, can be more and more finely differentiated; here again we can approach a theoretical limit of delicacy, at least in imagination, by progressive sub-classification of features of field, mode and style.

Ultimately, register and dialect meet in the single speech event. Here we have reached the UTTERANCE, the smallest institutional unit of language activity. In arriving through dialect and register at the 'piece of activity', we complete the circuit which led from this in the first place, via the description of substance and form, through context, to language in use. Viewed descriptively, the speech event was the occurrence of a formal item 'expounded' in substance. Viewed institutionally, it is an utterance in a situation, identifiable by dialect and register.

In the last resort, since each speaker and each situation is unique, each single utterance is also itself unique. But, as we saw at the beginning, the uniqueness of events is irrelevant to their scientific description, which can only begin when different events are seen to be partially alike. We become interested in one piece of language activity when we can show that it has something in common with another.

It is possible to group together a limited number of utterances according to what they have in common in dialect and register. One way of so delimiting a language variety is to retrace our steps a little up these two scales, to where we meet the individual as a participant in numerous situations. We can then define a set of language events as the language activity of one individual in one register. This intersection of idiolect and register provides an institutional definition of individual style.

Some registers are extremely restricted in purpose. They thus employ only a limited number of formal items and patterns, with the result that the language activity in these registers can accommodate little idiolectal or even dialectal variety. Such registers are known as RESTRICTED LANGUAGES. This is by no means a clearly defined category: some restricted languages are more restricted than others. Extreme examples are the 'International Language of the Air', the permitted set of wartime cable messages for those on active service, and the bidding code of contract bridge. Less restricted are the various registers of legal and official documents and regulations, weather forecasts, popular song lyrics, and verses on greeting cards. All these can still be regarded as restricted languages.

The individual may still sometimes be recognizable even under the impersonal uniformity of a restricted language. This is often due to PARALINGUISTIC features: these are features, such as voice quality and handwriting, which do not carry formal contrasts. (In languages in which voice quality does carry formal contrasts it is not paralinguistic but linguistic.) Such features, like the phonetic and phonological characteristics by which an individual is sometimes marked out, will appear in a restricted language just as in an unrestricted register. Occasionally we even come across individual formal patterns in a restricted language: there is the bridge player who expects her partner, but not her opponent, to interpret correctly her private structural distinction between 'one club' and 'a club'.

Except in restricted languages, it is normally assumed that individuals will differ in their language performance. In spoken registers the individual may stand out within his own dialect community through idiosyncratic phonetic habits. That he would of course stand out in a dialect community other than his own is trivial, since it is no more relevant to his linguistic individuality than the fact that an Englishman would stand out in France by speaking English. Even phonology gives some scope to individual variety: the present authors pronounce 'transparent plastic' in three phonologically different ways. Graphological practice is more uniform: we no longer tolerate individual spelling, though punctuation is allowed to vary somewhat.

Nevertheless, even in written registers the individual stands out. His language is distinctive at the level of form. A person's idiolect may be identified, through the lens of the various registers, by its grammatical and lexical characteristics. This is how we recognize the individual qualities of a particular writer. All linguistic form is either grammar or lexis, and in the first instance it is the grammatical and lexical features of the individual writer's language, together with a few features of punctuation, that constitute his 'style'.

Individual style, however, is linked to register. It is the writer's idiolect, especially the grammar and lexis of the idiolect, in a given register. In so far as 'style' implies literary style, register here means literary, including poetic, genre and medium. Style is thus linguistic form in interrelation with literary form.

If we refer to 'the style of Pope' we presumably imply that there is something in common to the language of the *Essays*, the *Satires* and other works: that they constitute in some sense a single idiolect. In fact, 'style', like other, related concepts, must be recognized to be variable in delicacy: each genre, and each individual work, has its style. If it is assumed from the start that two texts are alike, the differences between them may be missed or distorted. It is a sound principle of descriptive linguistics to postulate heterogeneity until homogeneity is proved, and the study of literary texts is no exception. By treating the *Satires* and the *Essays* as different registers we can display the similarities as well as the dissimilarities between them.

Literature forms only a small part of written language, but it is the part in which we are most aware of the individual and most interested in the originality of the individual's language. At the same time it is of the essence of creative writing that it calls attention to its own form, in the sense that unlike other language activity,

4+L.S.L.T.

written or spoken, it is meaningful as activity in itself and not merely as part of a larger situation: again, of course, without a clear line of demarcation. This remains true whether or not the writer is consciously aiming at creating an individual variety. Thus the linguistic uniqueness of a work of literature is of much greater significance than the individuality of a variety of language in any other use.

The language activity of one user in one use: this concept will serve as the fundamental variety of a language. Such an individual variety is a product of both dialect and register, and both are involved in its study.

Dialectology is a long-established branch of linguistic studies. In Britain, which has lagged notably behind other European countries and the United States, large scale dialect survey work did not begin until after the Second World War; but the three national surveys now being conducted at the universities of Leeds, Edinburgh and Wales have amassed a large amount of material and the first results are now in course of publication.

Serious work on registers is even more recent in origin. Very large samples of texts have to be subjected to detailed formal analysis if we wish to show which grammatical and lexical features are common to all uses of the language and which are restricted to, or more frequent in, one or more particular register. Such samples are now being collected and studied at University College London, in the Survey of English Usage under the direction of Professor Randolph Quirk; and related work is in progress at the universities of Edinburgh and Leeds. The study of registers is crucial both to our understanding of how language works and in application to literary analysis, machine translation and native and foreign language teaching.

6

Languages in contact, dialects and registers are three of the major topics of institutional linguistics. The fourth and last to be considered is the observation of the attitudes of members of a language community towards their language and its varieties. Here we mention briefly some of the attitudes that are relevant to the present discussion, with commentary where necessary.

Most communities show some reverence for the magical powers of language. In some societies, however, this respect is mingled with, and may be eclipsed by, a newer set of attitudes much more disdainful of the language, or of a part of it. The value judgments that underlie these attitudes may be moral or aesthetic, or they may rest on a pragmatic appeal to efficiency. The degree of social sanction they carry varies according to the language community; but whether the judgments and attitudes are social or individual, the individual expounding them frequently claims objectivity for his opinions. A typical formulation is: 'Obviously it is better (or: 'Everybody agrees that it is better') to say, or write, this than that, because' either 'it's clearer' or 'it sounds better' or 'it's more correct'. Less common, and more sophisticated, are 'because the best people do it' and 'because I prefer it'.

The most far-reaching among such value judgments are those passed on whole languages. Those who argue that it is necessary for English to remain the language of government, law, education or technology in former colonies sometimes claim, in support of their view, that the national languages are not suitable for these purposes. This reason is even put forward by the native speakers of the languages concerned.

The arguments for and against the use of English in such situations are complex; but this particular factor is irrelevant, because it is not true. This misapprehension, that some languages are intrinsically better than others, cannot just be dismissed as ignorance or prejudice; it is a view held by people who are both intelligent and serious, and can bring forward evidence to support it. Nevertheless it is wholly false and can do a great deal of harm.

Essentially, any language is as good as any other language, in the sense that every language is equally well adapted to the uses to which the community puts it. There is no such thing as a 'primitive' language. About the origins of language, nothing is known; there is merely a tangle of conflicting speculation, none of it falling within linguistics. But there is evidence that speech in some form goes back at least a hundred thousand years, and quite certainly no society found in the world today, or known to us in history, represents anything but a stage long after language had become a fully developed form of social activity. If historians or anthropologists use 'primitive' as a technical term, to designate a certain stage of social development, then the term may be transferred to the language used by a community that is in that stage; but this is *not* a linguistic classification and tells us nothing whatever about the nature of the language concerned.

Among the languages in the world today, there is no recognizable dimension of *linguistic* progress. No language can be identified as representing a more highly developed state of language than any other. Worora, in Western Australia, is as well adapted to the needs of the community which developed it as English is to our own. Neither language could be transferred to the other society without some changes, because the needs and activities are different; in both cases new lexical items would have to be added. But only the lexis would be affected, and only a portion of that. There would be no need for any changes in the grammar. At most there might be a statistical tendency for certain grammatical changes to take place over a very long period; but no simple change would be predictable in any given instance, none would be bound to occur, and certainly none would be necessary to the continued efficiency of the language.

In other words, the changes that would be necessary in Worora, for it to operate as a full language in the modern world, would be those that were also necessary to English as it was before the modern period. Middle English, even Elizabethan English, was not adapted to the needs of a modern state either. One could no more describe an electronic computer in Middle English than in Worora. Different languages have different ways of expanding their lexis, determined by their own internal structure: Chinese, for example, coins scientific terminology in a very different way from Japanese, being a language of a very different type. But all languages are capable of incorporating the lexical additions they require.

Whether or not it is economically feasible for the language of a very small community to be used as a medium for all the purposes of the modern world is of course an entirely different question, which each community has the right to decide for itself. It is worth pointing out that in the next generation machine translation will probably have become efficient enough, and cheap enough, to overcome the problem of translating all the material such a community would need to have translated from other languages. Whatever considerations may affect the choice of a language for science or administration in a newly independent nation, this at least can be made clear: all languages are equally capable of being developed for all purposes, and no language is any less qualified to be the vehicle of modern science and technology than were English and Russian some centuries ago.

A type of language that particularly attracts adverse value judgments is the mixed language. As long as this remains a pidgin, it can be nobody's L1 and has not the status of a language; it exists only in certain restricted varieties. But in those communities which have developed a mixed language as their L1, the new language has thereby gained full stature and become a completely effective medium of language activity. *? note its lexical borrowing of nat lang?*

In any case a creole is only an extreme result of a normal phenomenon in the development of language: linguistic borrowing. There is no reason why a language with such a history should be less effective than any other. They are languages in the defined sense of the word; some of them are already used as literary media, and they would be fully viable as media of education and science. At present they tend to be more discriminated against than languages with a more conventional history. But there is no justification for discriminating against any language whatever. In most parts of the world today, including Britain, there has to be some measure of linguistic policy and planning; decisions may have to be taken, for example, to establish certain languages as the national languages of a new nation. What matters is that the real issues and problems should not be allowed to become clouded by false notions that one language may be objectively inferior to another.

Many speakers from communities whose languages is in some or other respect denied full status, while they would not maintain that their own L1 was in any way inferior, and might vigorously reject such a suggestion, nevertheless in their language activity, as speakers, accept and thereby help to perpetuate its diminished status. In countries where English, or some other L2, is the mark of education and social standing, conversation in the government office or college staff common room normally takes place in English. Alternatively, if the L1 is allowed into these surroundings, no sentence in it is complete without at least one item from English.

This is sometimes explained on the grounds that the speakers do not share a common L1, as indeed they may not. It often is in countries which face a really difficult national language problem that a foreign language flourishes as a lingua franca. As is well known, many speakers from minority communities, whose language is not a strong candidate for national status, so firmly oppose the claims of any other language from within the country that they prefer to assign this status to a foreign language, which at least has the merit of being neutral. Probably this is at best a temporary solution; moreover there is reason to suggest that shelving the problem makes it more difficult to solve in the future.

But the lacing of L1 utterances with L2 items is not confined to multilingual societies. It is likely to happen wherever a foreign language is a mark of social distinction and the sole medium of language activity in certain registers. English probably occupies this position more than any other language. There are of course no grounds on which the linguist, who observes and describes this phenomenon, could object to it as a use of language: it works. But he may also reasonably point out that the use of English in situations for which the L1 is adequately developed, and of English items in L1 utterances where L1 items are available, tends to inhibit the progress of the L1 towards regaining its full status in the community. *cf. 101 'borrowing'. same argum also applies to C16 England — & later.*

7

Within our own language community, value judgments on English as a whole are relatively rare. Occasionally one hears it compared unfavourably with French, by those who subscribe to the myth, sedulously kept alive by the French themselves, that French is a 'more logical' language. What are extremely common, however, are value judgments on varieties of English: sometimes referring to registers but principally to dialects. The English language community, especially the British section of it, is almost certainly unique in the extent to which its members pass judgment on varieties of their language. One of the few other communities that at all resembles us in this respect is the French. The English attitudes are of course bound up with the socio-regional character of our dialects; as such, they are class attitudes rather than individual attitudes. Nearly all the widely accepted value judgments can be traced to this origin, though some reflect it more directly than others.

It is at the new urban dialects, the varieties of the standard language with regional accent, that the most severe criticisms are levelled. The 'original' dialects, now confined to the rural areas, have become quaint. They are tolerated; sometimes they may be praised, as 'soft', 'pleasant', or even 'musical'. And, somewhat inconsistently, though it is the rural dialects which provide the only instances of pairs of mutually unintelligible varieties remaining in England, it is often on grounds of incomprehensibility that criticism is directed at the urban dialects.

Perhaps the most frequent complaint is that formulated in various terms implying some sort of linguistic decay. The urban dialects are said to be 'slovenly', 'careless' or 'degenerate'. Similar terms were used about English and French in the nineteenth century, by those who regarded all recent linguistic change as a process of degeneration and decay. It is implied, and sometimes stated explicitly, that in the urban dialects there has been some loss of the communicative power of language.

This is simply nonsense. All the dialects, including all forms of standard English, are subject to change, both through the normal tendency of language to change and as a result of external factors such as movement of populations. Rate of change in language varies considerably, between different languages, between dialects, and at different times and places; even at different levels within the same variety of a language. English has altered rather strikingly over the last thousand years; the dialect now functioning as standard English is one of those that has changed the most, though it is difficult to measure comparative rates of change very accurately.

To the way of thinking that these attitudes represent, probably the slovenliest people in the world would be the French and the north Chinese: Parisian and Pekingese are the result of a high rate of change over long periods. There is no difference between the type of change undergone by these two languages and that which has affected the dialectal varieties of English, including the dialect that has become standardized and its modern regional derivatives.

There is actually no such thing as a slovenly dialect or accent. That the dialect of Sheffield or Birmingham has evolved in a different direction from one's own is hardly a matter for reproach, and anyone who labels it 'debased' is committing two errors. First, he is assuming that one type of standard English preserves an earlier variety of the language from which others have deviated; this is not true. Second, he is claiming that there is merit in this imagined conservation; if there was, such merit might appropriately be claimed by the Italians, the Cantonese and the Germans in reproach to their slovenly neighbours the French, the Pekingese and the English.

Traditionally, this charge of debasement rested on straight-forward moral grounds: it was wrong and irresponsible to let the language fall into decay. More recently the same imputed short-coming has come to be criticized from another point of view, that of loss of efficiency. Since the fault is imaginary, the grounds on which it is censured might seem unimportant. But one comment at least is called for. Many people, including for a time some linguists, have been taken in by the spurious rigour of some pseudo-scientific 'measurements' of the 'efficiency' of language. There is no evidence whatever that one language, or one variety of a language, can be more efficient than another. Nor is there, either in our intuitive judgment or yet in mathematics or linguistics, any means of measuring whatever such efficiency might be. Information theory, which has a place in the quantitative description of a language, implies nothing about the relative efficiency of languages or the effectiveness of language activity.

A second accusation has been brought against the urban dialects that is somewhat different from that of slovenliness, in either its moral or its utilitarian form. This is an aesthetic criticism. The dialects are labelled 'harsh', 'grating', 'guttural'—this probably refers to the higher frequency, in some varieties, of glottal closure unaccompanied by oral stops—or simply 'ugly'.

Here the person judging is on safer ground, if he means that he personally does not like the sound of certain varieties of English: no one can dispute that. The formulation may be a general one, but there is a broad human tendency to generalize one's prejudices, and we probably all know people who would not distinguish between 'I dislike the sound of Cardiff English' and 'Cardiff English is ugly'.

It is true that there is often a wide range of agreement in these aesthetic judgments. What is not realized, however, is that they are usually learnt. An Indian brought up in the Indian musical tradition will not agree with European judgments on European music, and a European who does not know the Chinese language and Chinese cultural values does not appreciate—that is, agree with Chinese judgments of—the sounds of Chinese poetry. Whether or not the adult ever does produce an unconditioned aesthetic response, in general what we like is as much a result of what we have learnt to like socially as of what we have grown to like individually. In language, we know already that people from different language communities respond quite differently to the aesthetic qualities of the dialects of a given language: a Persian or a Japanese not knowing English would be as likely to prefer Birmingham to RP as the other way round. The chief factor in one's evaluation of varieties of a language is social conditioning: there is no universal scale of aesthetic judgment. Those who dislike the Birmingham accent often do so because they know that their children will stand a better chance in life if they do not acquire it.

It is thus the socio-regional pattern of English dialect distribution that gives rise to both the aesthetic and the moral or pragmatic value judgments on the urban and rural dialects, in so far as these judgments are held in common by a large section of our language community. In many countries such judgments either are not passed at all or, if they are, are regarded both by those who pass them and by those who listen to them as subjective expressions of personal taste. Foreign students in Britain listen in polite wonder while their teatime hosts in Leeds or Manchester explain how important it is that they should not copy the speech of their landladies: 'everybody agrees', they are told, that this is an ugly, distorted form of English.

Not everybody does agree, in fact: such views seem to be most general among speakers of mildly regional varieties of Standard English. But when these attitudes are shared by those who themselves speak the dialect, and no other, they become rather harmful. A speaker who is made ashamed of his own language habits suffers a basic injury as a human being: to make anyone, especially a child, feel so ashamed is as indefensible as to make him feel ashamed of the colour of his skin.

Various courses of instruction are available in spoken English, under headings such as 'Speech and Drama', 'Elocution' and 'Normal Voice and Speech'. In general three different kinds of instruction take place. The first is concerned with techniques of speaking on the stage and in public; this is a form of applied phonetics, and is often very successful. The second is concerned with personal attainments such as voice quality and clarity in speech, and is often linked to aspects of social behaviour under the general heading of 'developing the personality'; these aspects lie outside the scope of application of linguistics or phonetics.

In the third type of instruction, which is again applied phonetics, the individual is taught to use some accent of English other than

4*

the one he has acquired naturally. This may be for particular professional purposes, as in the schools where dance-band leaders and pop singers can acquire the pronunciation considered appropriate to their calling, and the courses in which actors, for the purpose of character parts, may learn reasonable imitations of regional accents or at least a conventional Mummerset. It may, on the other hand, be for general social purposes; classes are held where those who speak with a regional accent can learn a pronunciation which they have found carries greater social prestige and better prospects of employment. Here the teaching is catering for social attitudes to language; but they are still recognized as social attitudes.

In the extreme forms of such accent-teaching, however, the particular accent taught is extolled by those who teach it as 'more beautiful' and 'better' than any other. This accent is generally a variety of RP with a number of special vowel qualities and lip postures. Sometimes the speech of a particular individual is held up as a model for imitation; but more often an absolute aesthetic merit is claimed for the way of speaking that is taught. Some of the teachers have themselves been taught that there is a scale of values on which vowels may be judged, ranging from 'bad and ugly' to 'good and beautiful'. The teacher is thus attempting to alter the speech of her pupils for reasons which seem to her sensible and obvious, but which are inexplicable to most of the pupils. The view that some sounds are inherently higher or lower than others on an absolute scale of aesthetic values has no evidence to support it, though it is of interest to phoneticians to know how widely it is held.

Perhaps the most uncomfortable of all the conflicts of approach between linguists and phoneticians on the one hand and teachers of 'speech' (who may invoke the authority of these disciplines) on the other, are those centring on the subject commonly known as 'Normal Voice and Speech'. This subject is included within the curriculum for speech therapists, in which phonetics also plays a prominent part. 'Normal' here is used prescriptively; the assumption is that one particular accent of English is in some way 'normal', all others being 'abnormal', and that the 'normal' accent is RP. Such judgments, as we have seen, reflect no property of the accent itself, but merely the social standing of those who have acquired it.

If all the patients treated by speech therapists belonged to this group, the confusion would do no actual harm. But those with speech defects are a representative cross-section of the whole population, the majority of whom do not speak RP, so that the background provided by 'Normal Voice and Speech' is both culturally loaded and, for many, therapeutically irrelevant. Many phoneticians continue to provide courses for students of speech therapy because they hope to give an objective training which will counterbalance the prescriptive nature of 'Normal Voice and Speech'; but the harnessing of two such differently conceived subjects in a single course can only be likened to an attempt to combine astronomy with domestic science, or perhaps rather chemistry with alchemy.

8

The English tendency to linguistic intolerance is not confined to strictures on the sounds of language. Value judgments also flourish in grammar. In grammar, however, the features subjected to those judgments are on the whole not dialectal. Many dialectal grammatical patterns pass unnoticed in speech provided the speaker is using the phonetics of RP: even such a markedly regional clause structure as that exemplified by 'they've never been to see us haven't the Joneses' is tolerated in spoken English if the accent is an acceptable one. It would not on the other hand be tolerated in writing.

In grammar we have a set of arbitrary prescriptions and proscriptions relating to particular patterns and items. Some are applied to written English only, others to both spoken and written. Neither the prescribed nor the proscribed forms correspond to any particular regional varieties. As with the dialectal prescriptions, there are various ways of giving a bad name to the proscribed forms: they are called 'slipshod' and 'crude', sometimes simply 'wrong'. 'Incorrect', taken from a different register, is sometimes used as if it was an explanation of 'wrong'.

In this context 'slipshod' and 'crude' are meaningless, and a native speaker of English who happened not to know which of a pair of forms was approved and which censured would have no evidence whatsoever for deciding. As effective language activity, there is nothing to choose between 'do it as I do' and 'do it like I do', just as soup has the same food value however it is eaten (or whether it is 'eaten' or 'drunk'). 'Wrong' is a social judgment:

what is meant is 'the best people use this form and not that form'. These are in effect social conventions about language, and their function is that of social conventions: meaningless in themselves, they exert cohesive force within one society, or one section of a society, by marking it off from another.

As we have seen, all languages have formally distinct varieties. What is unusual about the language situation in Britain is the extent to which rules are consciously formulated for what is regarded as appropriate grammatical behaviour. Other communities have sometimes attempted to impose patterns of linguistic form, generally without much success; at the most, what is prescribed is the distinction between the spoken and the written language, some forms being rejected as inappropriate to the latter. Conventions in the spoken language are normally confined to lexical taboos: certain items are not to be used before children, strangers or members of the opposite sex. In Britain, rules are made for speech as well as for writing, and the speaker's grammar contributes, alongside his phonetics and phonology, to his identification on the social scale.

Since 'incorrect' linguistic behaviour whether dialectal or otherwise may be counted against one in many situations, the solution chosen by many speakers, in face of the prevalent attitudes, is to acquire a second idiolect. Indeed so strong is the feeling that there are correct and incorrect forms of linguistic behaviour that if one asks, as the present writers have asked many groups of university students, 'what is the purpose of the teaching of English in English schools?' a frequent answer is 'to teach the children to speak and write correct English'. The old observation that parents in the new dialect regions send their children to school so that they can be taught to 'talk proper' is by no means out of date. The subject of native language teaching is taken up in Chapter 8; suffice it to say here that if children have to learn new speech habits, it is the social attitude to their dialect, and no fault of the dialect itself, that is forcing them to do this: at least they need not be taught that their own speech is in some way inferior or taboo.

Some voices are raised against the prevailing attitudes, and some of the rules are occasionally called into question. Priestley once wrote, in *English Journey* (London, Heinemann in association with Gollancz, 1934, p. 290), 'Standard English is like standard anything else—poor tasteless stuff'. Hugh Sykes-Davies, in *Grammar Without Tears* (London, The Bodley Head, 1951, pp. 131–2), suggested reversing the polarity of prescription and proscription: 'the use of the indirect cases of *who* should be avoided wherever possible by putting the preposition at the end of the sentence, and making *that* the relative, or omitting the pronoun altogether. It is better to say "the man I found the hat of" than "the man whose hat I found"'. But here the speaker is still being told how to behave; there is still a right and a wrong in language.

Serious interest in dialectal varieties of the language is fostered by such bodies as the Yorkshire Dialect Society, which publishes both literary work in, and academic studies of, the Yorkshire dialects, urban as well as rural. Detailed surveys of the dialects of England, Wales and Scotland are, as has been mentioned, now well advanced. The Linguistic Survey of Scotland takes account of urban varieties of Scots; and although the English Dialect Survey has not yet turned its attention to the new dialects in England this is because the original, now rural, dialects are fast disappearing and must be recorded first. And teachers and university students seem to be becoming increasingly aware of the artificial and arbitrary nature of the conventional notions of 'good English' and 'bad English'.

Interwoven with the highly prescriptive attitudes towards the linguistic behaviour of individuals is a strong protective feeling for the language as a whole. Unlike the selective judgments, which are rare among language communities, the defensive 'leave our language alone' attitude is very commonly found. Perhaps the most striking instance of this in Britain is the fierce resistance to any suggestions for spelling reform. So strong is the feeling against it that it seems unlikely at present that any orthographic revision of English will be undertaken for a long time.

Here again China provides an interesting example for comparison. Because of the complexity of the Chinese script, and the fact that it acts as a barrier to linguistic unification, at various times during the last fifty years suggestions have been made for its replacement by a phonological script; a number of versions have been devised, some using the roman alphabet and others not. In 1956 one romanized version was officially adopted as an auxiliary script for limited purposes, and its use has been very gradually extending; whether it will ever generally replace Chinese characters remains to be seen.

It has been argued that if the English expect their language to operate as an international medium they should consider reforming the script in the interests of foreign learners. On the other hand any project for doing so would face enormous difficulties. The linguist, as a linguist, does not take sides in this issue, though as a private citizen he may; but he is qualified to act as a consultant, and to make suggestions as to how best to revise the orthography if it is once decided to do so. Apart from this, the role of linguistics at this stage is to help clear the air for rational discussion of the problem, as of all the other problems that are raised by the complex and deep-rooted attitudes of the members of a language community towards their language.

BIBLIOGRAPHY

See items 12, 24, 38, 45, 49, 57, 75, 88.

Chapter 5

Comparison and translation

1

Throughout at least the recent history of foreign language teaching there has been a conflict of opinion on the question whether it is useful, when teaching a foreign language, to make some comparison with the native one. One view rejects comparison altogether: it clearly has no place in anything like the 'direct method', where the language under instruction is also the language of instruction and no use is made of the learners' native language. Comparison may be excluded, of course, not only as a result of the deliberate application of a pedagogical theory but also from force of circumstances: where, for example, the pupils have no common native language, or where the pupils have a common native language but the teacher does not know it. There are numerous foreign language classes all over the world in which for theoretical or, more often, for practical reasons the use of comparison between the native and the foreign language does not arise.

Whether or not this situation predominates, there are also many classes in which regular use is made of the native language; and there are those who hold the view that, where circumstances permit, the native language has a positive and definable role in foreign language teaching. Again, a wide divergence of views is possible within this general approach. One may regard the native language as a medium of instruction standing in the same relation to the language under instruction as it does to a non-language subject such as mathematics or history: in this view the relation of L1 to L2 is the normal relation of medium to subject-matter. Or the relation of language of instruction to language under instruction may be regarded as a special and unique case of the medium to subject-matter relation, in that the two can be systematically compared. Such comparison may again take a variety of different forms: the explanation of categories of L2 by reference to categories of L1, the use of translation in either or both directions, the treatment of errors based on diagnosis as 'negative transfer' (the carrying over of inappropriate patterns from L1), and so on.

The issue of whether to use the native language or not is thus a matter partly of circumstance and partly of pedagogical theory; it cannot be resolved by reference to linguistics. If the native language is to be used, however, it is important to know what possibilities exist for using it. What can be answered within linguistics is the question how two languages can best be brought into relation with one another. The answer will suggest the possibilities that exist for using the native language in foreign language teaching; the teacher can select those that are appropriate to his own methods in the given situation. If comparison is to be done it should be done well; otherwise it may hinder rather than help. The theories and methods for the comparison of languages, including theory of translation, belong to the branch of the subject known as 'Comparative Linguistics'.

Comparative linguistics is probably more familiar in its historical dimension, comparative historical linguistics; and within that field especially the historical comparison of genetically related languages, known as 'comparative philology'. Comparative philology is an old-established and important branch of the linguistic sciences. It has provided a detailed picture of the evolution of the great and prolific language families, such as Indo-European, Semitic and Sino-Tibetan, as well as a general account of the nature of linguistic change. It is not, however, this kind of comparative linguistics that is relevant to foreign language teaching. For language teaching purposes the relevant dimension is not the historical one but the descriptive one: what is needed is a method for comparing languages according to how they work, not according to how they have evolved. The theory and method for comparing the working of different languages is known either as 'Comparative Descriptive Linguistics' or as 'Contrastive Linguistics'. Since translation can be regarded as a special case of this kind of comparison, comparative descriptive linguistics includes the theory of translation.

2

There are two fundamental principles of comparative descriptive linguistics: one is 'describe before comparing', the other is 'compare patterns, not whole languages'. The first is no doubt obvious: one cannot compare how things work if one has not first described how each of them works. It might be enough to have understood how each of them works, without having written a description down on paper; but there is a danger in this, of thinking one has understood more than one has. The teacher who wants to make use of the native language for comparative purposes in foreign language teaching must therefore know something about it. It is not enough that he should be able to speak it: he must also be able to describe it.

The second principle may seem equally obvious, but it is in fact often not understood. There can be no question of, say, 'comparing English and Urdu'. Each language is a complex of a large number of patterns, at different levels and at different degrees of delicacy: a 'system of systems', in one well-known formulation. There can be no single, general statement accounting for all of these, and therefore no overall comparative statement accounting for the difference between two languages. One may be able to compare, for instance, the nominal group of English with the nominal group of Urdu, or English clause structure with Urdu clause structure; but one cannot generalize from these two comparisons. In no sense can it be said that English clause structure is to Urdu clause structure as the English nominal group is to the Urdu nominal group. (Or rather it can be said only in the institutional sense, here trivial, that the first are used by English speakers and the second by Urdu speakers.) Each pattern-comparison must be made independently and in its own right. This is not to say, of course, that one cannot then put all such comparative statements together into a book and call it 'The comparison of English and Urdu'. But it is impossible to abstract from the comparative statements any general formulation of 'the difference between', or 'the likeness between', the two languages.

What can be done in comparative descriptive linguistics, then, is to make detailed and useful comparisons of particular patterns in two or more languages once these have been described. Every comparative statement presupposes three steps: first, the separate description of the relevant features of each language; second, the establishment of comparability; third, the comparison itself. The second step is worth making explicit: before comparing the nominal group in English with the nominal group in French it is desirable to establish that they are comparable. A brief illustration of the way comparison proceeds is given in the next few paragraphs.

Let us consider the personal deictics or 'possessive adjectives' of English, French and Russian. The systems can be briefly tabulated as follows:

English

PERSON:	
I	my
I +	our
2(+)	your
3 masc.	his
3 fem.	her
3 +	their

French

HEAD OF NOMINAL GROUP: PERSON:	SINGULAR		PLURAL
	masc.	fem.	
I	mon	ma	mes
2 ins.	ton	ta	tes
3	son	sa	ses
I +	notre		nos
2 outs., 2 +	votre		vos
3 +	leur		leurs

Russian

HEAD OF NOMINAL GROUP: PERSON:	SINGULAR			PLURAL
	masc.	fem.	neut.	
INTENSIVE	svoj	svoja	svojo	svoi
EXTENSIVE I	moj	moja	mojo	moi
2 ins.	tvoj	tvoja	tvojo	tvoi
1 +	naš	naša	naše	naši
2 outs., 2 +	vaš	vaša	vaše	vaši
3 masc.	jego			
3 fem.	jejo			
3 +	ich			

Notes: 1   speaker
2   addressee (person spoken to)
3   other participant
+   more than one participant
ins.   insider (addressee treated as familiar)
outs.   outsider (addressee treated as non-familiar)
intensive   participant already referred to in (nominal group operating as subject of) same clause
extensive   participant not so referred to
( )   with or without

To establish that these are comparable, we first need to show their contextual equivalence; this can be done most simply by reference to translation. If the items are not at least sometimes equivalent in translation, they are not worth comparing. Here there is a fair probability of translation equivalence, although we observe certain circumstances under which this is not fulfilled, as when 'I've hurt my foot' is translated into French or Russian. Having decided that the sets of items are comparable, we ask to what extent they are formally equivalent.

All three languages display the units 'clause', 'group' and 'word'; the 'group' is the unit entering into clause structure, and the 'word' is that entering into group structure. Although the elements of clause structure are not identical, we can recognize in each language a class 'nominal' of the unit 'group' which operates, among other things, as 'subject' of the clause. Each language has a word class 'noun', defined as operating normally as head of the nominal group; and a word class 'deictic' which may occur in the same nominal group together with a noun. The personal deictics form a sub-class within this class. They also form a closed system. So much for the likenesses; we can now note some formal differences.

(1)   In all three languages the personal deictics are in contrast with other deictics, such as the demonstrative ones 'this, that'; but the total ranges are different: Russian, for example, has no item comparable to 'the' or 'a'.

(2)   In Russian the personal deictic normally precedes, but may follow, the head of the nominal group; in English and French it can only precede it.

(3)   The Russian system includes the 'intensive' *svoj* in contrast to *all* the other personal deictics. (More delicately, three of the others,

moj, naš and *vaš*, vary with *svoj* as intensive; this is shown in the
subsequent table by a dotted line.) *svoj* never, except in the register
of proverbs, occurs in a nominal group which is the subject in a
clause. There is no comparable item in English or French.

(4)   Russian and French, but not English, show partial gender and
number concord—differently distributed in the two languages—
between the personal deictic and the head of the nominal group;
Russian also shows case concord.

Finally the principal contextual differences are as follows:

(1)   In Russian, but not in English or French, a participant already
referred to in the same clause is, with the proviso in (3) above,
indicated by a special 'second reference' item *svoj*: this is used
when the referent of the personal deictic in a nominal group *not*
operating as subject is the same as that of the subject of the clause.
So in 'I'm meeting my teacher', 'my' is translated by *svoj* (in the
appropriate case); in 'he's meeting his teacher', 'his' is translated
by *svoj* if the referent of 'his' is the same as that of 'he' and by *jego*
if it is not.

(2)   In Russian and French, but not in English, a distinction is
made between familiar and non-familiar address when one person
only is spoken to.

(3)   In Russian and English, but not in French, a distinction is
made between male and female when one 'other participant' is
referred to.

(4)   In English the personal deictics are regularly used in nominal
groups the head of which refers to a personal relation, a part of the
body, or an article of clothing or other 'intimate possession'. In
Russian they occur with nominal groups of these types only under
certain restricted conditions; likewise in French except with personal relations, where they are regular.

We can show the comparison in parallel tables, ignoring for the
sake of simplicity the categories determined by concord (page 117).
Similar tabulation could of course be used to show the difference in
the relations of concord with the head of the nominal group. If
transparent material is used, the tables can be superposed on one
another to show the foreign language student where he must make
a choice which is not made in his own language. The method
emphasizes that comparison is the display of differences against a
background of likeness.

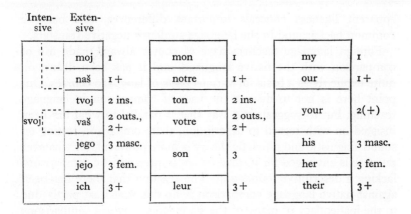

Intensive	Extensive						
	moj	1	mon	1	my	1
	naš	1+	notre	1+	our	1+
	tvoj	2 ins.	ton	2 ins.	your	2(+)
svoj	vaš	2 outs., 2+	votre	2 outs., 2+		
	jego	3 masc.	son	3	his	3 masc.
	jejo	3 fem.			her	3 fem.
	ich	3+	leur	3+	their	3+

3

Comparisons can of course be presented in a variety of different ways, corresponding to the different 'strata' referred to in Chapter 6. Since comparison depends on description, the better the underlying description the more successful the comparison is likely to be. It will be some time before full-scale systematic comparisons of languages are produced, if indeed they ever are: this will depend on how useful such overall studies would prove in the various applications to which comparison is relevant. But they are quite possible. As soon as any two languages have been described using the same theoretical categories, a work of reference could be provided to serve as a source for textbooks and other teaching materials; such a work would give a systematic comparison of the major patterns in the two languages at the level or levels concerned.

The levels primarily suitable for such overall systematic comparison are grammar and phonology. Systematic bilingual comparisons of this kind would do for grammar and phonology what the bilingual dictionary does, and a bilingual thesaurus could do, for lexis. At another stratum, the textbook for use in the classroom could draw on the general and more theoretical comparison, exactly as it draws on a general and more theoretical description, in dealing with particular problems. For example, 'faux amis' are not limited to lexis; drills may be called for at any level to cope with a feature comparable to one in the learner's native language where an apparent likeness conceals important differences, this being a common background to the language student's negative transfers.

Foreign language teachers have of course always made use of comparison with the native language, and it has been drawn on quite explicitly as a basis for various parts of language courses. Our point here is not to discuss the uses of comparison in language teaching, but to suggest, in a way that is parallel to what has been insisted on with regard to description, that comparison resting on sound linguistic and phonetic theory is more powerful, for whatever purpose is envisaged for it, than *ad hoc* impressionistic comparisons lacking a descriptive foundation. The reaction that there has been against native language comparison is no doubt at least partly due to the inadequacy of many of the statements of which comparisons traditionally consist. For example: 'The past definite, or preterite, *je portai*, corresponds to the English *I carried*' (Weekley, Ernest and Wyatt, A. J.: *Tutorial French Grammar*. London, University Tutorial Press, 1919, pp. 102, 103); this is subsequently modified by a 'fiction': 'The past indefinite is frequently used for the past definite in colloquial style'.

There is, however, one rather controversial use of comparison, in the discussion of which linguistic criteria are frequently invoked: this is in relation to error analysis and the 'interference' of the native language. There tends to be some misunderstanding here of the nature and role of comparison, and possibly some confusion between the diagnosis of errors and their prevention and cure. Certainly one can predict likely errors, and sources of error, by means of a good comparison. But when one asks what is the purpose of predicting errors, it becomes clear that three separate stages in the teaching are involved, and that comparison is relevant to only two of them.

In the first place, in the preparation of teaching material comparative methods can be applied both in finding out which features of the foreign language are the most likely sources of errors due to interference, and also in describing these features in such a way as to minimize their undesirable effect. For example, a good comparison of the tense systems of French and English would enable us not only to predict that here was a likely source of errors by English students of French, if we did not know this already from experience, but also to describe the French system in a way that would anticipate and forestall at least some of the errors. This is the preventive use of comparison. In the second place, comparative methods can be used in the explanation of errors which the student has committed and in the preparation of remedial exercises and drills designed to eliminate errors already observed. This is the stage of treatment and cure.

But the *diagnosis* of errors has nothing to do with comparison. Here the concern is with the analysis of an error, not with the study of its causes; and such analysis is a purely descriptive matter. Any error in English can be described with complete accuracy by reference solely to the description of English, without taking any account of the student's native language or even knowing what it is. Each error is stated as a specific deviation from a described English feature.

It is important to note that a given error can often be described in two or three ways, to each of which corresponds a different step that could be taken to correct it. For example, 'he asked a new book' could be corrected either to 'he asked for a new book' or to 'he requested a new book'; these will lead to two different analyses of the error, in this case as it happens at different levels: the one grammatical, the other lexical. Both analyses are valid.

It is extremely useful to construct a purely descriptive framework for the analysis and notation of errors, taking into account the level of language and the various categories involved. There are two ways of choosing between different analyses: this can be done either descriptively or comparatively. Descriptively, the analysis which yields a simpler correction will be preferred. 'Asked for' and 'requested' are each minimal corrections, in the sense that each involves only one step; but 'requested' involves a possible change of register and might therefore be inappropriate. It might, however, be decided that if an error can be shown to be explicable as native language interference, this explanation is to be preferred and exploited remedially. In this case the choice is made comparatively, that analysis being adopted which can best *be regarded as* due to interference. The teacher may regard this as the most effective way of treating an error even if he is not convinced that interference was the cause of it; in the last resort the cause is unknowable. Conversely the teacher faced with a class of students having different native languages may prefer the analysis which is most easily accounted for descriptively, since even if he thinks the error was due to interference he cannot exploit this in the classroom.

4

There is a special method for comparing the grammar of languages which differs somewhat from ordinary comparative descriptive; this is known as 'transfer comparison'. Comparison in the normal way brings together two languages which have been separately and independently described, with the categories appropriate to each; such comparison is therefore neutral, as it were, and gives equal weight to the languages concerned. In transfer comparison, on the other hand, one starts from the description of one language and then describes the second language in terms of the categories set up for the first. Traditional descriptions of English are in a sense transfer comparisons based on Latin; they might have been very useful for ancient Romans studying modern English.

Although a transfer comparison faces one way, as it were, this does not imply that it can be made effective without a prior description of both languages, since unless one has a clear picture of each it is difficult adequately to adapt the description of one to fit the categories of the other. What it means is that, both languages being fully understood, the picture of one of them is deliberately distorted by its being viewed through the matrix set up to account for the other.

It is doubtful whether it would ever be worth making a complete transfer comparison of one language with another. But the method has its uses in the treatment of particularly intractable language teaching problems, especially in cases of mutual exoticism, where the patterns being compared are so different that a straight comparison is always open-ended. It may happen, for example, that not only is it impossible to show one-to-one correspondence between the terms in the systems one wishes to compare, as for example between a particular tense in French and any single tense in English; but that there is even no correspondence between these systems, a system in the one language corresponding partially to two or more systems in the other.

An example would be the category of aspect in Russian, in a comparison with English. There is no exactly comparable system in English; but there is a correspondence with part of the English tense system. A straight comparison is of considerable theoretical interest, and useful, for example, in a machine translation programme. But for a language textbook it would be more useful to substitute a transfer comparison in which either the English verbal group was described as if it had aspect, or the Russian verbal group was described as if it had not. Either, that is, one uses the categories needed to describe both tense and aspect in Russian and distributes the English tense forms among them; or one distributes the forms operating in the two Russian systems among the terms of the English tense system.

The result is deliberately inaccurate, since the whole problem arises from the fact that one and the same form in one language may be the equivalent of more than one form in the other. But its value is that it highlights the areas and the extent of this non-equivalence more simply than a straight comparison would do. One can then concentrate on the areas of non-equivalence and attempt, by more delicate statements, to show the conditions under which one out of the possible equivalent forms may be preferred.

An example of a transfer comparison between English and French can be drawn from the systems of personal deictics already cited above (Section 2 of this chapter). This table shows the English system described in French categories:

HEAD OF NOMINAL GROUP: / PERSON:	SINGULAR		PLURAL
	masc.	fem.	
1	my	my	my
2 ins.	your	your	your
3	his/her	his/her	his/her
1 +	our		our
2 outs., 2 +	your		your
3 +	their		their

We have now distorted the description of English by foisting on the language a set of irrelevant categories and fictitious distinctions, exactly in the way that it was distorted in old-fashioned Latin-based grammars: for example in the statement: 'The noun or pronoun which forms the subject of a sentence is said to be in the nominative case . . . The subjects . . . "horse" and "master" . . . are in the nominative case.' (Palser, E. M. and Lewis, R. T.: *A New Outline Grammar of Function*. London: Harrap, 1923, p. 24.) But whereas

there are no ancient Romans learning English, there are many
French speakers doing so; and a comparison of this type may sometimes help them. In the present example we have left out, for the
sake of simplicity and clarity, several important features of non-
equivalence, such as the occurrence of the English items with
certain nouns which would not be found with personal deictics in
French. But the illustration shows how one can pinpoint the main
difficulty which the French pupil learning English will face: he must
select between 'his' and 'her', yet the selection is *not* determined
by any formal feature of the nominal group.

   The question arises in which direction to make the transfer.
Since the attention is being focused on the foreign language, the
natural procedure is to account for patterns of L2 by referring them
to patterns of L1. The transfer is thus L1-based: in other words, a
textbook of Russian for English students would describe some
Russian features by means of categories appropriate to English.
This corresponds closely to traditional practice in the writing of
textbooks; with the proviso that since in such cases the use of
transfer was unintentional and unformulated, no distinction is made
between description of the foreign language in its own terms and
transfer comparison in which the foreign language is made to look
like a strange variety of the native one.

   This latter point emphasizes the danger of L1-based transfer: it
may make the L2 in the long run more intractable by building in a
false appearance of similarity. Whatever happens the pupil must not
get the idea that he is learning an imperfect or misshapen copy of
his own language. For this reason there may be a place in foreign
language teaching for transfer in the opposite direction: for describing, at least in class if not in textbooks, parts of the native language
with the categories suited to the foreign one. The pupil can be
asked to imagine certain patterns of the foreign language operating
in his own, and to see what errors this leads to in the native language. It has often been pointed out that excellent practice in the
phonetics of a foreign language can be gained by learning to speak
one's own language with the appropriate foreign 'accent': imitating
a French accent in English is good for one's French. It would not
be possible to speak English with entirely French grammar. But it is
certainly possible, and useful, for an English pupil learning French
to look at the grammar of English as it were through French eyes.
This after all is partly what has kept traditional descriptions of

English grammar alive for so long; since they look at English through Latin eyes, they at least help the English pupil to learn Latin.

5

The relevance of comparative linguistics to foreign language teaching thus lies partly in this: that it makes it possible to compare features in different languages with a reasonable degree of accuracy and objectivity. There is, however, another matter falling within the field of comparative linguistics which is relevant here: this is translation. Translation again is a controversial topic, and its place in foreign language teaching is discussed below (Chapter 9). Here we are concerned with the nature of translation as language activity, and of 'a translation' as the product of such activity.

Translation as activity faces only one way; the translator observes an event in one language, the 'source' language, and performs a related event in another, the 'target' language. But the total result is two texts which stand in mutual relation: each is as it were 'a translation of' the other. A pair of texts related by translation stands to a comparative description of the languages concerned as a single text stands to a description.

If one says that a text is a special case of a linguistic description, in the sense that it is a description of itself, this is thought-provoking but in fact trivial: it is rather like saying that Beethoven's Fifth is a special case of a description of a symphony. But if one pursues the analogy, to say that a pair of texts in translation is a special case of a comparison, this ceases to be trivial, for this reason: that textual translation equivalence is itself one way of establishing comparability. That is to say, the occurrence of an item or pattern in language A, and of another item or pattern in language B, in actual use and under conditions that allow us to refer to these items as 'equivalent', is a piece of evidence of a kind that is crucial to useful comparative studies.

The nature of this equivalence is not formal but contextual. It is not formal correspondence that we accept as translation: if we are assessing whether an English text is an acceptable translation of a French one we do not judge it by whether each grammatical category has been replaced by its nearest formal equivalent, one clause always being rendered by one clause or an active verbal group always by an active verbal group. We regard translation as the relation between two or more texts playing an identical part in an identical situation. But this, like synonymy, is a 'more or less' not a 'yes or no' relation, since 'identical part' and 'identical situation' are not absolute concepts. In the first place, two situations in which the language activity is in different languages are *ipso facto* not identical: if a question is asked in German, the answer to that question is not operating in the same situation as the answer to a question in English, and both differ from a situation in which the question is asked and answered in German and the answer is then translated into English. More important, however, since less easily recognized and allowed for, is the second point: that situations vary across cultures. In thinking of the German translation equivalent of 'shall we go out for a drink?', one needs to consider the different drinking habits of the English and the Germans. What we can ask about two texts is therefore strictly speaking not 'are these in translation or not?', but 'how far are these in translation?'.

In practice in normal life we postulate a kind of threshold of acceptability for translations, at some point along the scale of 'more or less equivalent'. The point tends to shift with different registers: more 'accuracy' is required in certain situation types than in others, so that in these a translation must be 'more equivalent' before being accepted as equivalent at all. Since we have chosen to define equivalence by reference to the task performed by the language activity and not to its grammar and lexis, in other words by reference to contextual and not to formal meaning, we can neither measure the equivalence nor define the threshold. But the choice makes it possible to use translation as a criterion in the comparison of languages; it avoids the circularity that would arise if we assessed equivalence on the basis of formal similarity and then used this equivalence as evidence for saying that the forms were comparable. In other words it is only because we find that French 'j'ai soif' and English 'I'm thirsty' are *contextually* equivalent, at least in some situations, that we even begin to think of comparing them formally.

It is clear that only in relatively rare circumstances, usually in situations in which the language activity is playing only a small part, can we actually observe translation equivalence by direct reference to the situation. More often, and always in written language, we are dependent on other language activity for situational information. When we learn our native language, these two types of contextual evidence, from the situation and from the surrounding language or 'co-text', constitute all the evidence we have: the meaning of 'hot', for example, is that it is used, *inter alia*, (a) when we get too near the fire, and (b) in collocation with 'fire' and other such formal items.

Those who wish to make second language learning as much like native language learning as possible aim to construct teaching situations in which the pupil is confronted with the foreign language as he had been earlier with his native language. He then has the same kind of 'situational' help as is available to a child whose parents move to another language community. With those who are bilingual from an early age, it may happen that the two languages are never brought into relation with one another; even adults moving to a new language community may keep the new and the old language quite separate. In such cases one person is operating with two or more languages but without translating between them. If one is taught a second language, however, even by something approaching the 'direct method', one usually sets up patterns of translation equivalence. Either one is taught to do so, because the teaching uses the medium of translation; or, if it does not, one abstracts translation equivalence for oneself from the observation of the two languages in operation. Either I am told that 'chaise' means 'chair', or I arrive at this formulation for myself from observation of the objects to which 'chaise' is applied.

In one way or another translation equivalences come to be attached to grammatical categories and items, and to lexical items, as such. At first these may be thought of as one-to-one equivalences: 'chaise' = 'chair' in all occurrences. But the exact match is soon upset, and the more advanced learner substitutes a range of equivalents in both directions running from more to less probable. For example, I find I can usually replace 'avoir' plus complement by 'have' or 'have got' plus complement, but sometimes I must select 'be' plus complement instead, as in 'I'm thirsty'; similarly I can usually render 'chair' as 'chaise' but sometimes it will be 'fauteuil'. It is thus possible to view the *process* of translation as the progressive selection among categories and items in the target language that are recognized on contextual criteria as equivalent to categories and items in the source language, each category and item having a set of potential equivalents range on a scale of probability. We can then construct a model of this 'progressive selection', based on the grammatical scale of rank. Let us postulate for each item and category, at every rank, a 'most probable' equivalent that is the one selected in the absence of contrary evidence. For each item of, say, morpheme rank we first select this most probable equivalent. We then look at the rank next above, in English the word; here a new selection is made which may affect the previous selection, perhaps leading to the replacement of the most probable morpheme equivalent by a less probable one. This process is repeated through group and clause to sentence, each move leading to a re-examination of the selection just made. The sentence can be regarded as an upper limit, since it is seldom that translation at the rank of the sentence fails to produce an acceptable equivalent, whereas translation clause by clause does sometimes yield unacceptable versions which a move to the sentence will correct.

It is not of course suggested that this is how the translator actually proceeds: this is a model, not a description, of the process. The translator may never consciously formulate equivalents below the sentence. But the concept of equivalent items and categories at various ranks is a meaningful one; one can validly ask for English equivalents of 'chaise', 'pomme de terre', 'il', 'pourvu que' and the French imperfect tense. Which is 'most probable' in each case is at present impressionistic, although this could be established objectively by the study of large samples of texts in translation. The important point is that in each case translation at a given rank presupposes a choice and that the choice is made by reference to the rank above.

'Translation at ranks' can be displayed as in the following example. The sentence is from Colette: *Gigi* (Paris, Ferenczi, 1945, p. 73). The English translation by Roger Senhouse (Penguin Books, 1958, p. 48) has: 'She rubbed her cheeks with both fists, then ran to open the door'. The sentence is analysed here in written French, to avoid complicating the illustration by the use of a phonological transcription. Grammatical units are shown as in the table of 'Symbols'; each step in the translation corresponds to a particular rank in the French version, X indicating a grammatical category with no item equivalent at the rank in question. The example selected is a relatively straightforward one; nevertheless it demonstrates how for a particular translation problem, such as the rendering of 'se', one can formulate the nature and amount of information required for its solution.

Translation at rank of: ||| elle   se   frott+a+ | les+   joue+s |

rank									
morpheme	X	X	rub	X	X	X	X	cheek	X
word	she/her	X	rubbed			the		cheeks	
group	she	rubbed		herself		his/her		cheeks	
clause	she	rubbed				her		cheeks	

de   [ses+   deux   poing+s   ferm+é+s] ||

rank									
morpheme	X	X	X	two	fist	X	shut	X	X
word	of	his/her		two	fists		shut		
group	of	his/her	two		clenched		fists		
group	with	his/her	two		clenched		fists		
clause	with	her	two		clenched		fists		

et | cour+ut+   ouvr+ir | la   porte |||

rank								
morpheme	X	run	X	X	open	X	X	door
word	and	ran			open		the	door
group	and	ran	to		open		the	door
clause	and	ran	to		open		the	door.

This is a form of comparison, and it shows where in the target language a given choice is made; it also gives some indication of what factors determine the choice of one rather than another from among the range of possible equivalents. There is no need of course to start at the lowest rank in order to illustrate a given point; indeed the move from morpheme to word is of little interest except for special purposes and with certain languages, since no one would ever think of the morpheme as a unit of translation. What is called 'literal translation' turns out when viewed in this way to be translation somewhere between word and group. Since failure to look above the group is a common source of error in translation it is often worth examining the process from here upwards. But one can 'move in', as it were, at any rank wherever an important point arises: if a problem hinges on sentence structure, for example the choice of 'wenn' or 'als' in the German equivalent of 'when he went', one need not look below the rank of the clause.

A useful distinction can be drawn between two different ways in which selection at one rank is determined at the rank above. Either the selection may be referable to something in the source language, or it may not. For example, in translating 'a big house' into French, we have no evidence in the English text to show that 'big' should be 'grande' and not 'grand'; this arises from the fact that the French nominal group carries gender selected by the noun head and displayed in concord by other elements, a selection not reflected in any way in the English version. Even if the source language was German, gender could not be carried over, since there is no contextual equivalence between the terms in the two systems. The selection of 'grande' as opposed to 'grandes', however, can be referred to the English text. We must of course as always, in order to arrive at this equivalent, still take account of the relevant formal features of the target language, in this case the concord rules of French. But the selection of number is made in the English nominal group; moreover the selection can be carried over with a high probability of its remaining unaffected by considerations arising at a higher rank.

If this distinction is taken into account, the stages of the translation process could be summarized as: (1) selection of most probable translation equivalent for each category and item, and (2) modification of this selection at the unit next above, either (a) from evidence in the source language or (b) from internal features of the target language. Once again it should be stressed that this analysis represents a purely theoretical construct whose value, if any, lies in its usefulness in application. In so far as foreign language teaching is one possible field for the application of translation theory, this in turn rests on the place accorded to translation in a foreign language course.

6

It is not only through the place assigned to it in the foreign language course that translation is relevant to language teaching. As well as being a means to the learning of a foreign language it may also be the end towards which this study is directed. Some of those who learn a foreign language do so mainly in order to put it to one or another of the uses commonly labelled 'translating', a label which can now reasonably be extended to include at least the linguistic component of the human participation in a machine translation programme.

If we leave aside the latter for the moment, translation as an occupation is usefully separated into the two activities of translating and interpreting, according to whether the medium is written or spoken language. The two activities are of course very different. In translating it is much easier, and much more usual, to translate into one's own language than into a foreign one: professional translators often translate in one direction only, many of them from a large number of different source languages. Those skilled in this respect often learn languages primarily by eye and can operate in written language without any awareness of the spoken form; it is not unknown for someone to be able to translate from as many as thirty languages of which he does not speak any.

Perhaps the major field of translation activity is the translation of scientific texts. Some of the translators are themselves qualified scientists taking time to help their less polyglot colleagues; others work in collaboration with specialists in the subject concerned. An important point for scientific translation is that, of all the components of language, technical terminology has the highest probability of one-to-one equivalence in translation. The correspondence is, it should be stressed, by no means complete; but once terminological equivalents are established they cause relatively little trouble. It is not true, however, that the whole of the language of a scientific text, including its grammar and non-technical lexis, is similarly likely to yield one-to-one equivalents in translation.

Scientific texts, like those in any other register, constitute a selection from the total resources of grammar and lexis, resources which the writers thereof have to take as they find them. Languages do vary in the extent to which they have institutionalized scientific registers; the use of quasi-formulaic grammatical patterns, such as some of the passive forms in scientific English, goes much further in some languages than in others. Such conventions in source or target language help the translator; they could be much more consistent, and more rigorously adopted, than they are. The planned development of scientific registers is an important task of applied linguistics, and must be treated as such; it could be successful only if worked out by scientists and linguists in collaboration. Some subjects of course lend themselves more readily than others to such planning; but the more the register which is used has the properties of a restricted language the quicker and more effective will be the dissemination of new material.

At the other end of this scale is literary translation, where the translator is not working within conventions of the restricted language type. Moreover a feature of literary registers is that, more than in any other use of language, the translator has to look beyond sentence boundaries to guide him in the choice of equivalents. In the last resort the only ultimately valid linguistic unit in a work of literature is the whole text, and in theory at least no selection of an item or grammatical category can be regarded as final until the context of the whole work is taken into consideration.

We have not seen the Russian translation of John Wain's *Hurry on Down*; but we wonder whether the two occurrences of the sentence 'They looked at each other, baffled and enquiring' (Penguin Books edition, 1960, pp. 142, 252) have been translated identically or not. This is an extreme example, because the two occurrences in different parts of the novel are completely identical in the English, and they should presumably be identical also in the translation. But such identity is merely the endpoint on a scale; and the numerous echoes of grammatical structure and collocation, and the controlled lexicogrammatical variation, characteristic of a work of literature, need to be reflected in a good translation: this, moreover, possibly in a language which either lacks formally equivalent patterns or, if it has them, exploits them in a different way. In Chinese, for example, the repetition of a lexical item, and the occurrence of high frequency collocations of the type that would in English be labelled clichés, have a status in literary registers which is quite different from their status in corresponding registers in English.

The interpreter's professional use of language is very different from that of the translator; he is more likely to be a person whose skill in language learning is oriented primarily towards phonic substance. There is a remarkable range of variety in the language-learning aptitude displayed by different people: some seem to learn almost entirely by eye, others almost exclusively by ear; while perhaps the most fortunate are those with a fairly even balance between the two channels. Whatever his personal approach to learning a language, the interpreter requires a highly developed skill in his use of the spoken medium.

He operates at high speed, with speakers who may throw at him anything from a morpheme to a 'paragraph', may demand anything from group by group translation to long range abstracting and may even exercise the privilege of correcting him if they think he has made a mistake. For accurate interpreting the unit easiest to operate with is the sentence; as has been pointed out, it rarely requires subsequent revision, unlike clauses or smaller units, but it is usually not too long to be readily memorized. In 'simultaneous translation', where there are no translation pauses, the interpreter keeps rather less than a sentence behind the speaker; this is the most difficult kind of interpreting and one that requires a very high degree of skill.

The training of translators and interpreters is a specialized branch of applied linguistics. This does not mean that translators need to study linguistics and phonetics as such, just as to regard language teaching as applied linguistics does not imply that linguistics is to be taught to the language student. But translators who have in the course of their training studied something of the relevant aspects of the linguistic sciences have found it useful. Whatever the detailed pattern adopted, however, what is urgent is the need to provide adequate specialized training at a high level for those taking up these professions. At present provision for this kind of training in Britain is totally inadequate; and whatever we may think of the status of English as a world language this does not relieve us of the obligation to contribute to world resources of translators and inter-preters, resources now quite insufficient to meet the ever-increasing demands.

7

Meanwhile we cannot predict how long such demands will go on increasing before machine translation develops to the stage where

an electronic computer can take over at least some of the work now
done by human translators. There is little doubt that this will happen
eventually; if the results of the first few years' work led many people
to become sceptical about its prospects, this was because research
in machine translation began with a rather one-sided approach.
Whether or not the interpretation put on Warren Weaver's famous
remark 'When I look at an article in Russian, I say: "This is really
written in English, but it has been coded in some strange symbols.
I will now proceed to decode"' was as he intended it, the approach
that it was generally understood to recommend is a very partial one.
For a time machine translation was treated as a problem in electronic engineering and linear coding, with no regard for the nature
of language and the specific properties of language patterning.

Machine translation is a problem in applied linguistics. It is not
of course a question of programming a computer to perform
operations in linguistic theory, nor even just of inserting a linguistic
description into the store, although the latter is in one sense part of
the total operation. What does go into the programme, however, can
be found out only by linguistic methods. Moreover two basic distinctions made in linguistics are both relevant: that between
description and comparison, and that between analysis and recognition.

At first it seemed to be expected that a computer could translate
between languages that had not yet been described—described, that
is, in terms suitable for a computer programme. But in fact a great
deal of preparatory work was needed simply in the description of
the languages concerned, partly in order to restate known facts in an
appropriate form but partly also to find out more facts about them.
The computer itself is indispensable for this stage of the work, both
for devising methods for the syntactic analysis of texts and for
acquiring more detailed information than is accessible to the
unaided human investigator. Whether or not statements of probabilities have a place in machine translation is still controversial; but
even without these there are limitations which only the computer
can overcome. One is the size of sample required for some studies:
in order to construct a thesaurus of a language based on collocations,
for example, it may be necessary to examine tens of millions of
orthographic words of text. Another is the multiple correlations that
are involved as soon as we take grammatical classification beyond a
certain degree of delicacy.

The distinction between analysis and recognition is not an easy one to grasp, but it is crucial to the success of machine operations on language. A computer operates on what is put into it. If every text has to be 'pre-edited' by a human being before the computer can accept it, the human being might as well have translated it in the first place. It must be possible for the computer to 'recognize', from the text and the text alone, the grammatical and lexical patterns and items in the source language that are necessary for the selection of target language equivalents; this means that there must be information stored in the computer against which portions of the text can be matched for identification.

Early suggestions as to what should be stored included lists of words, lists of morphemes and even lists of sentences; but the simple view of language as a string of beads, whether called words or morphemes, arranged into patterned sequences called sentences, is not an adequate model for a translation programme. On the other hand the process by which a human being recognizes exponents of the categories required by a more powerful model are exceedingly complex. For example: it is useful to be able to talk about the category of 'subject' in an English clause. A human being can be taught to recognize the subject, if there is one, in any clause in a text in the language; in doing so he brings to bear all he knows of the description of English. He can immediately marshal the relevant criteria for deciding if something is or is not a subject. But there is no *simple* instruction to a computer: 'find the subject in the next clause'. The category of subject depends on a long chain of abstraction; that is precisely why it is so useful. The text supplied to the computer, however, is not a set of categories; it is a chain of letters, spaces and punctuation marks. It does not even indicate where a clause begins and ends.

As we have stressed throughout, any attempt to account for language directly in terms of strings of letters, or of sounds, is prohibitively complicated. A machine translation programme, to function efficiently, needs to work with categories of a high degree of generality. This is the key problem of machine translation. It needs powerful descriptions of the languages concerned. But the better the description, the more abstract the categories; and the more abstract the categories, the more difficult they are for a machine to recognize. Therefore the description of a language for computer purposes must differ to a certain extent from a linguistic description for other purposes. The formulation of such descriptions is an important part of current research, directed not only towards machine translation but equally towards information retrieval, the storing, classifying and retrieving of information from written documents.

When the results of current, more linguistically oriented research are added to the already considerable achievements in the U.S.A., the U.S.S.R., Britain and elsewhere, in using programmes with a relatively low degree of generality for the translation of specific texts, it should not be too long before machine translation can produce translations of acceptable quality. Meanwhile there is likely to be no lack of employment for human translators in the foreseeable future. The day may come when computers can handle the vast output of scientific literature and translate it into everyone's native language; and one of the most important reasons for speeding up work in machine translation is that it will make it possible for everyone to be educated entirely in his native language. The day may even come when we have machines capable of translating from spoken as well as written input. But the human translator will not have been displaced. The problem of translating literary texts by computer is probably so vast as to be for practical purposes insoluble. For our part we are content that it should remain so.

BIBLIOGRAPHY:

See items 12, 14, 27, 38, 58, 78.

Part 2

The Linguistic Sciences in relation to Language Teaching and Language Learning

Chapter 6

The basic role of linguistics and phonetics

1

The purpose of having a theory is to use it; if a theory is devised to account for how language works, this is in order that it may be used to describe languages. Such a theory, it is clear, could only come into being after many generations of linguists had studied many languages, some of them in great detail; and a long time was needed before models could be constructed which were general enough to apply to 'language' (and thus to all languages) and to give real insight into their complex patterns. Nor is there any one moment when this stage is reached; rather there is a long and continuous process of setting up and testing hypotheses, of constructing models, and of using them and replacing them by better models, a process that will continue for many years to come. But once such a general theory has been formulated the events we call 'language' can be regarded afresh in the new light shed on them by the theory.

A theory is not of course a set of instructions for describing a language; no mere knowledge of theory is a substitute for the descriptive insight into language that can only come from a thorough training in linguistics. The theory increases our understanding of language by enabling us to make statements that are accurate, consistent and powerful: powerful in the sense that each holds good for a large number of different events. It thus demonstrates that language events are not random: they follow recognizable patterns.The patterns can be thought of as predictions about language events, predictions which first distinguish between what is possible and what is impossible, and then, within what is possible, show what is more likely and what is less likely; but the line between 'impossible' and 'very unlikely' is often difficult to draw.

The description of a language is the formulation of such predictions. They relate, as we have seen, both to the internal, formal patterns of language and to its external, contextual patterns. Sometimes, in grammar and phonology, we can state absolute restrictions on what may occur: we will not find a syllable /loɪŋθ/ or a verbal group 'does been' in a text in English.

An absolute restriction, however, is merely a special case of a probability, and other features are described as more or less probable: in English, for example, 'easiest' is more likely than 'most easy', although both are possible. Furthermore, probabilities may be stated conditionally: for example, given that the nominal group acting as the subject of an English clause has 'this' as deictic, it is unlikely that the verbal group acting as predicator will be plural, but 'this committee are hopeless' might nevertheless occur.

Given suitable facilities, we can count the actual occurrences of items and categories in a corpus of text. This provides a basis for stating probabilities quantitatively: the text is treated as a sample and statistical inferences are drawn from it. We can then predict, for example, the ratio of affirmative to interrogative clauses in a passage of English in a given register, and assess the probability that interrogative will occur under various definable sets of conditions, such as when following another interrogative clause. Such statements accord with the normal principles of statistics and probability theory; they have parallels in the study of many aspects of human activity, and have nothing to do with questions of freedom of choice. Nor do they challenge the uniqueness of the individual. Shakespeare's stature is not diminished when we find that the resources he was exploiting had their own intrinsic patterns.

The use of linguistic theory to describe language is not itself counted as an application of linguistics. If a language, or a text, is described with the sole aim of finding out more about language, or about that particular language, this is a use of linguistic theory but it is not an application of linguistics. Applied linguistics starts when a description is specifically made, or an existing description used, for a further purpose which lies outside the linguistic sciences.

Until fairly recently it was often assumed that linguistics had no applications; the subject was thought of as knowledge for its own sake. Now that it has turned out, on the contrary, to have very specific and practical applications affecting the lives of large numbers of people, it is worth remembering that its usefulness is entirely due to the hard work and insight of scholars who were simply seeking knowledge. In this respect linguistic theories are like many other scientific theories, which turn out later to have applications never envisaged by those who originated them.

The conclusion to be drawn is commonplace but important: that even after theories have come to be usefully applied, there must still be some people working in the theoretical or 'pure' side of the subject. Theories can always be replaced by better theories, new facts elicited and new syntheses made. The applications themselves are an important source of feedback: a theory is constantly re-examined in the light of ideas suggested in the course of its application. If a theory is allowed to stand still, it soon ceases to be useful.

Quite naturally, it is when a theory turns out to have applications that it becomes of general interest. Until that time, it will impinge on only a small minority. Even some of its applications may remain very much a field of specialist activity. One of the principal applications of linguistics today is in machine translation; this involves many people besides linguists, but they are all specialists of some kind, mathematicians, computer programmers and others. Until we can programme a computer to translate quickly and cheaply any scientific text that is fed into it, machine translation, even though itself an application of linguistics, will remain of limited interest.

There are other applications of linguistics, however, which have a wider public. Of these the most important is undoubtedly the teaching of languages: both the teaching of the native language and the teaching of foreign languages. If linguistic theory can be used to make better descriptions of languages, as it can, then this theory has a contribution to make in any situation in which language is being taught.

Languages have been being described for teaching purposes for a very long time. If linguists claim that the modern theories which have been worked out for phonetics, phonology, grammar or lexis yield better descriptions of languages than those which have been being used up till now, this is because they feel that a great deal more is now understood about how language works; and that the earlier descriptions, which still form the basis of the great majority of our language textbooks, are by contrast defective in the picture they present both of language in general and of the particular language being described.

No linguist or phonetician thinks that the last word has been said; no doubt by 1980 our theories will have been extended, and in part replaced, by newer ideas. Meanwhile, we do know considerably more than was known in 1880. Today, moreover, millions of people of all ages are struggling to learn one, two or even more foreign languages, and many others would like to know more about how their own works; they have a right to benefit from what has been done in linguistics and phonetics to make their task easier. Let there be no mistake here: it will presumably always be hard work to learn a foreign language, because language is a highly complex form of activity and the process of replacing patterns learned from early childhood which have long since ceased to be the object of attention, by a new set of patterns differing *at every level*, as they do in all languages, is bound to need careful observation, concentration and control. But at least it need not be made more difficult by an inadequate representation of the processes and activities involved.

The adult especially, whose native language patterns interfere more than do the child's, but who has in compensation the power to understand, make and apply generalizations, ought not to be faced with unsatisfactory descriptions of language such as are current in many textbooks today. These descriptions not only fail to make use of the very powerful generalizations about each particular language that linguistic and phonetic theories make possible; they frequently offer instead vague and unintegrated statements which reveal all too little about the language being described. These may then be coupled with 'generalizations' of the wrong kind, in which certain features are assumed to be universal which are in fact special properties of one language: the writer's native language perhaps, or a language he learnt at school, but certainly not the one he is describing.

The basic defect of the descriptions we are criticizing is that they are too complicated; and this is because the theory on which they are founded is too simple. Of course to someone accustomed to an old description and an old approach it may be daunting to be faced with a new description and a new approach; and this may obscure the fact that the new account is simpler than the old. But this is no reason for perpetuating the language-learning difficulties of those who have not yet been faced with either alternative. It is a commonplace of science that the more complex the theory, the simpler the description: the simpler, that is, the explanation of the events which the theory is devised to account for. It has happened in the history of many sciences that a new and more complex theory has been constructed which has allowed a given set of events to be accounted for (those already observed being explained, and those not observed being predicted) by a much simpler set of statements. The gain in simplicity may be obscured by the fact that the new theory accounts for many more events than the old: it still takes a hundred pages to write about them, but whereas previously the hundred pages were all taken up in accounting for a set of events x, the new statement accounts both for the set x and for a new set of events y, and only fifty pages would have been needed to account for x alone.

Linguistics has taken exactly this path. We may still write our hundred pages, or thousand pages, about English grammar; but in the given space we can account for much more of English grammar, achieving much more delicacy, than we could before. Nor are the descriptive statements themselves any more complex in character; they are merely more rigorous, being subject to constraints imposed by the theory. All this is made possible by the construction of a more complex and elaborate *theory* about the nature of the patterns of language.

2

The deficiencies of many earlier descriptions, which render them inadequate for language teaching purposes by comparison with those that can be produced today, are perhaps best examined in the context of the history of language studies. Both linguistics and phonetics have a very long history, not only in Europe but in India and China also. Several centuries before the Christian era, Indian linguists were making highly sophisticated and accurate descriptions of Sanskrit; both their theory and their observation was of a merit probably not surpassed by any descriptive work on language until well into the twentieth century. In Europe, the ancient Greek grammarians analysed Greek and disputed vigorously about order and disorder in language.

Both in India and in the Hellenic world, as also in China, where linguistic studies began at about the same time, interest was focused on those forms of the language which were the vehicles of classical literature. Changes in the spoken language, and dialectal diversity, led to difficulties in the interpretation of the classical texts which the descriptions served to elucidate. Moreover the classical and pre-classical varieties of Sanskrit, of Greek and of Chinese tended to be regarded as a model of what language should be, and thus in describing them the scholar was describing the presumed ideal state of his language.

The central theme of the studies of Greek was grammar. 'Grammar' was regarded as an applied science, and the description was formal, in the technical linguistic sense: categories were defined by formal criteria and referred to phonological or graphological features as their exponents. Morphological analysis was separated from syntactical, but the two were made congruent by the use of morphologically identified categories of the word as syntactic classes. A noun in Greek, for example, was identified as a class of word displaying inflexion for number and case; this class was then shown to enter into certain structural relations with other classes such as the verb.

To their formal definition of the category, the Greek grammarians added observations about the contextual meaning it carried: a noun was the name of a person, living being or thing. But this was not presented as a defining criterion: the noun was defined by its form. The attempt was made to explain certain structures, notably that of subject and predicate, in terms of logical relations. These were assumed to represent inherent properties of the external world, and thus to determine the primary structure of sentences in all languages. In fact they had been derived from the Greek language in the first place, and as we now know they are not universally valid for all languages. But in the description of Greek, and particularly of the written texts in which the grammarians were interested, even those categories formulated in logical terms were not inappropriate; while the categories identified on morphological criteria still stand, with minor modifications, in a good description of classical Greek today.

When the Roman grammarians adapted the descriptions of Greek to Latin, they were fortunate in that Latin and Greek were very much alike. The two had not long diverged from a common ancestor, and retained a great many similarities. Consequently the categories established for Greek were in most cases also valid for Latin, and their assumed universality did not need to be called into question. It could still be supposed, for example, that the subject-predicate relation was a constant property of all languages, and that 'tense' and 'case', 'subjunctive' and 'passive', 'preposition' and 'subordinate clause' were indispensable to human speech.

Throughout the medieval period in western Europe, interest in language was almost entirely confined to Latin. But as long as linguistic categories continued to be regarded as universal, however much the items might vary, statements about Latin were accorded the status of statements about language. Latin, however, was no longer anyone's native language. Its grammar had ceased to evolve, and its phonetics now followed in the wake of its users' native language, undergoing English sound changes in England, French in France and Italian in Italy. Medieval grammarians were very little interested in phonetics; at the same time they had very little new to say about Latin syntax or morphology. Their major preoccupation was with the linguistic reflection of logical categories and relations.

From the modern standpoint, both the classical and the medieval European linguists, like the Indian linguists over the same period, were in some respects strikingly successful. They saw language as a system of interrelated categories, and set themselves the task of observing it accurately and describing its operation. The Indian linguists had the further merit that in their work language was studied independently as a phenomenon in its own right, without the appeal to logic, which is now seen to be invalid. Not that there is no connection between logic and *linguistics*: linguistic theory, like all scientific theories, gains from being formulated in terms of a suitable logic if such can be devised. What is invalid is the imputed connection between logic and *language*: the attempt by the medieval grammarians to explain language as a reflection of certain logical relations which had been derived, originally by Aristotle, from the very linguistic patterns they were being used to explain.

Renaissance scholarship wrought two fundamental changes in European linguistics. In the first place, Latin was ousted from its position as the unique object of language study. Many of the modern European languages had for a considerable time been recognized as literary media; they now became acceptable also as vehicles of learning and education, and thus began to occupy the attention of linguists. In addition the European overseas conquests and Christian missionary activities brought new languages from every continent within the vision of European linguists. This widening of the horizons might reasonably be expected to have led to a new understanding of the nature of language. It was not necessary even to go to China or South America to find a language which worked very differently from Latin; English would serve equally well to demolish the universality of the Latin-based categories. But the potential benefits of this enlarged scope of observation were largely lost as a result of the second of the two changes referred to above. This was a change in attitude towards the whole phenomenon of language.

Certain of the early humanist scholars fiercely attacked the medieval learning, and in their general condemnation of the works whose tradition they sought to overthrow they found especial fault with medieval grammarians. These grammarians had concerned themselves with language; they should, it was argued, have studied the ideas behind it. In the extreme views of some advocates of the new learning it was a mistake to analyse language in its own terms at all; the only reality lay in ideas, and language was at best a clothing for these ideas. Indeed it was worse than mere clothing: language might make a naked idea fit to move in society, but it also might disguise it, since language could be used to lie, to suppress and to falsify.

There was substance in the objection that the medieval grammarians had paid too much attention to minute details of language. Their preoccupation with logic, and the restriction of their attention to one language, had led them to concentrate on linguistically marginal features, and they lacked a coherent view of the working of the language as a whole. What was needed was an understanding of the part played by language in life. In place of this understanding, there came to be substituted what amounted to a denial that it played any significant part at all. In the new ideology it was reality that was considered to be structured, and thought reflected reality; language was merely the imperfect expression of thought.

This was the view with which the new languages were approached. The entire notion of language had changed, and with it the basis of description. The categories were no longer formally defined. In classical linguistics the Latin noun had been defined as that class of the word which was subject to inflection for number and case; the observation that the noun was generally the name of a person, living being or thing was added as an associated feature to explain the contextual meaning of the category. In the new view of language, 'name of a person, living being or thing' became the defining criterion, with the formal features treated as incidental. Linguistic categories were replaced by conceptual ones, linguistic relations by relations among objects and events and among ideas. This meant that the beam of linguistic scholarship, instead of being widened in focus, was in effect switched away from language on to something else.

Since the new languages did not display the same formal categories as Latin, the conceptual view was useful: it avoided the problems raised by the fact that languages differ. There is no word class in English that inflects for case and number; if a word class corresponding to the Latin 'noun' is to be identified in English, the Latin definition will not serve. The principle that every category must be defined afresh for every language is a commonplace of linguistics today; but this conclusion was not faced until the twentieth century. What had made it possible to avoid it in the earlier period was the use of conceptual criteria as the defining ones. 'Name of a person, living being or thing' serves as well, and as badly, to define the noun in English as in Latin.

As long as language was considered to be merely an imperfect reflection of reality, any inadequacy of such definitions could be regarded as the fault of language. If they seemed less apt for other languages than for Latin, this could be taken merely to show the superiority of Latin in more nearly approaching the standard to which a language was required to conform. Conceptually defined categories can be held to be universal precisely because they are incapable of exact application; some of the definitions have survived to this day, protected by a cosy unreality. But it is doubtful whether any English schoolboy, having to find out whether a certain word is a noun or not, asks: 'Is this the name of a person, living being or thing?' More probably he will test whether it has a plural in -s, or whether he can put the definite article in front of it. Since he is probably required to decide that 'departure' is a noun whereas 'somebody' is not, he is more likely to reach the right conclusion by this method.

So it happened that, when the new languages came within their field of vision, few European scholars had any real interest in language as a unique and vital human activity. Language for them was only an outer covering, a skin to be peeled off to let the ideas show through. Instead of asking how each language worked, and noting the '-s's and the 'the's which (though not the only basis for identifying the class of 'noun' in English) are immeasurably more powerful and revealing than conceptual or referential criteria, they seem to have assumed that they knew the answer. Instead of gazing in wonder at the miracle of language through which we exist as social beings and at the complexity of each language and the diversity of language types, and instead of using that capacity for observation of which the age was so proud to examine and understand it, they took it for granted and treated it as unfit for serious study. In place of linguistic theory they erected a logic of relations among ideas and entities; they sought rules for how language should mirror reality: they were critics of language, not analysts. So speculative, and so divorced from observation, was this view of language that it seems explicable only in the context of a reaction against scholasticism; or perhaps the very lack of interest of the age in the patterned activities of man was in some way inseparable from its brilliant insight into the orderly workings of nature.

3

It was four hundred years before linguists once again paid full attention to explaining the patterns of language. Four trends were perhaps most significant in leading up to this recovery of interest. First, in the two and a half centuries between 1550 and 1800 many accounts were written of modern European languages, and these highlighted the problems of describing a language even in failing to solve them. In the kind of approach to language which was inherited from early humanist works there were four main barriers to scientific linguistics: the study of language tended to be logical rather than linguistic, conceptual rather than formal, comparative rather than particular (that is, based on a language other than the one being analysed) and prescriptive rather than descriptive. Sometimes a writer broke through these barriers, bringing fresh ideas into theory or description; even those who did not at least added to the observations that linguists had to be able to account for.

Second, at the end of the eighteenth century a new dimension was introduced into linguistic studies: that of the history of languages. Against a general background of evolutionary thinking in science, nineteenth-century linguists developed theories of how a language changes in time; and showed by careful comparison that distinct languages might be 'genetically' related in the sense of their having diverged from a common 'ancestor' language. Since language is neither an organism nor a species, some of the analogies drawn from biological evolution proved misleading, as they did in other social sciences. But it was through this branch of linguistics, known first as comparative philology and more recently as comparative historical linguistics, that language was restored to its place as a field of scientific inquiry. Most of the basic concepts formulated in the last century are still accepted as valid, and the accounts of the Indo-European and other language families, though they have been modified in various ways, were and remain the foundation of all historical study of language.

Third, while linguists were attending exclusively to the study of the history of languages, others who were not professional linguists had taken over the task of describing them. Those who in this way maintained the continuity of descriptive linguistics were neither teachers of language nor research workers, but soldiers and missionaries, and men in the consular and colonial services. Europeans were penetrating into every continent, and these people came across and learnt languages that Europeans had never previously heard of. They had no methodology for describing a language. But they had a very good command of the languages they were describing, and they used the categories of classroom Latin to classify and expound their material. We may smile at these descriptions today, but the smile is sympathetic and admiring. The material they collected is invaluable, and their accounts of it can often be re-interpreted. Moreover some of the languages have yet to be better described.

The fourth and latest of the developments which made modern linguistics possible was the emergence of phonetics as an exact science in the last decades of the nineteenth century. It had taken linguists a long time to free themselves from the tyranny of the written language and to observe speech sounds accurately and objectively. Once this stage was reached, the first task was to classify speech sounds according to types of articulation and to devise a transcription for noting them down. The I.P.A. alphabet made it possible to transcribe the sounds of all languages objectively and with varying degrees of delicacy. In the 1920s phoneticians took up the instrumental analysis of the acoustic properties of speech sound waves; this has been followed most recently of all by the instrumental study of articulation. Phonetics has vastly increased the scope and accuracy of linguistic observations, and provided a general theory for the description of speech sounds. Linguistics and phonetics both play an essential part in modern descriptive studies of language whether pure or applied, and neither flourishes as a subject of teaching and research if divorced from the other.

At the beginning of the twentieth century linguists once again turned their attention to the study of the working of language, opening the way to descriptive theory as we know it today. The progress made in the last fifty years has not of course followed a single track, any more than in psychology or anthropology. There have been advances on many different lines, and widely divergent views have been put forward; nor is there any reason to fear that argument will not continue. Meanwhile the area of agreement has been widening all the time. Since the scope of the problems with which linguists concern themselves widens perhaps even more rapidly, there is an ever increasing number of topics about which they can disagree. This means that the extent of what has become generally accepted in linguistic theory and method tends to be lost sight of; yet in fact it is striking. One factor leading to convergence is that the validity of new theories has often been confirmed both by extended observation and by application.

The first major contribution to the renewal of progress in descriptive linguistics came from a few scholars such as Baudouin de Courtenay, Henry Sweet and Ferdinand de Saussure, who in a sense founded modern 'general linguistics' as an overall science of language. Saussure is best known for his posthumous 'Course in General Linguistics', in which appear his theory of linguistic symbolism and his view of the nature of language events in relation to a language as an acquired potential common to all its speakers. Saussure stressed that language can only be understood through the set of systematic relations that make up its internal structure; and that these in turn must be studied by abstraction from accurate observations of phonetic data.

Emphasis on the development of a rigorous and integrated theory to account systematically for all patterning of language is the keynote of the work of the Danish linguist Louis Hjelmslev. Modern theories in phonology were first developed by the 'Prague circle' founded by the Russian linguist N. S. Trubetskoy, whose work has been followed up by Roman Jakobson and many others. In the

United States, Edward Sapir stressed the link between linguistics and social anthropology, the study of a language being part of the total study of a community.

Perhaps the most influential contribution has been the work of a large number of linguists, mainly American, who developed strict procedures for the analysis of language on the basis of ideas first formulated by Leonard Bloomfield. The work of these linguists, especially in 'phonemics' and 'morphemics', marked a great advance and a shift of emphasis. Recognizing that what had stifled linguistic theory and made it impossible to describe languages accurately and usefully was exclusive concentration on meaning to the neglect of language form, some of them attempted to exclude all considerations of meaning from linguistics. Meaning, they said, could not be observed or described; the linguist should analyse only form and substance, without reference to context or to the part played by language in life.

This view was never held by all linguists, and is probably not held today in its extreme form by any. But it exerted a great deal of influence, precisely because it was a necessary corrective to the earlier view that concepts, not forms, were what mattered. Although all modern descriptive linguistics is 'structural', in that description is centred round the internal patterns of language, it was mainly work based on this approach that was given this label; and if such work has often been taken, by those newly acquainted with the subject, to represent the whole of linguistics, this is a tribute to its progress and achievements.

In its earlier form this approach appears mechanistic and, as a theory, lacking in explanatory power. In application, though immeasurably more useful than the 'mentalistic' view which it replaced, it has serious shortcomings. Descriptions based on this approach have been used in language teaching; they have been found unsatisfactory largely because of their neglect of contextual meaning and their inability to present an integrated picture of a language as a whole. It is a pity that this has led some language teachers to continue to rely on the older methods. These 'structural' descriptions are many times more useful than those that went before them; and if they are deficient, the answer is to move forwards, not backwards.

An important forward move of recent years has been the introduction of a new model and method of description known as 'transformation theory', associated particularly with the work of Noam Chomsky. In the past, descriptions of language have been mainly of two types: they have proceeded either by text or by example. Either the linguist has described the language of a particular text, recognizing the categories necessary for that text alone and analysing it item by item; or he has described 'a language', giving a comprehensive outline of categories and illustrating them by examples. The first has a narrow range of validity but a greater accuracy than the second: it gives more exact information about fewer events, since it accounts only for those observed in the text.

Transformation theory carries the second approach a stage further: it is a 'generative' model, in which description takes the form of sets of rules for generating the sentences of a language with descriptions attached. Its special purposes are to account for the native speaker's ability to produce, identify and interpret correct sentences in his language; and to yield descriptions which can be rigorously validated or invalidated. To attain these ends the linguist must decide what is and what is not a 'grammatical' ('well-formed') sentence in the language, since testing involves seeing whether the rules in fact generate all and only the sentences required.

The descriptions used in this model have taken over many features from earlier structural linguistics (for example 'constituent analysis' in sentence structure); but it has moved sharply away from the 'mechanistic' standpoint and is in this respect closer to the models that have been being developed in Britain. It does not, however, present an integrated theory to cover all levels of language; it is not easily adapted to the description of texts, as required for example in the study of literature or the comparison of different registers (whereas the model represented in this book is partly designed precisely for textual purposes); it does not readily lend itself to statistical statements about language, where we need to distinguish 'more and less probable' rather than 'possible and impossible'; and it requires one particular type of descriptive statement. But linguistics has various aims, and different types of statement are appropriate to different purposes: a grammar for the teaching of a language does not look like a grammar written for linguists, while a grammar written for a speech pathologist would differ from either. The transformational model achieves with unique success certain of the aims of linguistic theory; but it is not comprehensive or adaptable enough for some of its other purposes.

The earlier 'phonemics and morphemics' model, therefore, which is often identified with 'structuralism', and through which linguistics first became known to many people, does not represent the only model within linguistic theory developed in the United States or elsewhere. It was in any case little used by most British linguists, the majority of whom have been more closely associated in their methods with the work of the late J. R. Firth, Professor of General Linguistics in the University of London from 1942 to 1956. Linguistics for Firth was the study of 'how we use language to live'. He rejected both extremes of 'mentalism' and 'mechanism', and indeed distrusted the whole dichotomy of language into 'form' and 'meaning'. What Firth emphasized was that meaning was a property of all the types of patterning found in language; one could not describe language without describing meaning. But in order to describe with insight, one had to recognize the various levels— grammar, phonology and so on—which represented the different 'modes of meaning' of language. The categories for the description of a language must be based on formal criteria and be ultimately relatable to their exponents in phonic or graphic substance; but no description was complete which did not leave both the formal meaning and the contextual meaning fully accounted for. It is Firth's general approach which the present writers have found to be most fruitful in application.

In our view, arguments about 'structuralism' are essentially out of date. All linguistics is structural, in the sense that a description must account for the internal patterns of language, and this can only be achieved if the criteria are drawn from within and not from outside language. At the same time all statements about language are statements of meaning, and the task of the linguist is to work out, from observations of language in action, theories of how language works which will enable him best to make such statements. Linguistics today thus inherits directly the traditions of its earliest times: the work of the linguists of ancient Greece and Rome, traditional Chinese scholarship in phonology and lexicology, and above all perhaps the achievements of the Sanskrit grammarians of India. Modern theories are more powerful and illuminating than theirs, modern descriptions more accurate and useful; we have profited not only from the general advances in scientific theory and method but also from the synthesis of divergent views on language through the ages. But it is their work that we look back to, as a model of clear thinking about language, rather than the curiously indifferent and almost arrogant treatment of language bequeathed to modern Europe by the early propagandists of the 'new learning'.

4

Today, when an Indian schoolboy learns English or an English schoolboy French, or when an English child studies the grammar of his native language, what is the view of language with which they are presented in their textbooks? Far too often they are faced with the conceptual or 'mentalist' view in an extreme and restricting form. Language is defined as the expression of thought, and various metaphors put across the same view: language as clothing for naked ideas, language as a vehicle for the conveyance of meanings, language as a body for the temporary incarnation of each conceptual soul. The approach is often implicit rather than explicit. It lies behind such statements as these:

'A sentence gives expression to a subject to which the speaker wishes to draw the hearer's attention, and also to something which he wishes him to think with reference to that subject ... Any utterance which calls up in the mind of the receiver these two linked things is a sentence.' (Grattan, J. H. G. and Gurrey, P.: *Our Living Language*. London, Nelson, 1925.)

'While we say, "This room needs *cleaning*", when we mean "This room needs to be *cleaned*", a speaker of a Latin language will say, "It is much *to desire* that you should come", when what he really means is, "It is much *to be desired* that you should come"'. (Kelly, Brian: *An Advanced English Course for Foreign Students*. London, Longmans, 1940/47.)

'Look more closely at the sentence:
"The wolf was imprisoned where the harness held him."
The writer starts by giving us the main fact that the wolf was imprisoned. "The wolf was imprisoned" is therefore the Main Clause.' (Ridout, Ronald: *English Today*, vol. iii. London, Ginn, 1947.)

'Consider this sentence:
   "The old lady gave the boy an apple."
... The noun "apple" directly suffers the action of the
giving, and is therefore the direct object of the verb "gave".
What work, then, does the noun "boy" do in the sentence?
If it does not suffer directly the action of the giving as the
noun "apple" does, it at least suffers the action indirectly,
since the giving is done for the sake of the boy. The noun
"boy" is therefore called the indirect object of the verb
"gave".' (ibid., vol. ii.)

This view of language, which attempts to define linguistic forms
by the criterion of the ideas they are supposed to express, still
persists and predominates in many textbooks of languages, whether
native or foreign. It is often not realized how aberrant and unusual
this view is in the total perspective of the history of serious thinking
about language. The fact that a view is unusual is not of course a
reason for condemning it. The relevant question is whether in this
case it leads to useful statements which throw light on language in
general and present a clear picture of a particular language to those
who are learning it or learning about it.

It is all too seldom that this question is seriously faced. So much
did the conceptual view of language become part of the climate of
European thinking that even today, when the linguist suggests that
there are other ways of accounting for language and that this may
not be the most fruitful one, he often faces an aggressive incredulity.
He is assumed to be saying either that language 'has no meaning'
or that ideas 'do not exist'. Both these charges need to be considered.

The first rests on a disastrous narrowing down of the notion of
'meaning' so that it excludes the meaningfulness of formal patterns,
a narrowing down for which the conceptual view is itself responsible.
Once the separation of 'form' and 'meaning' is accepted, then
'meaning' comes to be regarded as an independent entity outside
language; and it follows, in this view, that if one is talking about
form one is not talking about meaning. As we have seen, some
linguists took over this opposition and prolonged its life for a time,
saying in effect: 'We agree that form and meaning are opposed; but
whereas in the earlier view meaning was the essence of language,
we say that the essence of language is form'. Whatever the role of

the latter view as a corrective, there is no longer any place for this rigid dichotomy. We cannot accept that 'form' and 'meaning' are independent entities, the one somehow carried by the other like turnips in a goods wagon. If the linguist today insists on describing the forms of language, and defining his categories formally, this is because form is itself meaningful. We cannot talk about language usefully and accurately if we continue to treat the internal, formal patterns as subordinate to, and definable by, the external, contextual patterns.

To say that meaning cannot be isolated from form is not, however, to say that ideas 'do not exist', whatever that may mean. It is not the province of a linguist to discuss the nature of an idea. The linguist is trying to explain language; he cannot use ideas for that purpose, because the reasoning becomes circular. The only way that we can observe an idea is through the language that has been used to 'express' it. How then can we use the idea to explain the language? The intelligent schoolboy, faced with the observation that 'this is put into the main clause because it expresses the main idea', dismisses it as useless, knowing perfectly well that the only way he can tell which is supposed to be 'the main idea' is by looking to see which is the 'main clause'; and consider the example 'I might if you would give me a year off with full pay'. Nor is he likely to apply the definition 'person, living being or thing which suffers or undergoes an action' in order to find the 'object' in 'I don't like dishonesty'. One cannot argue whether statements of this kind are true or false. They are simply irrelevant, and add nothing to our understanding of how English works.

Linguists therefore do not say that language has no meaning or that it is to be described as if it had no meaning. They do say, on the contrary, that the meaning of language is more than a mere bundle of concepts and referents: it is a property of language as activity and must be described in all its aspects through the study of language at all levels, including the situations in which it operates. Linguists do not say that there is no place in the universe for concepts or ideas or that there is no relation between language and thought. They do say, on the other hand, that since concepts cannot be observed, but only postulated through the observation of particular events in particular languages, they cannot be used to define linguistic categories; this applies equally whether such concepts are offered as supposedly universal factors determining for all human speech or are set up *ad hoc* to explain the language being described.

If a language textbook is based on a narrowly conceptual approach, and presents a view of language that falls far short of the level of knowledge and insight reached by modern linguistics, it can fairly be criticized on theoretical grounds. But we are concerned here with an application of linguistics; and if the linguistics being applied is of three generations ago, perhaps the only relevant question is: does it work? Of course it works. So do candles; but we nevertheless use electric light. In our opinion the old approach does not work well enough. We cannot hope to teach languages successfully on the scale required in the world today if we continue to display them in the candlelight of last century's linguistics.

5

The teaching of foreign languages is now one of the world's major occupations. The content and method of the teaching varies, or should do, with the purpose of the learner, and the range of different purposes is very wide. In many countries educational theory and practice require that a secondary school pupil should learn something of at least one foreign language. In addition to this, millions of children and adults all over the world are studying one of the languages with international status, especially English, Russian and French, as a means to a variety of practical ends. The numbers are constantly increasing. At a conference called by the British Council in December 1960 it was suggested that, in the teaching of English as a foreign language, 'we should think in terms of 700,000 "teacher-years" within the next decade as a global—if impracticable —requirement'.

The number of people to whom it is important to succeed in the language-learning task is thus immense. Whatever the different purposes involved, there is one general aspect of the task which is common to all learners: they are trying to acquire certain skills which, although new in themselves, are of a type already familiar. How well, if we look at the world as a whole, do they succeed? If the answer is 'not as well as they might', then we should seek the possible reasons. Let us concede that some of the students are not good students. This does not, in our opinion, account for more than a small percentage of the relative failures. Let us concede further that some of the teachers are not good teachers. Since in some countries there are inadequate facilities for training teachers, this is certainly another relevant factor. But it remains true that, in countries where there are excellent facilities for training teachers and the training given is of a high standard, the results of years of hard work spent in teaching foreign languages, with sound *pedagogical* methods and classroom practices, are often depressingly disappointing.

It has been argued that in this case the reason is that the teachers themselves are not skilled enough in the languages they are teaching. Again, this no doubt plays a part in accounting for the poor results, especially in some countries abroad where there had been a huge and rapid increase in the demand for English. But again, in our opinion, it is not the whole of the story, even in these countries; and in foreign language classes in English schools it is today a very minor factor.

What is mainly at fault, in our view, is the approach to language, and the descriptions of languages, on which the teaching is grounded. It is difficult to assess the relative importance of this factor at all accurately. But if it is true that there is something wrong with the account given of a language being taught, then it is important to put this right even if the teacher is a highly qualified person, well skilled in the foreign language and teaching under ideal conditions. It is even more important if he is imperfectly trained, lacks proper teaching facilities and has an inadequate knowledge of the language he is teaching.

It is not only the teaching of foreign languages that is adversely affected by the attitude to language. Native language teaching also suffers. Here the purpose is clearly different, although there is a wide divergence of opinion as to what the purpose actually is. Some would say that every citizen should know something about how his native language works, just as he should know something about music, electricity and local government. Others would stress rather the acquiring of skills, maintaining that a child has to be taught to use his native language properly. In the latter view the study of the native language is not so very different in aim from the study of foreign languages. Whatever the aims against which performance is measured, it is probably fair to say that there is a general dissatisfaction with the results, at any rate of the teaching of the English language in English schools. Some teachers have denied altogether the value of teaching English language, and have suggested that it should be cut out of the syllabus.

We have a great deal of sympathy with a teacher who rebels against the teaching of the grammar of the native language. So often, what he is expected to teach is thoroughly bad grammar, in the sense that the analysis he has at his disposal rests on an inadequate understanding of how English works. It does not throw light on the 'Englishness' of English or display systematically the meaningful resources of the language. It does not show how we use English to live. Similarly we sympathize with those who play down the importance of grammar in the learning of a foreign language: again, it is often bad grammar, and does not help the student understand how Frenchmen use French or Germans German. The answer is not, however, to abandon grammar. The answer is to use good grammar, and to re-examine its role in the teaching of language. If we claim to teach a child his native language, we must at least understand our own model and be capable of revealing to him how a native English speaker may exploit the versatile resources of English. If we expect him to learn a foreign language, we must be able to show him likewise something of what a Frenchman can do with French, and from that what an Englishman might be able to do with French.

If the approach to language is unsound, a grammar based on such an approach will be a bad grammar and of little use to the student. It will offer him categories he cannot handle and statements he cannot interpret or apply. At the worst it may misrepresent the facts of the language, although this is rare. As we have seen, the charge against such grammars is not of error but of irrelevance: they do not give insight into the language or describe it most effectively. We do not learn from them what the language really means to those who use it.

Criticism of the linguistic theory that lies behind such grammars can be summarized under five headings: unclear categories, heterogeneous criteria, fictions, conceptual formulations and value judgments. To these could be added two more which lie outside grammar but contribute to the total picture of the language: inaccurate phonetics, and confusion of media. Below are some examples of the kinds of statement exemplifying this approach, which we feel are open to criticism. Such statements are to be found even in the best textbooks; indeed it is precisely in the work of writers of the highest professional qualifications and experience, who therefore make the most demands on a linguistic theory, that the theory will be shown to be an inadequate instrument for their purpose, where its deficiencies might be masked in a less ambitious work until the teacher actually came to use it. It has thus caused us some difficulty to know how to illustrate our criticisms. In some cases, where a point could be made without a specific example, we have attempted a generalization showing the kind of statement that is made, though always with actual examples in mind. In other cases, however, more specific illustration was required. It seemed invidious to paraphrase existing works without acknowledgement; on the other hand by inventing our own examples we would have run the risk of paraphrasing or even quoting unintentionally. We have felt it more appropriate, therefore, to cite illustrations from a small set of representative textbooks of English in current use and by writers of unassailable reputation, where it would be clear that no criticism was intended or implied of the quality of the work and that no unfair selection of examples had been made. What is being illustrated is the linguistic theory, at its best, that until very recently has been the only one readily available for the teaching of languages. The books quoted are:

(1) Eckersley, C. E. and Eckersley, J. M.: *A Comprehensive English Grammar for Foreign Students*, London, Longmans, 1960. (E. & E.).
(2) Kelly, Brian: *An Advanced English Course for Foreign Students*, London, Longmans, 1940/47. (K.).
(3) Ridout, Ronald: *English Today*, 5 volumes: London, Ginn, 1947–48. (R. i–v).
(4) Thomson, A. S. and Martinet, A. V.: *A Practical English Grammar for Foreign Students*, London, Oxford U.P., 1960. (T. & M.).

(a) Unclear categories. A clause is sometimes defined as a sentence which acts as a word. In the same theory it is also held that an infinitive, such as *to make*, can be used as a clause; that an infinitive is a kind of verb; and that a verb is a kind of word. All these observations may be found on different pages in the same work. If they are taken together, we are presented with a description in which a sequence of two words is one word which is used as a clause, a clause being a sentence which acts as a word.

The same point can be brought out by an illustration. We find the statement: 'These doing or being words are called *verbs*' (R.i. 39). On the following page there is a list of 'seven verbs', *one* of which is 'has won'. But if *has won*, like *to make*, is *one* word, how is this unit *word* defined? Similarly 'Prepositions are words used with nouns . . . Prepositions may be . . . two or more words' (E. & E. 277). In this case it seems reasonable to ask how many words, and how many prepositions, there are in *in front of*. The relative status of the categories of 'word' and 'phrase' is perhaps the most widely confused, but there is often uncertainty at other ranks also. For example, are we to take it that the whole of any text in the language is divisible into clauses; and if not, what is the status of those parts that are left over?

The nature of a 'class' is often similarly loosely defined, for example: 'The following classes of verbs . . .: Verbs of the senses, Verbs of emotion, Verbs of thinking; The Auxiliaries; Some others' (T. & M. 117–8). Compare with this 'There are four kinds of nouns in English: 1 Common nouns, 2 Proper nouns, 3 Abstract nouns, 4 Collective nouns' (T. & M. 6). We are not told whether 'kinds' are the same thing as 'classes'; these are not defined, and the labels do not seem to be used elsewhere. Other groupings, however, are used which are not mentioned in this list: for example 'nouns which are countable' (T. & M. 1). It is not clear whether these are a 'kind' of noun, in the same sense as those previously distinguished; in this instance a definition is given, a 'singular noun which is countable' being explained as '(i.e. of which there is more than one)' (T. & M. 1). Compare further '*like* is an adjective and preposition, and can be treated as a preposition' (T. & M. 63); and below 'Some words can be used as either prepositions or adverbs'. But we need to know whether, if they are assigned to different classes, they are then the same item in the language or two different items: in other words is there just one word *like*, or are there two, or three?

The status of some categories used in this theory is impossible to determine. For example, 'English genders are extremely simple, because all inanimate things are neuter: 1 Masculine; 2 Feminine; 3 Common; 4 Neuter . . . The moon is usually considered feminine, so are ships and sometimes trains, while the sun is masculine' (T. & M. 6). However, 'Adjectives in English have only one form' which is used with singular and plural, masculine and feminine nouns' (T. & M. 12): are they not also used with common and neuter ones? Since nowhere in the theory is the category of gender defined, it is not surprising that what is said about it is rather confusing.

There is confusion also in the ranging of contrasts in systems and in the assignment of systems to the units where they belong. For example, there is in English a system of mood, operating at the rank of the clause, whose terms include affirmative, interrogative and imperative. This is quite distinct from the system of polarity, whose terms are positive and negative and which operates at the rank of the group: it is the clause which is affirmative or interrogative, the verbal group which is positive or negative. Traditionally (as for example in T. & M. 76 ff.) affirmative and positive are conflated as 'affirmative', and this gives rise to some uncertainty about the place of this conflated category in the language: compare 'when the sentence is affirmative' (T. & M. 76) with 'an affirmative verb is used . . .' (T. & M. 28). Moreover although the term 'interrogative verb' occurs (ibid.), it is clear from such formulations as 'The *interrogative* is formed by inverting subject and auxiliary' (T. & M. 115) that it is not the verb that is regarded as interrogative here but some unspecified higher unit.

(b) Heterogeneous criteria. The traditional definitions of the so-called 'parts of speech' are based on a mixture of largely incompatible criteria: conceptual, for example 'Words that are the names of things or people or places . . . are called NOUNS'; formal syntactical, for example 'Words that are used to join words, phrases or sentences . . . are CONJUNCTIONS'; or mixed, for example 'Words that qualify a noun by making its meaning clearer, fuller or more exact . . . are called ADJECTIVES' (E. & E. 3–4). Some writers, including those just quoted, in a praiseworthy attempt to overcome this weakness of traditional theory, have tried to define 'parts of speech' consistently according to 'function' (for example, E. & E. 5). The difficulty is that 'function' has then to be used as a cover term with two quite separate meanings: that of 'place (of the category concerned) in the language', which is a matter of form, and that of 'relation (of the category concerned) to the non-linguistic situation', which is a matter of context and altogether different.

It is fair to point out, since these authors refer to 'time and effort . . . spent in trying to settle what names should be given to these categories' (E. & E. 3), that we entirely agree with them in being concerned with the categories rather than with what they are to be called. But they then go on to say, 'there is little point in giving anything but the most general definitions of the parts of speech, in the first place because it is almost impossible to give a definition which is exact and comprehensive; secondly because it is hardly necessary, since the conception of "Noun", "Verb", etc., will almost certainly be familiar to the student in his own language' (ibid.). Here we feel that there is a cry for help: the theory has not proved adequate to the demands that the language teacher must make of it.

This type of difficulty constantly arises. Compare 'A word that tells us about (or modifies) a verb is called an adverb' (R.iii 30), which again shows the mixture of linguistic and non-linguistic components that is imposed by the theory. In 'Participle adjectives which have *not completely lost their verbal nature*' (K. 288) the criterion, though linguistic, is not defined, and is certainly not self-evident enough to be readily capable of application; while in statements such as 'Nouns or pronouns that are in the subject are in the NOMINATIVE CASE' (E. & E. 9), followed later by 'The case of nouns is shown not by inflexion but by word order' (E. & E. 98), 'case' is a pseudo-category which merely complicates the description without adding anything to it. A final example in this connection is 'A subordinate clause is a group of words containing a subject and verb and joined to the main sentence by a conjunction or relative pronoun or adverb' (T. & M. 158): here the theory can offer only a number of unrelated linguistic criteria, which yield a definition that is full of loose ends. If the subordinate clause is not part of the main sentence, as presumably it is not if it is 'joined to' it, of what sentence, if any, is it a part? Is the relative pronoun part of the subordinate clause? Is the 'main sentence' a clause? If the status of the defining categories is in doubt, the definition itself is likely to be of little value.

(c) Fictions. 'A finite verb must have a subject, expressed or understood' (R.iii 13). Such statements and definitions, which depend on the presence of something that is absent, are accepted by tradition, though their scope is undefined: compare 'The subject (which is always in the second person) is not usually expressed with the

6+L.S.L.T.

imperative' (E. & E. 226); 'In conversation it is often possible to use *have to/had to* alone, the infinitive being understood but not mentioned' (T. & M. 84).

Sometimes a form is said to be 'suppressed' or 'omitted': '*To* is *suppressed* before the infinitive in the following cases . . . After *better*, in sententious remarks . . . Sometimes the whole infinitive is suppressed' (K. 168). 'When an infinitive is used to replace another verb, often . . . the infinitive itself and its complement are *suppressed*' (ibid.). Since there is no infinitive, how can it be said to be used to replace another verb? 'In indirect speech the conjunction *that* is often omitted' (T. & M. 205): why should its absence be regarded as an omission? Is a simple sentence really a complex sentence with subordinate clauses omitted?

As always it is the theory that is deficient: fictions are required to sustain definitions that create their own difficulties. For example: 'Below is a list of condensed sentences. They are really complete, though certain words are omitted and have to be understood. When these understood words are inserted you will see that each sentence has its usual subject and predicate. Thus (1) really means (You be) quick!' (R.ii 41). This kind of manipulation is not, however, always permitted: compare what is said about 'The mole' under (d) below, where one might have expected a similar appeal to something 'understood'.

Sometimes a form is said to 'replace' or to 'be used instead of' another: 'The passive, with *it* as subject, is used in English instead of an impersonal pronoun construction or a reflexive verb' (T. & M. 202); '*It* is used to replace an infinitive phrase at the beginning of a sentence; e.g. instead of: "*To be early* is necessary" we usually say: "It is necessary to be early"' (T. & M. 33). It is not clear what is gained by 'explaining' one pattern by reference to another which it is held to 'replace'. (Here, moreover, *to be early* has been moved rather than replaced.)

It is sometimes asserted that a form is something other than what it is: '"If I saw him I should speak to him" . . . The past tense here is really a subjunctive' (T. & M. 162). This seems to imply that it is not a past tense; compare 'If it [a clause] stands on its own it ceases to be a clause' (R.iii 13). The danger is that this suggests that much of the language may be rewritten without change of meaning: compare for example '*Should* in *indirect* questions may be replaced by the infinitive. E.g. "*To be* or not *to be*. That is the question", *i.e.* the question is, *whether one should exist or not exist*' (K. 161).

(d) Conceptual formulations. Examples of these are: 'Every word has a job of work to do in clothing our thoughts' (R.i 39); 'A sentence is a complete thought put into words' (R.i 12); 'If Kenneth Grahame says, "The mole", he has not made a sentence, for the thought is not complete' (R.I 29); 'A clause is a group of words which . . . does not by itself make complete sense' (E. & E. 320).

Such definitions, which rely on the concept of 'incomplete thoughts' or 'incomplete sense', are open to all kinds of logical objections, as philosophers are continually reminding us. Scarcely less so are statements denying any meaning at all to certain linguistic items; for example, 'link verbs' are said to be 'verbs which have no meaning *unless followed by a noun or an infinitive.* Such verbs are: . . . to turn, . . . to go' (K. 289). The *turn* in question is as in 'apples turn red'; this is presumably, though it is not stated, regarded as a different item from the *turn* in 'he turned the corner', but even if it is assumed that this *turn* cannot occur without a following complement (and one might cite 'the milk has turned'), this is a very different thing from saying that it 'has no meaning' unless so followed. One may wonder why, since 'he killed' likewise rarely occurs without a complement, the theory would not require 'kill' to be said, in the same way, to 'have no meaning unless followed by a noun'.

Sometimes a clash is implied between form and meaning: '"We have nothing to wear" . . . Note that the meaning here is passive but that the active infinitive is used' (T. & M. 181). Compare 'In sentences like this (e.g. "it is possible that I may not be able to come"), *it* is called the FORMAL SUBJECT; the real subject is the noun clause' (E. & E. 334). Quite apart from the confusing opposition of 'formal' and 'real', neither term seems to fit very well the definition 'The subject of a sentence is the word (or group of words) denoting the person or thing about which something is said' (E. & E. 8).

Finally we meet examples like 'The passive voice is used in English when it is more convenient or interesting to stress the thing done rather than the doer of it . . . "This chapel was built by Henry VII"' (T. & M. 201). It is difficult to accept that the reason for using the passive here is to stress the fact that the chapel was built, rather than the fact of who built it; one can invent similar examples such as 'it was painted by a very good friend of mine whom I'd love to have you meet some time', where no such explanation would hold. The difficulty arises in this instance because the theory does not provide the means for distinguishing among the different kinds of passive in English; but the real point here is that conceptual definitions, as used in the theory, are allowed to stand even when they are inappropriate, because they cannot be disproved.

(e) Value judgments. 'To say, "This is *a* good silk" is *shop English*, and should not be imitated' (K. 215); 'An over-use of the passive makes a narrative stilted, and *must be avoided*' (K. 148); 'The split infinitive is, however, often heard on the lips of educated people in conversation. Its use in speech cannot, therefore, be absolutely condemned' (K. 169); 'The banality of a good many North American writers and speakers is in part due to their failure to understand that the genius of the English language does not lend itself to the generous use of superlative adjectives. The English prefer *adverbs*' (K. 303). Opinions of this kind are surely debatable, and if propounded without due discussion and qualification may have a very daunting effect, especially on a foreign student.

The Americans come in for frequent criticism, for example: 'Americans are especially fond of slipping in redundant prepositions. They will talk about checking up on figures, when checking figures means exactly the same' (R.iii 41). We wonder whether many Americans, or even many English people, would agree that these two expressions are synonymous. Another doctrine which is perhaps not very helpful without full discussion is of the kind exemplified by: 'It is a good rule never to use a word of foreign derivation, especially Latin or Greek, *when an Anglo-Saxon one will do*' (K. 426); compare 'Latin borrowings tend to be too long and clumsy' (R.iii 90).

In phonetics the desirability of RP as a model is often taken for granted: 'What is this good speech like when it is finally developed? ... It is the B.B.C. speech at its best' (R.iii 114). The word 'pure' is frequent in phonetic observations, for example: 'What is the best position of lips, mouth and tongue for making the sound a pure one?' (R.iii 44). It is very rare to find any attempt to define what is meant by 'pure' in such cases.

(f) Inaccurate phonetics. It might be thought that in the previous example 'pure' referred to a phonetic property of the vowel sound and meant simply that the vowel in question was not a diphthong. If so the example should be transferred to the present paragraph, since the sound in question was 'the OH sound in "mole"', which in B.B.C. speech *is* a diphthong, although in many dialects it is not. If on the other hand what is meant by 'pure' here is merely 'as similar as possible to that heard in B.B.C. speech', this is likely to be very misleading, being in this case in direct conflict with the usual sense of the word in popular phonetics. Equally misleading are some of the general statements that are made about phonetics, for example 'Whilst concentrating upon vowel sounds we must not forget that it is the consonants that most carry the voice' (R.iii 117).

Perhaps we might include under this same heading a tendency to undertake complex orthographic contortions in an attempt to indicate clearly the sounds of speech. Examples of this practice are numerous; as throughout this section, quotations are given merely in order to make clear what is being referred to: 'Examine the difference of ŏŏ (as in look) from OO (as in moon)' (R.iii 32) and 'OI is compounded of AW plus ĭ . . . EW is compounded of ĭ plus OO' (R.iii 175). The intention, namely of representing speech sounds unambiguously, is of course admirable; but the attempt to do so while avoiding the use of the symbols of the I.P.A. alphabet may lead to serious misunderstandings. Moreover since the method still requires its own unfamiliar notations and conventions, such as ŏŏ and OO, the I.P.A. alphabet would seem the simpler as well as the more reliable alternative.

(g) Confusion of media. H. E. Palmer's *Grammar of Spoken English on a Strictly Phonetic Basis* was first published in 1924, and marked a great step forward towards ending the tyranny of the written language, and the confusion of writing and speech, in the language-teaching field. But the older tradition is still strong; here is an example: ' 1. Form. The indefinite article is *a* or *an*. The form *a* is used before a word beginning with a consonant, or a vowel sounded like a consonant' (T. & M. 1). The difficulty here is that we are not told what a consonant is. Is it a letter, a sound or a phoneme? Here, as so often, the theory is that associated with the old-fashioned type of grammar of the written language; compare the rules for the plural of nouns, which not only relate solely to the written forms but also

take this restriction for granted, without explanation. But this
approach is difficult to maintain consistently; note for example:
'*One-syllable adjectives* form their comparative and superlative by
adding *er* and *est* to the positive form' (T. & M. 13). This appears
to suggest the forms *safe, safeer, safeest*.

When 'dice' and 'sixpence' are stated to be 'plural in form'
(K. 403–4), this could be regarded as another instance of the same
approach, in which only the written language is taken into account,
since it is difficult to see how these items could be plural in modern
spoken English (unless perhaps *dice* were the plural of '*douse*').
Spoken English has /z/ in the plural after a vowel or a nasal consonant, whereas these forms have /s/. But the statement is equally
inappropriate from the orthographic point of view, since regular
plurals are written with s and not c. Hence it is probably to be
explained as a relic of an approach which is now rarely met with,
one which fails to distinguish clearly between the description of a
language as it is and the study of the facts of its history. The fact
that *dice* and *sixpence* were once plural is not relevant to a description of Modern English, as Henry Sweet saw and made clear as
early as 1884.

6

The role of linguistics and phonetics in language teaching is not to
tell the teacher how to teach. The teacher of the language is as much
a specialist in his field as the linguist is in his, and will remain so.
He is not teaching linguistics. But he is teaching something which is
the object of study of linguistics, and is described by linguistic
methods. It is obviously desirable that the underlying description
should be as good as possible, and this means that it should be based
on sound linguistic principles.

This is the main contribution that the linguistic sciences can
make to the teaching of languages: to provide good descriptions.
Any description of a language implies linguistics; it implies, that is,
a definite attitude to language, a definite stand on how language
works and how it is to be accounted for. As soon as the teacher uses
the word 'sentence' or 'verb' in relation to the language he is
teaching, he is applying linguistics, just as when he says 'open your
mouth wider' he is applying phonetics. It is a pity then not to apply

the linguistics best suited to the purpose. The best suited linguistics is the body of accurate descriptive methods based on recent research into the form and the substance of language. There is no conflict between application and theory; the methods most useful in application are to be found among those that are most valid and powerful in theory.

In Chapters 2 and 3 we gave a very brief sketch, in terms of one model, of some aspects of the relevant descriptive theories and methods. Not very long ago, it seemed that it might be many years before detailed and accurate descriptions along these lines, whether of English or of other languages widely studied as foreign languages, could be made available. Linguistic analysis is a long and laborious process, and even in such a well-described language as English there are many features about which little was known; these including some fundamental features which, far from belonging to a very delicate stage of the analysis, are crucial to a description of English from the very beginning. Moreover the number of people engaged in research in this field was exceedingly small, though in this respect some countries, especially the United States, were far ahead of Britain: in 1955 there were hardly a score of people in posts in descriptive linguistics in all the universities of the United Kingdom, and probably no more in phonetics.

In the last few years, with the discovery that the linguistic sciences have an 'applied' as well as a 'pure' side to them, some increased provision for research and teaching in linguistics and phonetics has been made, and more would seem to be likely. In both subjects most of the early developments in this country took place within London University, at University College and the School of Oriental and African Studies; now there is research and specialist training also at other centres, principally Edinburgh, Leeds, Cambridge, Manchester and the University College of North Wales. The overall facilities are still quite inadequate, but they are better than they were; the number of people being trained in at least the rudiments of the linguistic sciences is probably ten times what it was a decade ago.

In phonetics, English and the major European languages have always received considerable attention in Britain, ever since the subject was brought to maturity by the great Oxford linguist and phonetician Henry Sweet. After Sweet's death Oxford abandoned the subject, but continuity was maintained in the famous

Department of Phonetics at University College London under Professor Daniel Jones. Here the work covered a wide range of both Indo-European and non-Indo-European languages; in particular English, French and German were studied intensively and the results applied in the teaching of these languages.

In descriptive linguistics, however, the main concentration of work in Britain has been on languages outside Europe. Just as, in America, linguists working in the North American Indian languages found themselves unable to continue to operate with the haphazard categories of traditional description, so in Britain precisely the same situation arose when Asian and African languages began to be seriously re-examined in the 1930s. It was thus no accident that the first linguistics department in this country was at the School of Oriental and African Studies of London University, and that it was here, among a small group of linguists working under J. R. Firth, that many of the basic concepts of descriptive theory were formulated. Until quite recently the School was the only centre of such studies in Britain, and of the now extensive writings in modern descriptive linguistics it is still probably true that the greater proportion is concerned with non-European languages.

Far from this being a matter for regret, it is very useful that such a wide variety of languages should have been described first. Attention can now be paid to English and other more familiar languages with, behind it, a vast store of experience of different languages and a general theory of language built up on the basis of this experience. This does not mean that we describe English so as to make it look like Chinese or Yoruba; to do so would be as bad as making it look like Latin. (Perhaps not quite as bad in practice, since English is in some ways more like Chinese or Yoruba than it is like Latin; but still unacceptable.) It means that we now know much better what really are the essential properties of language as such, and what are features specific to one language or to a certain group of languages. That is to say, we have a picture of how language works, as well as different pictures of how different languages work: we have a 'general linguistic' theory.

Much research is now being done in the, to us, better known European languages, including English. This work consumes a lot of time, since it involves collecting and examining a large amount of data, spoken and written, as well as a great deal of thought and discussion of theory. Since 1945, however, important new facilities have become available. Not only the tape recorder and the instruments of the phonetics laboratory, which have revolutionized the collection and observation of data, but also the electronic computer are now essential implements for describing languages. It is now possible to examine far larger samples and to examine them much more accurately.

The descriptions of English and other languages which are being produced by linguists will not be textbooks of languages. The linguist can say what is a good description of a language, and can produce such a description. But he cannot say how the language should be taught. That is a matter for teachers and for those who train the teachers. Textbooks can be based on the descriptions written by linguists; but the writing of a language textbook is again a specialized activity and is not the same thing as describing a language. The textbook writer, however, needs to have some acquaintance with the attitude to language and the foundations of linguistic theory which underlie a good description; otherwise he will almost certainly fail to make the best use of whatever pedagogical methods he is seeking, in his books, to apply. Language teachers likewise may find such knowledge useful.

This is the background to the subject that has come to be known, somewhat misleadingly, as 'applied linguistics'. This term covers the whole field of research and training in the teaching of languages, including but not restricted to general linguistics and general phonetics. It is misleading because it excludes other activities which are just as much applications of linguistics, such as machine translation and sociological linguistics. At the same time it includes parts of certain subjects which lie outside the linguistic sciences, such as those aspects of psychology and educational theory that are relevant to language teaching. The aim of courses in applied linguistics, such as are now available for example at Edinburgh, Leeds and London, is not to produce specialists in linguistics and phonetics—separate courses are given for these purposes—but to give a solid grounding in those aspects of these and other subjects which lie behind the language class. This should enable the 'applied linguist' to evaluate both descriptions and textbooks of languages, to produce his own teaching material, to plan and teach a language course, to test his pupils' attainments and, as a background to all these, to understand as much as possible of the working of language.

Thus even before new descriptions have been written and placed

6*

on the market, it is already useful for teachers of language to have some acquaintance with linguistics and phonetics to the stage that is reached in these subjects in an applied linguistics course. This will help them to evaluate textbook and other material on language, such as for example studies of the language of literary texts; and give some insight into the nature and operation of language. It will not do to assume that because we all speak and write we know how language works, any more than the fact that we eat and drink gives us an insight into the physiology of the digestive system. The main role of linguistics and phonetics in language teaching is, as we have said, to produce good descriptions of languages. But an insight into linguistic and phonetic theory, which a good description also helps to impart, is itself of value to those who are applying these subjects in an important and difficult task.

7

This then is the principal contribution of the linguistic sciences in application to language teaching: they enable a good description to be made of the language being taught. Whether this is a foreign language or the learner's own native language, a good description is the first essential. In foreign language teaching, there is the further possibility of comparing the foreign language with the native one. The subjects involved in these applications are descriptive and comparative descriptive linguistics.

Institutional linguistics, though less directly applicable than descriptive linguistics, is nevertheless also relevant to both native and foreign language teaching. In the first place, description is itself interdependent with institutional studies: any description of a language which is at all delicate is bound to be specific in the sense that it relates only to a certain variety, or certain varieties, of the language; and institutional linguistics is needed to define and identify these varieties. For example, if we want an accurate account of the English of medical textbooks, we cannot expect the description given to be valid in detail also for the language of political speeches. In the second place, decisions have to be taken about which varieties of a language, both dialectal and 'registral', are to be taught; it is through institutional linguistics that we can survey the full range of possible varieties, classify them and estimate the uses of each.

For the student learning about his own language, the picture is not complete without an account of its varieties and of the linguistic differences among them. If the teaching of the native language is conceived of as, at least among other things, educational in purpose, in the sense of contributing to the citizen's total understanding of his world, the study of its varieties in their appropriate uses is likely to figure prominently in the course. An examination of the registers of Modern English can be fascinating and instructive. The language used in advertising, in headlines and news reports, in recipes, dressmaking patterns and the instructions for fitting and using manufactured products, in technical manuals, official forms and notices: all this enters into our experience of language in use, and it is a valuable exercise to try to discover the grammatical and lexical features that characterize and distinguish such varieties.

If the concept of 'literature' is meaningful, such that some language activity is regarded as literature and some not, there must likewise be linguistic features which are characteristic of literary uses of language. It may be possible after more research to make certain generalizations about the language of literature as a whole; it is certainly possible to make revealing statements about the language of particular works of literature. At the same time a work of literature makes its impact against the background of our total experience of the language. One can compare the language of, let us say, a modern novel not only with that of another modern novel but also with a sports commentary and a report of a directors' meeting; and it is useful to observe not only how they differ but also what they have in common. In all such work, description is made more effective by the concept of varieties of language.

When native language teaching is prescriptive, institutional considerations become central, since the theme is the placing of value judgments on what are treated as different varieties of the language. As we have seen, such value judgments are 'institutional' in the sense that there are no linguistic grounds for choosing one form rather than another; it is the speakers' attitude to language that is the determining factor. More than anything, what matters here is that the teacher should have access to the facts, so that he can concentrate on productive rather than prescriptive teaching, and so that he does not condemn as 'ugly' or 'ineffective' certain patterns or items in the language whose only fault is to have been used by the wrong people.

It is true that many people, including many teachers and probably most phoneticians and linguists, deplore the social value judgments that tend to be passed on varieties of English. The linguist, of course, has the responsibility of observing and describing the attitudes to language as well as that of observing and describing the language; and just as he does not pass judgment on language, so also he does not, *quâ* linguist, pass judgment on those who pass judgment on language. This does not mean that linguists merely put language under the microscope and never make recommendations concerning what they observe. On the contrary, we are here precisely making recommendations about the teaching of languages; and in other applications such as machine translation, script reform and the development of languages as scientific and educational media linguists are likely to hold definite views about what to do, and to enjoy giving advice as much as the next man. What they will not do is award marks for merit to what they are describing, or judge the forms and varieties of a language, or its speakers, according to a ready-made scale of values.

But as private citizens, so to speak, the present authors are among the deplorers; and it would be disingenuous not to admit that our positive rejection of value judgments on language is closely derived from what the linguistic sciences have found out about language, both how it works and how it is modified through time. In other words, the more one learns of linguistics and phonetics, the more one is likely to consider it undesirable that a person should be required to alter his native language habits or that he should be judged and assessed according to his conformity to a particular variety of the language. Such attitudes may be harmful; not because they represent personal preferences but because they have the apparent objectivity of social sanction. A teacher who shares our view may of course still decide, albeit reluctantly, that in his pupils' own interests he must 'do something about' their language. But this will be both less dangerous and more effective if as much as possible can be taught productively and not prescriptively: not 'it is bad to do this', but 'in these particular circumstances we do that'. One does not have to condemn English in order to teach French; why should one condemn one English accent or set of grammatical habits in order to teach another?

In foreign language teaching, the question what variety or varieties to teach arises already at the start. Of course, there is much in common to all varieties of a given language, and it might be assumed that this is what should in all circumstances be taught first. But even this assumption needs examining.

As far as dialect is concerned, there is often an initial selection to be made. This, however, rarely presents a problem; there is usually some dialectal variety agreed upon by the native speakers as 'standard' in one sense or another. Occasionally there is a problem of selection between two or more 'standard' varieties, for example British and American English; but in most countries where English is taught as a foreign language the teaching is oriented towards one or the other, and since either in its 'standard' variety is acceptable to all native speakers of English the problem is not so much which to select as that sooner or later the student will probably have to cope with both. He may in some areas meet with both among his teachers, even at a relatively early stage.

Formal distinctions between the two are slight, and when they arise the student usually learns at least to recognize both versions without much trouble, even if he selects one for his own use. Differences such as that between 'You've got a class now, haven't you?' and 'You have a class now, don't you?', though they may affect a large number of utterances, involve only a few recurring patterns; only a small proportion of the total resources of English grammar and lexis shows consistent divergence between British and American usage. The most far-reaching distinctions are in phonetics and phonology; here it is probably advisable to select one variety or the other, at least for the elementary stages of language learning.

In some countries, such as India and Pakistan, where instead of a native variety of English local L2 varieties are often accepted as a standard for teaching purposes, confusion is caused by the fact that, once an L2 variety has become 'standardized' in this way, it is thought to be equivalent to a native language. The teaching of English then comes to be regarded as a native language teaching problem instead of as a foreign language teaching problem, and the whole task is made more difficult for all concerned. English is not a native language in India or Pakistan for more than a tiny minority of the populations; to treat it as such merely complicates the problem for those learning it, however early they start.

The doctrine that there is an 'Indian English', to which Indian and Pakistani speakers should conform rather than aiming at a native model, whether British or American, is one which commands sympathy on general liberal principles because of the way it is usually formulated: why, it is asked, should Indians 'be expected to' adopt a British or American model when English is an Indian language? The same point of view was adopted by the Russian aristocracy about French in the nineteenth century: French was regarded as a Russian language. But there is a risk here, of creating an implication that the native languages are somehow inferior. Those who favour the adoption of 'Indian English' as a model, from whatever motive, should realize that in doing so they may be helping to prop up the fiction that English is the language of Indian culture and thus be perpetuating the diminished status of the Indian languages.

In addition to dialectal selection there may be another selection to be made among varieties of the foreign language, that between different registers. Foreign languages are learnt for a wide range of different purposes, and for some of these purposes it is appropriate to teach selectively one or more specific varieties. There is no reason why the student of a foreign language should be required to study 'the whole language', which in any case is an aim impossible of achievement, if the uses he wishes to make of it are restricted and defined; nor why he should study certain registers, such as the language of literature, if his need is for quite other ones. There has already been a considerable trend towards language courses much more specifically related to the varying needs of the student; but the potentialities of such courses are still not widely recognized.

One striking example of the success of specialized language teaching was provided during the Second World War, both in Britain and in the United States. Numbers of British servicemen were taught, in a very short time, a restricted language of Japanese: for example, the language used by Japanese pilots in communicating with each other and with the ground. Those who learnt this variety of Japanese did not at the same time learn to order a cup of tea in a Tokyo café or to hold an informal conversation with a Japanese citizen; such skills they were not going to need. The British courses were worked out on linguistic principles under the direction of Professor J. R. Firth, who had himself first formulated the concept of restricted languages in his work in general linguistic theory.

There are of course many degrees of 'restriction' in between a restricted language such as, for example, the International Language of the Air and anything conceived of as 'the whole language'; and to these correspond the different requirements of the language learner. There are those who learn a foreign language in order to read scientific papers, often in one or two specialized subjects only; they need not learn to speak the language or to read its literature. An export manager in an industrial firm may need to speak and be spoken to in the foreign language, both in a technical register and in informal conversation; but in the written language he might only require technical and commercial registers. For secretarial purposes, the restricted language of commercial correspondence may be the only requirement in a foreign language; it can be effectively taught in secretarial colleges in quite a short time.

If one can formulate clearly the aims of a particular foreign-language teaching operation, it becomes possible to specify what registers of the foreign language are relevant. Here we must again stress, however, that the description of particular registers and restricted languages, even in well-described languages such as English, is still very little advanced; much of the basic linguistic research remains to be done. The number of people employed to do the necessary work, while still seriously inadequate, is now at last beginning to increase.

What is important is that those undertaking such studies should be trained as linguists and phoneticians. Otherwise, a great deal of time and energy may be wasted on work that proves to be invalid, as has happened in the past for example when statisticians have turned their attention to language and counted occurrences of 'words' or 'syllables', without knowing what a word or a syllable is or what function the word or syllable fulfils in the language concerned.

It has long been realized, especially by those engaged in the teaching of English overseas, that an approach is needed which takes account of differences of register; and some excellent attempts have been made to devise textbooks directed towards such specialized aims. Methods of analysis drawn from general linguistic theory, and statistical techniques developed within linguistics, enable us to make and handle quantitative statements about the large samples of text that are required. It is not beyond the powers of quite small research groups, given the facilities available today for the processing of large quantities of linguistic data, to make detailed studies of important varieties of English, or of other languages. These would provide material for courses more closely adapted to the needs of particular language students than is much of the teaching material at present in use. At the same time such studies would be very relevant to other applications of linguistics, from medicine and psychiatry to machine translation and information retrieval.

BIBLIOGRAPHY

See items 5, 9, 15, 29, 35, 62, 65, 72, 79, 82, 85.

Chapter 7

Language teaching and language learning

1

Before we can properly consider the problems and techniques of teaching languages we must first take account of the other side of the coin, language *learning*. The relation between learning and teaching is one that defies close analysis. 'Did he learn or was he taught?' is an unanswerable question. Just how extensive a person's skill has become—that is, how well he speaks or reads or writes the language in particular situations—is itself very difficult to discover precisely, since our methods of testing language ability are little more than rudimentary. As for being able to say whether any specific changes in the course of instruction would have been followed by any specific differences in his performance in the language, here we are still very largely in the dark.

If we knew more about the nature of learning in human beings we should be better equipped to prescribe methods of teaching. In fact, we know rather little about learning in human beings, although a lot of information about learning in other animals, for example rats and pigeons, is being amassed. No one assumes that what is valid for rats is also valid for humans; but it does seem to be true that many of the observed facts about learning in experimental animals can be transferred to human learning without much change. At the same time the average human pupil exposed to language-teaching procedures exists in a situation much more complex than that enjoyed by the psychologist's experimental animals.

In recent years one of the most stimulating and illuminating controversies in the realm of language study was an incursion into descriptive linguistics by the behaviourist psychologist, B. F. Skinner, who used the concepts and categories of his psychology to describe language behaviour as he believed it occurred in total situations. Few linguists accepted Skinner's thesis as a whole, and one linguist, Noam Chomsky, having first devoted a great deal of time to the study of psychology, added to his criticisms on linguistic grounds others that attacked the psychological foundations of Skinner's theory. There are a number of interesting sides to this episode. For instance, Skinner pinpointed an aspect of one model in linguistics which had come to be regarded as less than satisfactory to many linguists in the United States, just as it had long so appeared to linguists in Britain. This was the way in which the consideration of meaning was continually side-stepped through concentration on the description of substance and form. But Skinner's intervention brought together more closely than had been achieved during the previous fifty years the disciplines of psychology and linguistics. The central point here is that Skinner's views on language were congruent with his experience in experimental psychology, as a specialist in the investigation of the mechanism of learning in animals.

What do we know about language learning in humans? We know that all normal human infants are born with the potentiality of acquiring language. Grossly subnormal intelligence or defective hearing can prevent an individual child from realizing this potentiality, but in the typical case a human child acquires the ability to perform in the two basic language skills of understanding speech and speaking understandably, and the language in which he so performs depends on his experience during the first two or three years of his life.

Heredity and race are irrelevant to the infant, except where physical characteristics affect such features as voice quality. The child of Finnish-speaking parents inherits no inborn facility for learning to understand and speak Finnish rather than some other language; he will learn the language that is being used around him, no matter what that language is. Of course, it is usual for the child to hear the language of its parents, which accounts for the term 'mother tongue'; but it is by no means necessary or universal that it should be the parents he hears.

It is useful to remember that the notion of language is irrelevant to the baby. He is assailed from birth by a kaleidoscopic variety of sensations, some of them visual, some auditory, some tactile. The process of growing older provides him with a store of memories,

memories of the sequence in which some of these sensations were perceived, and memories of which sensations habitually go with others. The baby early discovers that some of the sounds it hears are made by itself; there is a stage of development in which the baby rehearses the process of noticing that it has stopped making a noise, then starting to make it again, then stopping once more. Later, the noticing, like the sound production, becomes steadily more sophisticated. Instead of somewhat random babbling with a repertoire that is sometimes supposed to include all the sounds found in all the languages of the world and some that are to be found in no language, the child selects out some of the sounds and sound-sequences that it has noticed in its own vicinity and imitates those, practising and repeating and imitating his own efforts until a semi-deliberate control of speech production gradually becomes more and more automatic. These habits are largely *phonetic*, but as the child grows older he begins to organize his speech into patterns of grammar, to acquire a stock of items, lexical and grammatical, to operate ni these patterns, and to fit his speech to the appropriate situations. He makes many mistakes, and it takes a long time before his command of the whole apparatus of language is sure and acceptable, but the process of habit-making is similar for all children, in all human societies.

This process of acquiring linguistic habits is familiar to most people, and there is little we could add that is not either common knowledge or accessible to everyday observation. It is worth making one point, nevertheless: namely that the young child knows, and needs to know, no linguistics or phonetics. When we acquire our primary language, or L1, we do so by learning how to behave in situations, not by learning rules about what to say. Whatever the place of phonetics and linguistics may be in language *teaching*, the formulation of linguistic statements is by no means essential to language *learning*.

2

A minority of children, but still a large number, learn two or even more languages simultaneously if they are exposed to them during this formative period. These are the bilinguals or (occasionally) ambilinguals (see section 2 of Chapter 4). But the great majority of children do not learn a secondary language until they have first acquired some degree of mastery of their primary language. All normal children learn *one* language: those who later learn a secondary language, or even several of them, may do so at any later period of life, but one of the facts about language learning is that a secondary language is more readily acquired very young; neurophysiology confirms that it is at about the age of eight or nine that maturation begins to render it somewhat more difficult to learn a language.

Quite apart from this inherent increase in difficulty there sometimes arise factors of learned behaviour that make it more difficult for children in some communities to learn languages than would otherwise be the case. Great Britain is an example of this. There is a piece of folklore about language learning that many British people are perversely proud of and which they teach as a fact to the young: namely that British people are inherently less well able to learn languages than are the natives of most other countries. This we do not believe. There is no evidence to support the notion that the inhabitants of any one country are less talented in respect of learning languages than the inhabitants of any other. Such statements cover up feelings of inferiority or superiority about language ability on the part of those who make them, or they are made to justify the conventional attitude towards languages in an educational system which places little value on practical language ability. In the circumstances of the present-day world children should be given every encouragement to regard the learning of several languages as normal; to suggest the contrary seems to us both prejudiced and harmful.

Perhaps it is even worse when this myth enters the teacher's patter. It is not unknown for French people teaching French in British schools to inform their pupils that 'of course English children can never pronounce the French vowel in *tu*' (or other habitual difficulties). Acting as if this were a statement of fact, the teacher then makes no attempt to teach the pupils how to overcome the problem. Here the statement is doing two things: it is reflecting poor teaching methods, and it is covering up the teacher's incompetence. Unhappily, parallel examples can be met in the teaching of other languages, including the teaching of English to foreign learners.

Children learn their primary language without systematic instruction in it. It is perfectly possible to acquire one or more secondary languages in the same way, a fact that is sometimes obscured by the manner in which we organize foreign-language teaching as part of the general education system. In other words, because most foreign languages are learned in the secondary school this does not mean that this is the only way in which they could, or even should, be acquired. And even if they are *best* acquired during the school career, looking at the matter from the point of view of the interests of the state as a whole, it is not true that they can only be learned in the manner in which they are acquired in school at present, namely through deliberate instruction of a formal nature. It is important to separate the consideration of how languages can be *learned* from how they can or should be *taught*; we are concerned for the moment with the individual human being who is doing the learning rather than with the discussion of deliberate procedures to be followed by the person who is attempting to do the instructing. The learner does not have to have a teacher, any more than an expectant mother has to have a midwife. There are a small number of circumstances that will favour the process of learning the language; and if these are not present in the ordinary course of events, then one of the useful functions of the teacher, like those of the midwife, can be to provide the physical conditions that will render more bearable and expeditious a process that could nevertheless take place without them.

What are these propitious circumstances that can favour language learning? One is youth, as we have seen already. The earlier learning begins, the better. Another is the amount of experience of the language received by the learner, provided that this experience is meaningful. In other words, learning takes place more readily if the language is encountered in active use than if it is seen or heard only as a set of disembodied utterances or exercises. But quantity of experience alone is not the only factor which determines the rate of learning; the rate at which this experience is taken in is also important. It seems to be the case that, for language, the memory span of the learner is relatively short, so that learning is more certain and rapid if lessons are frequent and hence there are correspondingly fewer opportunities for forgetting what has been learned so far. This is one of the places where the experience of the classroom teacher is borne out by the evidence of the experimental psychologist; reinforcement of what has been learned should take place with as little delay as possible.

Another favourable factor is that elusive quality, *motivation*. Human beings, whether they are children or adults, learn more rapidly and effectively if they have a reason for doing so. The reason may not be consciously known to the learner; it may be simply another feature of the social pressures that impinge on every individual in a community and impel him to develop as he does. Or it may be a deliberate wish or intention to acquire a particular skill and ability. The converse is also true: a child who has been antagonized in some ways towards a skill or a subject learns with only the greatest difficulty, if indeed he learns at all. Acquiring a positive reason for learning a language will thus help a pupil to learn it, while a negative motivation may make it impossible for a pupil to learn at all effectively. (Incidentally, popular superstitions such as the view that the English cannot learn languages may act as just such negative motivation.)

All these favourable circumstances—an early start, extensive experience at frequent intervals, and strong motivation—are present in the highest degree for the normal child, during his acquisition of the primary language, at least for the understanding of speech and the ability to speak intelligibly and acceptably. When the time comes for society to require of the individual that he should add to the skills of speech those of reading and writing there remains a strong motivation for doing this, since the child generally discovers at an early age that those who do not become literate are relegated to membership of an unfavoured group within the community.

When it comes to learning any secondary language, on the other hand, the reasons for doing so are often less obvious. For the majority of children the only motivation for learning French or German or any other language is in order to make up the right number of examination subjects, if indeed the matter is consciously considered at all. It has commonly been remarked in the past that more people tend to learn languages more effectively in those countries which depend to a great extent on commercial and political intercourse with a large number of different language communities. The motivation is there, in fact, on a national scale, and there is a precedent too: there is a national language-learning habit. It seems certain that developments such as the entry of Britain into the Common Market would produce a rapid increase in national motivation towards the more effective learning of languages.

By 'learning a language' we mean 'learning effective and acceptable language behaviour in situations in an unfamiliar culture'; we
do not mean 'learning *about* a language'. This is one further distinction which, familiar as it is, must be taken into account if the
processes of language teaching are to be effectively related to those
of language learning.

3

In Chapter 4 we discussed the concept of 'a language', and showed
that this cannot just be taken for granted as something clearcut and
homogeneous. In this section we shall re-examine the concept of
'teaching a language', and suggest that this too may need drastic
reformulation.

A study of the titles of papers and articles on the subject of
English language teaching for overseas learners during the past
fifteen years shows a steady process of analysis, of breaking down
the task into smaller, more manageable components, and applying
a specialized solution to each component. But the analysis itself has
not been a consistent or a planned one; individual writers, many of
them gifted teachers with wide experience and the initiative and
flair to make a contribution to their profession, have each written
on a separate problem, while a small number of those with wide
experience have occasionally brought together a group of related
ideas and applied them to the field as a whole. Two main trends
can be discerned, both of them relevant to our theme. The first is
the realization that the teaching of literature to learners for whom
English is a secondary language is necessarily a separate job from
the teaching of language, and that to maintain this implies no denial
of the value or importance of literature. The second is the swing
towards the fuller application of linguistic theory to the business of
teaching.

We should consider the first of these trends in detail, because it
is, in some ways, one of the most fundamental of all the changes that
have taken place in language teaching during this century, and
because it is a change that is in train in the teaching of English as
a foreign language.

To a great many teachers of English, both in Britain and abroad,
'the teaching of English' still means 'the teaching of English

literature'. In countries such as India the pattern of education has been exported so successfully from British school and university practice that syllabuses exist which are nowadays *plus royaliste que le roi*. From such countries students come to Britain for training that will fit them to join the teaching profession in their home country and teach English literature (or rather, a version of literary history and criticism); yet in many cases it is painfully clear that there are many among them whose command of English as a language is not sufficient to enable them either to discuss and teach great works of literature or fully to understand or appreciate them. In such cases the superstructure is more weighty than the foundations can support, and the only sensible solution is to repair and strengthen the foundations.

Unfortunately, prejudices and opinions are such that proposals of this kind are often taken as being a threat to the superstructure itself, instead of a means of saving it from eventual collapse. The reasons why this should be so are complex, but one factor that recurs frequently is that the whole teaching of English is often in the hands of people whose training is in literature alone, and who sense a danger to their livelihood, or at least to their prestige and influence, if a new generation of teachers is inducted into their profession who have mastered another and different aspect of English studies. Others regard the importance of literature as being not only transcendent but self-evidently so to all those who come into contact with it, and they do not even question the ability of students to handle it. Whatever may have been the effect in British schools and universities of denying or playing down the importance of language and linguistics in English studies, the effect abroad has been to encourage a process of self-annihilation, in which more and more literature has been accompanied by less and less language ability until in many overseas countries the study of 'English' in the sense of 'English literature' has become a practical impossibility in the present educational circumstances. The result is that from more than one country in Africa students now go to the Soviet Union, Czechoslovakia or France for the purpose of acquiring a better practical ability in English, because most of the channels to 'English' offered in their country or in Britain are concerned above all with literary studies.

The solution is not to exclude literary studies, but to ensure that no student is pushed into literary work until he has sufficient linguistic ability to understand, enjoy and appreciate the literary texts that he will be studying, and that above all no student who wishes to extend his practical ability to *use* English should be forced into accepting a kind of 'conditional sale' in which he can only continue in English if his studies are of a literary nature. Matters are steadily improving in these respects. Overseas teachers who have reached a high standard in teaching English in the way British expatriates used to teach it, often represent a vested interest which it may be hard to overcome. But as a result of the first of the two trends referred to above teachers began to be trained in Britain along lines which recognized the importance and necessity of studying and teaching language as well as literature, and who now teach and train others along these same lines.

It was chiefly among secondary school teachers, rather than those in primary schools whose task was in any case a 'practical' one, that the swing towards the practical teaching of language ability had the greatest effect. This advance took place in a fairly short period of time, largely between 1945 and 1950 as far as British-based teaching of English is concerned. Since that time, 'English teaching' has very largely evolved into 'English language teaching', and for several years further developments have consisted mainly in improvements in classroom techniques and materials. It seems to us that the profession is now ripe for yet another big advance; it is largely since 1950—that is to say, since the change towards practical teaching— that the main developments in linguistics have taken place in Britain, and it is only since 1955 that the relevance of linguistics to language teaching has been properly considered here. What we have learned about this in recent years is described in outline in various sections of this book, and indeed one of our aims in writing it has been to help language teachers to know more about those methods and techniques in which linguistics and educational practice combine to increase the effectiveness of teaching. Many teachers are already doing what we advocate; but they are still far from being in the majority. This second wave of linguistic advance is already upon us and is still gathering momentum.

What we have said about the two waves of linguistic development could be summarized in this way: the first change was to pay more attention to *language*, and especially to the spoken language; the second change is towards more attention to *linguistics*. The second change, in fact, continues where the first left off and leads to greater sophistication in the study of languages. This introduces a problem of its own, the problem of satisfying the sudden explosive demand among language teachers already in the profession for opportunities of keeping up with the new developments.

The problem arises because up to the present very few books have been published in Great Britain of a kind which could answer this demand for material on linguistics; but, on the other hand, teachers in Britain in the 1960s have suddenly gained access to some of the books and teaching courses illustrating one particular linguistic approach which were published in large quantities during the 1950s. These were books developed out of the great American effort in teaching English to the armed forces, to immigrants, and to school children in the Philippines and in Puerto Rico. Their approach is for the most part rigorously in accord with that version of structural linguistics which holds that syntax must be based on morphemics and morphemics on phonemics, an approach with which the names of Trager, Smith, Fries and Lado are associated.

Many of these textbooks and language courses have been used with great success all over the world. Where, then, does any problem arise for teachers in Great Britain? Why do we not supply a booklist and encourage our readers to dig deep into these works? There are two parts to the answer: the first part concerns linguistics, the second part concerns teaching method. As to the first, there have been considerable advances since the time when works of this kind first appeared. They were great pioneer works, but they have been in operation long enough for their shortcomings to be seen and for other ways of thinking to evolve. In the United States, many of the foremost specialists in the application of linguistics to language teaching (though not all of them) have begun to use techniques based on *transformational grammar* in preference to *phoneme-morpheme grammar*. In Britain, some form of the model which we have outlined is widely regarded as more applicable to the problems we are concerned with than either the *phoneme-morpheme* or the *transformational* approach. The practical snag is that we are only just beginning to see the publication of the large store of books, handbooks, teaching courses and ancillary materials that are essential if language teachers as a whole in Britain are to have access to the newer ways of thought.

The methodological problem is that the American teaching materials do not make use of the particular tradition of classroom method of which the British teaching profession is so justly proud. Their own methods are different from ours, and while we can certainly learn a great deal from American practice in this respect, we believe that the British tradition has its special merits, too. There are very many books available which illustrate American linguistics and language-teaching practice between 1940 and 1960, but few which illustrate the more recent developments taking place in both the United States and Great Britain. It is rather like the position people would be in who suddenly decided to go in for building railways; until recently they would have found plenty of books on how to build steam engines, but relatively few on how to make use of either diesel or electric power. We hope that in the present demand for books on linguistics and language teaching teachers will remember that changes have recently taken place in linguistics which are equivalent to changes away from steam towards the use of diesel and electric locomotives.

4

The basic question is: at what points should linguistics operate in language teaching? It is sometimes assumed that linguists are simply advocating the use of linguistics as such in the school class-room; but this is not the case. Replacing good teachers with no linguistic knowledge or training by teachers trained in linguistics does not of itself make much difference to the effectiveness of the language teaching taking place in their classes. It has been tried, of course; in the early days of the linguistic renaissance many people, especially in the United States, thought that linguistics could be given a direct classroom role, just as many people in Britain once thought, and perhaps still do think, that in the teaching of modern languages the science of phonetics could be given a direct classroom role. In fact, the place for both phonetics and linguistics is *behind* the classroom teacher, in the training that he received for his job as a teacher, in the preparation of the syllabus according to which his teaching programme is organized, and in the preparation of the teaching materials of all kinds that he makes use of in class. These are the points at which the linguistic sciences affect language teaching.

However, before these matters are considered in detail there remains a further general point to be made: that is the need to provide for each separate teaching situation the syllabus and the teaching materials most appropriate to that situation. Courses for teaching English, until comparatively recently, were like courses for teaching French or German: they were intended for use at a particular age level, but in all other respects they set out to teach a generalized 'English', the same course for all learners, anywhere in the world. Courses for adults were somewhat similar, the framework making some degree of allowance for maturity on the part of the learner. What was rarely attempted, but is now becoming more general, was a study of the needs of the learner in close detail and the preparation of a course that was specially designed for one particular group of learners.

There are numerous reasons why this was so. Many teachers have for long agreed that such specialized courses were desirable, but they were not attainable for economic reasons: it costs a lot of money to publish a teaching course, and the publisher needs an assurance that it is suitable for a group of learners large enough in numbers to make his investment worth while. There was also the drawback that in order to prepare textbooks reflecting the special needs of groups of learners, someone had first to make a detailed analysis of just what those specialized needs were, and few had both the experience and the time to do this. Above all, the most obvious specialization was along the lines of courses adapted to learners with a particular mother tongue: English for Urdu-speakers, English for Spanish-speakers and so on; but here the writing of a course demanded a high degree of linguistic sophistication that few textbook writers possessed.

We should not leave this point without referring to some of those who early saw the need for specialization of this kind in the teaching of English to foreign learners. In the domain of phonetics, Professor Daniel Jones and, later, members of his staff at the Department of Phonetics of University College London have for more than thirty years laboured along just these lines. The late Dr. H. E. Palmer and his colleague Mr. A. S. Hornby, basing their doctrine on the results of many years of work in Japan, also pioneered specialization and a measure of bilingual comparison. There is also the large group of teachers who have worked within the framework of English-teaching operations of the British Council, a group which has at some time or other included most of those who are in leading positions in the English language teaching profession today. Between them, working either in isolation or in small teams, they have supplied the profession with large numbers of careful analyses of difficulties experienced by specific kinds of learners, and with proposals for overcoming these difficulties in classroom teaching. The most useful source of such contributions is the journal *English Language Teaching*, which was started by the British Council in 1948 and has grown steadily more influential and authoritative.

A different kind of specialization, which has been less common but which is now already beginning and will clearly become widespread, is specialization according to the use to be made of the language by the learner. The generalized educational use of language teaching within a school system varies very little from one country to another—or rather, it has in the past varied very little; there are signs that in some countries within the coming decade a distinction may come to be made even within the school system between language teaching for general educational and cultural purposes and language teaching directed solely towards practical ability. Until 1950 or thereabouts, languages were taught in more or less the same manner in schools all over the world, and relatively few teachers were engaged in courses of other types. Since then, however, there has been a vast increase in the demand for English to be taught to learners, mainly adults, outside the normal school educational system; these learners have aims manifestly different from those of the average secondary school child.

Most of these new special needs for English are connected with the emergence into independent political status of former colonial territories in the Commonwealth. It is not surprising that the needs should relate to national requirements of an institutional kind: English for civil servants; for policemen; for officials of the law; for dispensers and nurses; for specialists in agriculture; for engineers and fitters. These are the kinds of learners who have suddenly become an urgent problem to the language-teaching profession, and for whom it is obvious that a highly specialized content to the courses will be needed. The job of writing a complete course is a long and expert task even when the writer has all the necessary data available to him; and in these cases the facts are not yet known. Only the merest fraction of investigation has yet been carried out into just what parts of a conventional course in English are needed by, let us say, power station engineers in India, or police inspectors in Nigeria; even less is known about precisely what extra, specialized material is required.

This is one of the tasks for which linguistics must be called in. Every one of these specialized needs requires, before it can be met by appropriate teaching materials, detailed studies of restricted languages and special registers carried out on the basis of large samples of the language used by the particular persons concerned. It is perfectly possible to find out just what English is used in the operation of power stations in India: once this has been observed, recorded and analysed, a teaching course to impart such language behaviour can at last be devised with confidence and certainty. This process has already been carried out on the English used in aviation; specialized teaching courses have been prepared for pilots, air traffic control officers, meteorologists and others who are concerned with using English in this specialized profession.

We have said that two distinct stages have taken place in the application of linguistics to language teaching. The first was a stronger awareness of the importance of practical language ability as an aim of teaching, and the second was the development of more advanced techniques in linguistics. An illustration of what is meant by this second kind of change is provided by the technique of *vocabulary selection*, which in the 1940s was regarded by many people as a high water mark in linguistic sophistication. By vocabulary selection is generally meant the deliberate choice for teaching purposes of particular sets of words, and the consequent deliberate rejection of others. Vocabulary selection in fact illustrates the difference between the first and the second waves of linguistics; it developed out of the need which language teachers felt for principles to guide them in the choice of the material they were teaching in the classroom, yet it does not provide the complete answer to the problem. Some teachers, reacting in a pessimistic way to the shortcomings of vocabulary selection as the be-all and end-all of preparing teaching materials, came to doubt the ability of any technical linguistic processes to help them. But the majority realized that vocabulary selection was a step in the right direction and that by recognizing the virtues of these techniques and extending them even further the benefits might be greatly increased.

5

The techniques of vocabulary selection reached their most sophisticated form in the work which led to the devising of *Le Français*

Fondamental; the team of workers responsible for this research have not only uncovered and recognized the advantages of vocabulary selection but have also identified some of the disadvantages. We shall have some criticisms to make of this programme of research; but first, since the work is a good example of the application of a certain amount of linguistic theory to language teaching, it may be helpful to describe it in some detail.

The aim of this particular project was to provide foreign learners of French with an indispensable minimum vocabulary; by eliminating all words outside this minimum the learners would avoid wasting their time on unnecessary items. The obvious criterion for choosing one word and rejecting another seemed to be frequency of occurrence—'the useful words are the frequent words' was the slogan—and, indeed, all vocabulary selection is based on lexical frequency counts of one kind or another. When the French group started work, in 1951, they proceeded to analyse in critical fashion the various frequency counts that had already been carried out on French. One feature was common to all of them: they were based on written texts and took no account of the spoken language. The written texts concerned were largely drawn from literature, from textbooks or from works of reference. As the aims of the French work were to produce a basis for instruction in the spoken language as well as (and before) the written, the distillation of a vocabulary from materials of this kind seemed unpromising. They decided to abandon written sources altogether (as Fries had done in 1946 for the study of American English, which he published in 1951 in his book *The Structure of English*), and to build their first-stage vocabulary on a basis of words actually occurring in speech. For this purpose they collected tape recordings of 163 conversations in which 175 different individuals took part. A very wide range of topics was covered in the conversations. All the recordings were transcribed into written form and a detailed count was made of every word that occurred. Facts such as the following were then elicited: how many times a given word occurred in the conversation of each speaker and how many times in the total corpus; in how many of the 163 different conversations a given word appeared (this figure is called the *range* of that word); how the distribution of various words was related to the profession and the social class of the speakers; and many other details.

One unusual feature of this work compared with previous

frequency counts was that every word spoken was counted, instead of the more usual practice of ignoring words such as the articles, personal pronouns and the parts of the verbs *to be* and *to have*. At a later stage it seemed desirable to reject certain categories of words for specific reasons, but until it was known just what words had occurred *all* words were included because there was no valid objective basis for excluding some rather than others.

Once they had completed the great labour of counting and listing the occurrence of all the 312,000 words of the spoken texts, the researchers prepared two lists: the first consisted of all the words used, arranged in decreasing order of frequency of occurrence with information about the range and the total frequency of each; the second consisted of all the words arranged in alphabetical order with an indication of how many times each had occurred in the total corpus. The basic material for a selected vocabulary was now in existence; it remained to study the evidence and decide on principles for making the selection.

Not surprisingly, the parts of the verbs *to be* and *to have* were the most frequent words of all, occurring 14083 and 11552 times respectively. Below them, the next ten most frequent items were these:

Rank order	Word	Range	Total no. of occurrences
3	de	163	10503
4	je	162	7905
5	il, ils	160	7515
6	ce (pronoun)	163	6846
7	la (article)	163	5374
8	pas (negation)	158	5308
9	à (preposition)	163	5236
10	et	161	5082
11	le (article)	163	4957
12	on	128	4266

Words occurring less than twenty times in the total corpus of 312,000 words were then eliminated on the grounds that they could reasonably be termed 'rare' and regarded as outside the scope of a basic vocabulary for teaching foreign learners. The ten least frequent words among those retained were the following:

Rank order	Word	Range	Total no. of occurrences
1054	éducation	11	20
1055	garage	11	20
1056	période	11	20
1057	pointe	11	20
1058	tableau	10	20
1059	programme	9	20
1060	château	8	20
1061	excursion	5	20
1062	guide	3	20
1063	inventeur	3	20

A study of the 1063 words that occurred twenty times or more showed at once that a number of words were included that would be hard to justify in a basic vocabulary for foreign learners, while other words that teachers needed to be able to use in class were absent from the list because they did not occur at least twenty times. Among the items included in the list with a high frequency were exclamations and 'fillers' such as *oh, ah, quoi!, eh bien*; the Commission in charge of the selection of the vocabulary from the lists produced for them by the research team originally excluded these words, but subsequently agreed to their inclusion in the list eventually published. This seems to us a wise decision, because adult learners in particular often feel an acute need for exclamations during the stage when their foreign language behaviour is becoming habitual through practice and use. Very little teaching is required to translate to the equivalent items in the foreign language.

Another group of words eliminated from the original lists contained slang words or words from an inappropriate style, like *type* (in the sense of *chap*), *gars, gosse, copain* and a few others, together with technical words like *micro* and *enregistrer* whose frequent occurrence could be traced to the mechanics of recording the conversations. Of a different kind were rejections when near-synonyms were found; thus *avoir peur* and *craindre* both occurred, as did *avoir mal* and *souffrir*. In these two cases the first member of the pair was the more frequent. A number of such pairs turned up; with an eye on the total size of the vocabulary projected, which was fixed provisionally at 1300 'words', the more frequent item was retained and the other rejected. Names of foreign countries and

peoples were rejected (although *français* was kept); technical terms
were eliminated, while on several different grounds a small number
of words like *confiance, doute, assurer, évidemment, simplement* were
also excluded, all of which reduced the original list of 1063 words
to 805.

There remained the problem of words absent from the list which
were nevertheless intuitively felt to be necessary. Two of the names
of days of the week, for example, *mercredi* and *vendredi*, failed to
appear in the texts, yet that could hardly justify their omission from
a basic teaching vocabulary. The biggest single group of words that
seemed to the researchers to be inadequately represented in the lists
was the category of concrete nouns. French people obviously knew
a great many words of this kind and therefore had them available
for use, but it seemed that they might not use any particular noun
very frequently. To judge from the occurrence of words in conversation on different topics, the use of such words depended very
closely upon the situation in which the speech was taking place.
An adequate stock of such words for teaching purposes could not
be assessed simply by waiting for them to come up by chance in
the course of conversation, especially when the conversations themselves were deliberately arranged to take place in the agreeable but
restricted surroundings of a private home; other techniques must
be tried, and since the words sought belonged to specific situations,
the approach must be to decide which situations were the most
relevant for the foreign learner, and to investigate the concrete
nouns that French people associated with those situations. The
research team drew up a list of topics (centres d'intérêt) that seemed
to them to be a minimum list for their purposes:

parts of the body	clothing
the house	furniture
food and drink	the kitchen
things put on the table at mealtimes	heating and lighting
the school and the classroom	the city
the country town	transport
farming and gardening	animals
games	occupations

A large number of people were selected as subjects for this stage
of the research, and in respect of each topic they were given the
following instructions:

'Think of . . . . . (a topic). Think carefully and write down the 20 nouns, but only common, everyday nouns, that you think are the most useful to know. They can be any nouns you wish as long as they relate to . . . . . (the topic).'

By asking several thousand schoolchildren in widely separated regions of France to carry out this simple task on each of the topics, the team collected a very large number of word-lists and then analysed them in close detail. The differences between town and country, between boys and girls, and between different social groups were studied in so far as they were reflected in the choice and order of words in the lists. But the main operation was to establish for each topic which words occurred with the greatest certainty in the various lists. Under the heading of 'furniture', for example, *table* was universally given, but *vitrine* was rather rare. The quality of being mentioned by a high proportion of those answering the questionnaire for a given topic was termed *disponibilité*, which might be translated as 'availability'; thus the word *table* is more *disponible* as a word relating to furniture than is *vitrine*. From these lists the words of greatest *disponibilité* were selected for each topic, and those words were added to the basic vocabulary list. This list in its final form has been used for making dictionaries, textbooks, courses in elementary French, and above all for the famous audio-visual courses in French for adult beginners associated with the language-teaching research programme of the École Normale Supérieure at St. Cloud, near Paris (see Gougenheim, Michéa, Rivenc and Sauvageot: *L'élaboration du Français élémentaire*, Paris: Didier, 1956).

Le *Français Fondamental*, and the research work that led up to it, are great pioneering efforts which have helped to bring about and to accelerate modern developments in the application of linguistics to language teaching. At the same time, although this highly sophisticated vocabulary selection programme illustrates the advantages of the technique, it also permits us to see clearly what its deficiencies are, and to guess how much better it could have been if it had been undertaken with a less limited framework of linguistic categories. The following are some of the most obvious criticisms.

To begin with, vocabulary selection in general is haunted by an underlying paradox. It seems to concentrate—almost by definition, the observer might think—on one single and obvious linguistic entity, the *word*, easily identifiable by the fact that it is written with a space on either side. But this simplicity is an illusion. Some items, it is true, are 'fully lexical': examples are *table, garage, question*. For items of this kind the assumption that vocabulary selection is a lexical process can be sustained. But at the other end of the scale a number of items are 'fully grammatical', e.g. *de, les, dont*. The patterns which fully lexical items enter into are different in kind from those of fully grammatical items and the use of the same criteria for both types produces confusion. But not all items are either fully grammatical or fully lexical; there is a scale between these extremes and some items fall more towards one polarity than the other. Thus there is a sense in which *un*, with its related forms *une*, and *-uns, -unes* (in *quelques-uns* and *quelques-unes*) is 'more grammatical' than *deux*, even though both are numerals and therefore incorporate a possibility of choice that is to some extent lexical. The point at issue is that an item is not solely and simply lexical: it may also be more or less grammatical. And this makes it necessary to state what grammatical notions are being used.

In any case, to take the orthographically defined *word* as the unit to be studied, instead of the *lexical item*, is to walk straight into a number of problems about what constitutes a word, especially in French. What, for example, about *Qu'est-ce que c'est*? How many words does that consist of? And how many of the items in it are relevant to vocabulary selection? Another problem is how to treat the word when it is clearly less than a lexical item; *avoir* is a word, *peur* is a word, each may be a lexical item, but so may *avoir peur*, and if *avoir peur* is taken as a lexical item what is the status of the discrete words of which it is composed? We are not attempting to give answers to these questions because we regard them as instances of general theoretical questions that would be handled from the beginning by a comprehensive array of linguistic categories.

In the Table cited on p. 192 the most frequent items are given as *être* and *avoir;* but this means, in fact, 'the parts of the verbs *être* and *avoir*', so that *suis* (in *je suis*) is taken together with *est, sommes* and all the others to give a gross total of occurrences. In the same way, *ai, as, a, avons* and so on were all counted together as if they were in some way identified with *avoir*. And of course they are—by grammar. The point is not that these words are unrelated, nor even that this procedure of counting them together was wrong, but simply that here is an example of grammatical rather than lexical criteria being used without this being admitted and without any basis of grammar having been stated.

Other examples of similar inconsistency may be quoted, e.g. *bonne*. The word *bonne* (as in *une bonne soupe*) is counted together with *bon* (as in *un bon moment*), for reasons which any schoolboy will appreciate; and the reason can fairly be called a grammatical one, reflecting the grammatical category of gender in French. Another *bonne*, the one meaning 'a daily help', is counted separately. The two different entries for *bonne* are labelled 'adjective' and 'noun' respectively. But *français* is not treated in the same way. This word, too, exists in forms that can be labelled 'adjective' and 'noun', and it too has forms differing according to a system of gender. But both sets of occurrences are grouped together under a single entry. This may be justifiable *ad hoc*, but no general criteria are given; nor is it clear whether these would be grammatical, lexical or semantic. A further example is provided by the treatment of *que*.

Seven different items occur, each spelt *que*: they are distinguished from each other by undefined but largely grammatical labels:

que	(conjunction)	3537 times
que	(relative)	1136
que	(after a comparative)	328
que	(in *ne . . . que*)	219
que	(interrogative)	83
que	(exclamatory)	30
que	(indeterminate)	25

The items which make up vocabulary lists need to be placed in groups; the criteria for setting up such groups are frequently grammatical, but are not disclosed as such to the reader. The only remedy, in linguistic analyses of this kind, is to accept from the outset the premiss that vocabulary selection entails attention to several levels of language; and that, although interest may be concentrated on 'vocabulary', the specification of a vocabulary list is certain to require the use of descriptive categories in grammar, in lexis, in context, and probably also in phonology.

These criticisms of the linguistic principles which underlay the preparation of *Le Français Fondamental* are made simply to illustrate the fact that such vocabulary selection, far from being all that linguistics can contribute to the preparation of teaching materials, is only a beginning; all praise is nevertheless due to a piece of work which was a great advance in the application of linguistic techniques to the devising of language teaching courses. Linguistics has evolved very rapidly and the research team concerned cannot be criticised for not having avoided, in 1952, shortcomings evident in 1964; they are certainly now well aware that the original scheme suffered from inadequate treatment of grammar. In consequence a large-scale grammatical analysis of modern spoken French is being undertaken with the aim of supplementing the lexical data with further information about the occurrence of grammatical items. Further programmes of lexical analysis are also under way, making use of modern punched-card and computer techniques for the preparation of specialized vocabularies in a number of scientific, technical and academic registers.

6

The work just described is probably the most sophisticated example of vocabulary selection. At the same time it demonstrates that satisfactory materials can be prepared only if account is taken of several levels of language, and if the techniques and procedures of teaching are married to the basic categories of linguistic description.

Postwar developments in Britain have followed a somewhat similar line, though without any single vocabulary selection project being completed of the calibre of the one we have described for French. The British developments have sprung in large part from the great experience which we have in this country in practical teaching of English to foreign learners; and in order to illustrate and explain the nature of these developments we shall begin at the point where they began, namely by considering the nature of the language teacher's job.

Everyone knows that the language teacher is imparting a skill, or rather a set of skills, in the strictly technical sense in which 'skill' means behaviour that involves muscular control. It is also clear that he is imparting a certain number of facts to be learned, at least in the sense that the singular/plural opposition *bed/beds* and the related yet different oppositions *child/children* and *sheep/sheep* can be called 'facts'. But at an earlier and more mundane stage of his job, before he goes into the classroom on any specific occasion to give a lesson, he has carried out a process which is fundamental to all language teaching: he has drawn up a list of items to be taught, a list of pieces of language behaviour that the individual members of his class cannot or do not perform before the lesson begins but which he proposes to help them to be able to perform by the end of it. For any one lesson the list of items is bound to be short, perhaps no more than a couple of points: for example the difference between the plurals of words that take the sound [z] (*beds, birds, bells,* etc.) and those that take the sound [s] (*cats, clocks, caps,* etc.). Some such deliberate choice of teaching items must be made by someone before systematic teaching can take place.

Two comments are needed here. First, there are classroom techniques that do not bind the teacher to the discipline of having to prepare a list of items to be taught, and then to stick to it. One such technique is reminiscent of the French 'explication de texte', in which a literary passage in the language being learned is set before the class and the teacher leads his pupils through it, making such comments and discursions upon the language used in the text as his own experience and his pupils' errors may suggest. There are those who contend that for studies of a literary and cultural nature this technique has something to commend it; nevertheless for language teaching in general, and particularly with learners at an early stage, it is a haphazard, hit-or-miss kind of instruction that wastes the time and energy of teacher and pupil alike.

The second comment is upon the statement that a deliberate choice of teaching items 'must be made by someone'. That someone need not be the classroom teacher himself, or at least not *only* the teacher. It is an axiom of good teaching that every lesson must be carefully prepared so that the teacher knows beforehand what he proposes to impart and can make some assessment by the end of the lesson of the extent to which he has been successful. But the classroom teacher is not alone in his profession. He has syllabuses, textbooks, readers, wall charts and other aids to choose from (or imposed upon him) which have been prepared by others specially qualified to do this, and the teacher's responsibility is to make use of these aids in the most effective possible way.

In many countries, including some where English is taught as a second language, education is expanding rapidly and teacher training facilities have been unable to keep pace with the numbers of teachers needed; as a result professional courses have grown shorter and shorter. Inevitably, large numbers of teachers of English have received only a small amount of professional training and therefore rely very closely upon the syllabus and the textbook. Yet even so someone, in this case someone other than the classroom teacher himself, has carried out the task of choosing certain items to be taught in particular lessons, and other items to be taught in other lessons. When we talk about 'the teacher', therefore, we need to distinguish between the person who confronts the pupils in the classroom, textbook in hand, and the person who has written the textbook or designed the syllabus which is being used.

If a choice of items for teaching needs to be made for each separate lesson, it needs to be made also for a course of teaching instruction viewed as a whole. Here is a crucial fact about systematic language teaching; any course, of whatever length or aims, pre-supposes a major task of preparation in which the limits of the course are set and the inventory and sequence of the teaching items is decided. This is the operation that can be so greatly improved by a suitable framework of organization, a 'check-list' of the peda-gogical processes of language teaching on the one hand against the major categories of language on the other. The development of such a framework of organization is one of the chief British contributions to language teaching in recent years. The fact that it has been applied so far only to English as a foreign language is irrelevant: this approach is as valid for teaching French in Britain as for teaching English in Iraq.

We need a label for the techniques and procedures which cluster round the point where linguistics and classroom teaching fuse together: a label which is sufficiently close to conventional terms for its general meaning to be self-evident, yet sufficiently different to avoid confusion with previous labels which implied little or no attention to linguistic theory. The term that has come into use here is METHODICS. Methodics is a framework of organization for practical language teaching, in which pedagogical techniques and linguistic theory cross-fertilize each other. It is not the same as *methodology*, which refers to pedagogical aspects of language teaching without necessarily any reference to linguistic categories. Methodics thus does not supersede methodology, but relates rather to a different area of the total operation.

There remains the term *method* to be related to the other two. It enters with a capital letter into specific terms such as 'the Direct Method', 'the Bilingual Method', referring to particular well-defined sets of teaching procedures, and into the names of specific textbooks and other teaching materials. Its lower-case equivalent is somewhat variable in its usage and of doubtful value as a technical term: it is very often a more conversational, less professional substitute for *methodology*. The sentences 'I used to go to old Smith's method lectures' and 'my colleague Dr. Smith looks after the methodology course' illustrate the type of register relation that exists between them.

The lexical set made up by these terms may be summarized in this way:

Method   (as in 'Direct Method'): a specific set of teaching techniques and materials, generally backed by stated principles but not necessarily having any reference to linguistics.

method: an alternative term for *methodology*, often less technical and less specific.

methodology: principles and techniques of teaching, with no necessary reference to linguistics.

methodics: a framework of organization for language teaching which relates linguistic theory to pedagogical principles and techniques.

The consideration of these terms leads us back to the cardinal issue: that a teaching course must be constructed round an inventory of teaching items, and that the preparation of this inventory necessarily involves both delimiting the items which it contains and arranging them in an appropriate sequence. This in turn leads to a number of questions such as the following, formulated here with special reference to English:—What kind of English is being taught? What uses will the pupils make of their ability in English once they have acquired it? How much English do they require in order to be able to carry out these particular purposes? How long will the course be? How many hours of teaching will it comprise? How long is each lesson? How well qualified are the teachers? What examinations will be imposed, and how closely are they related to the aims of the teaching? What teaching methods are to be used?

These and a great many other practical questions of the same kind may seem at first sight to have little to do with linguistics and to be solely the province of the expert in classroom teaching, in methodology. Indeed, this is how the British tradition has looked at them

7*

until recently. But most of these questions have at least one aspect
that is linguistic in nature. All of them, of course, lead at the same
time to the conclusion that preparing a language-teaching course
involves establishing a list of teaching items and arranging this list
in a suitable manner. This is a general statement, applicable to the
teaching of *any* language as L2. In the following discussion, the
illustrations are drawn from the teaching of English to foreign
learners; but the same principles apply to the teaching of French
or Russian in Britain.

Let us take as examples the questions 'what kind of English?'
and 'for what purposes?' The items to be taught are absolutely
determined by the answers to these questions, and obviously the
reply 'we should teach the whole of English'—which would imply
English as spoken and written at all times, in all places, about all
subjects—is an unreal one and therefore useless for teaching.
Suppose, then, the answer is: 'We should teach such English as is
needed for the purposes of airline pilots in the 1960s'. The inventory
of teaching items must include a number of technical terms like
runway, degrees, undercarriage, boost, emergency. The ability to
understand spoken English through noisy radio channels and to be
understood when speaking on them is far more important than the
ability to write English acceptably, while the ability to spell
correctly is hardly important at all. The present tenses and the
imperative are likely to occur with great frequency, while tenses like
might have been being talked down are likely to be so rare that they
can be ignored. The total range of situations for which language
behaviour must be taught is restricted and can be analysed,
described and taught as a finite operation. But if we answer the same
questions by saying 'We should teach English as needed to pass the
Overseas G.C.E. Examination in English Language and Literature', then our inventory of teaching items will be very different;
it will include few technical terms from flying but many from
literary studies; the ability to understand speech and to speak
acceptably will carry little weight; a great many stylistic devices
(such as are used by writers going as far back as Shakespeare) must
be included; the total range of registers will be rather wide and not
related to any great extent to the practical use of the language by the
individual in an English-speaking situation.

The question of the appropriateness of present-day public
examinations in English for overseas candidates is a separate one

and will be treated in a later chapter. But the catalogue of abilities just listed strikes us as being a very poor target indeed, and we deplore the fact that the shape of these examinations leads to such emaciated forms of English teaching. But with regard to the effect of the kind of English selected upon the stock of teaching items, in the contrast that has just been made between 'English for airline pilots' and 'English for G.C.E.' the former represents one of the few cases where a deliberate and studied answer has been given to the questions about the kind of English that should be taught. For the vast majority of learners no choice appears to have been made at all, and yet, of course, a choice must have been made by someone, however unknowingly. What has happened in practice is that the normative standards of teachers and educational administrators brought up in Britain have been taken over and applied without question to all overseas English teaching situations, so that what is right (or at least what is done) in teaching English in Britain is regarded as right for teaching English overseas. Thus the selection of teaching items for overseas use has generally been made, how-ever unwittingly, by the requirements of British examinations, such as G.C.E. and School Certificate, which were originally conceived for English-speaking children but were later transferred without modification to situations of a totally different kind.

One of the most important changes that took place in the period between 1950 and 1960 was the acceptance that 'to speak like an Englishman' was not the obvious and only aim in teaching English to overseas learners (as far as speaking ability was imparted at all): in this respect British acceptance of variations of accent in English used overseas has run ahead of American views. Although linguistic theory was applied to language teaching by American workers long before it became a widespread practice to do so in Britain, the linguistic consequences of social and political changes, and especially of newly won political independence, have been recognized and accepted by the British while many American language teachers re-main troubled but unconvinced. Some American language teachers accept only American forms of English, but in the eyes of the British language-teaching profession one or other of the varieties of English that are growing up may in specific cases be of a kind more appropriate to the local educational systems than any form current in the British Isles. This acceptance is accorded to varieties of English such as those labelled 'Educated Indian English', 'Educated

West African English' and so on; and obviously such acceptance makes a difference to the inventory of language-teaching items.

Let us assume that in a given case it has been decided to teach spoken and written English of the present day, based upon the usage of educated people brought up in England, in registers appropriate to discourse between people of this kind, and in the context of the general education of the young. We have now restricted this amorphous notion of 'English' to a more workable corpus, but we are still a long way from having prepared an inventory of teaching items. The next process is to look at this kind of English, to consider for teaching only items occurring within this variety of the language, and then to select from these only a practical, workable number of items. Such a further filtering of the potential stock of teaching items is essential, since whatever guess one might make as to the total number of words (to consider only lexis here) in this one kind of English, it would certainly be very much greater than any normal teaching course could contain. Even more important is the question: how is this further selection to be made?

Some criteria for selection must be found; each individual author or educational administrator may have his views on what he prefers as a basis for a teaching course, but if other, external bases for selection exist they should be discovered and used whenever possible. One obvious criterion is frequency of occurrence, another is *disponibilité*, or 'availability'; the analysis of French which we have described provides us with a valuable guide to procedures of this kind. At least two other criteria exist: *teachability*, and *classroom needs*, which are essentially pragmatic in nature. Clearly, some items are easier to teach in the classroom than others; the practical experience of the classroom teacher in any given cultural and linguistic region must feed back to the syllabus design in such a way that, where a choice has to be made between two items, one of the factors considered is how easy they are to teach. To take an obvious example, the use of the word *cold* is fairly easy to teach to young children in Europe but is much less easily teachable in tropical Africa. On another plane, except where exact equivalents can be found, *in front of* is more easily teachable than *instead of*. The needs of the classroom situation, too, must not be forgotten. This means not only including items like *blackboard* (which is extremely rare outside the classroom) but also commands like *Silence!* and expressions like *to leave the room* (or some equivalent euphemism).

Throughout this process of limitation, whether in choosing which register to teach or in selecting the items within that register, the process must be carried out at all levels of language. It is not enough to decide that the variety of English to be taught shall be one which employs Standard English *grammar*, the kind which is used with little variation by educated and professional people speaking English throughout the world; a decision also has to be made about the accent (that is to say, about *phonetics* and *phonology*) as well as about vocabulary (which brings in *lexis*) and about the areas of contextual meaning and the range of situation types to be included in the total course or syllabus. It would be impractical to reproduce here the whole of a syllabus in which these criteria had been applied, but we consider it worth quoting the first few items from a good example of such a syllabus. The following extracts are from the *Alternative Syllabus in English for Classes VI, VII and VIII in East Pakistan*, by R. Mackin.

'The following orders and expressions may be used by the teacher at his discretion before unit 59 is reached (i.e. during the first main section of the Syllabus):

Good!	Listen!
Again!	Yes!
Together!	No!
Stand up!	Be quiet!
Sit down!	Be quick!
Come here!	Be careful!
Go back to your place!	Silence!
Go on!	Thank you!
Good morning.	I'm sorry!
Good afternoon.	
Good night.	
Good evening.	

'The pupils may use the following when addressing the teacher:

Good morning.	Thank you!
Good afternoon.	I'm sorry!
Good evening.	Please, Sir!
Good night.	Please, Miss . . .

Yes!   Present, Sir!
No!   Present, Miss . . .

1. This   This is John.   That is Ahmad.
    That   This is Ahmad.   That is John.
    is   This is Mary.   That is Mary.

    Vocabulary, unit 1: Names of pupils.

2. my   This is my arm.
    your   This is your arm.

3. his   a) This is her . . . . .
    her   This is his . . . . .
                 This is my . . . . .
                 That is her . . . . .
                 That is his . . . . .
                 That is my . . . . .

              b) This is his name.

              c) His name is Ahmad.
                 His name is John.
                 Her name is Rashida.

4. 's   This is Ahmad.
              This is his book.
              This is Ahmad's book.
              This is John's book.

    Vocabulary, units 2 3 and 4.

    A. (parts of the body: 20 words)

    B. bag   name   C. beak   nail
       ball   pen   body   neck
       book   pencil   chin   shoulder
       box   place   chest   throat
       country   rubber   heart   thumb
       friend   knee   toe

5. a   This is a . . . . .

    Vocabulary, unit 5 . . . . . '

                                          etc.

To summarize the discussion so far: a process of limitation must be undertaken, since 'the whole of English' is neither teachable nor appropriate. There are two parts to the process: first, the *restriction* of the language used to a particular dialect and register; and secondly, the *selection* from within this register of the items that are to be taught, according to criteria such as frequency of occurrence, *disponibilité*, teachability and classroom needs. The whole process must be applied at all levels of language, so that unlike conventional vocabulary selection, which deals only with items labelled 'words' but in fact having no clear linguistic status, the inventory of teaching items is reached by considering phonology, grammar, lexis, context (semantics) and extra-linguistic situation at every point in the process.

Once an inventory of teaching items has been arrived at, it must be arranged in a way suitable for teaching. It is easy to forget that even when the full process of limitation has been carried out, a separate set of operations is necessary in order to decide which items shall be taught before which others. For instance, granted that both *I come* and *I'm coming* will be taught at some stage, how do we decide which shall precede the other, and by what extent in time and in number of lessons?

7

The process of arriving at an inventory of teaching items we have called *limitation;* the process of putting these into the most appropriate order for practical teaching purposes is generally called *grading*, and it can be subdivided into two distinct operations. The first of these takes the list of teaching items and arranges it into blocks of the right size for the various years, terms, months, weeks, days and classes of the teaching course; while the second operation deals with the problem of the sequence in which the items in the blocks are to be taught. It is useful to give a separate label to each of these subdivisions of the total process of grading, and so we shall use the term *staging* to refer to the division of the course into time segments, and *sequencing* to refer to the problem of deciding the order in which the items should be taught.

The subject of staging takes us squarely into the field of language teaching methodology. Suppose a course has been divided into three years, each of two terms, each term of fourteen weeks, each week having four classes, each class lasting forty-five minutes; these are non-linguistic factors, imposed upon the teacher by the practical and administrative needs of the situations in which he works. Another course might be only six weeks long, with twenty-four classes per week, each lasting an hour and a quarter; here, too, the shape of the course is a non-linguistic fact that has to be accepted by the classroom teacher: if he disagrees with it his arguments are more likely to be administrative and practical than linguistic in their nature. In both cases the teacher must distribute his list of teaching items in the most effective way over the periods available to him, making sure that he neither crams too many into a given period of time, which would overload the pupils and render some of the teaching ineffective, nor provides too little to be learned, and so wastes the time of both teacher and pupil alike. Such practical matters might appear to have nothing to do with linguistics, but in fact linguistics has a dual contribution to make here: firstly, and behind and throughout the whole task, linguistics provides the description of the language being taught and shows the teacher what the place of each component is in the sum total of what is being taught; secondly, and specifically in this area of grading, linguistics reminds us that the items being subdivided into units of teaching time belong to different levels of language and are being taught in relation to four different skills. This reminder affects the process of staging in a number of important ways.

To begin with, the different skills themselves do not make equal demands on the different levels of language. A learner who has acquired mastery of all four skills (understanding speech, speaking comprehensibly, reading and writing) must have made the acquaintance of all levels, however unconscious he may be of the fact. But for certain purposes one may learn, and even teach, a language without acquiring all four skills in it, and therefore without necessarily coming to grips with all levels of language. Courses exist in spoken English and in spoken French which make no use whatever of written forms of the language, while other courses have long been taught which set out to impart only a reading and writing knowledge of the language; in such cases either the phonological or the graphological level may be ignored or at least played down. In courses of the more conventional kind where both the spoken and the written forms are in use it is common practice for the one to lag behind the other and for the introduction of the spoken forms to precede by some margin, which may be either very small or quite large, the introduction of written forms of the same language items. All these considerations affect the total grading of the course. *Staging* will be affected because the teacher must decide the point in time, measured from the beginning of the course, by which a given standard of attainment in each skill must be reached; but *sequencing* is also affected because he must decide to introduce items from one aspect of language before or after items from another.

Examples of these consequential effects are easy to find. Some modern syllabuses in English for learners in schools overseas prescribe an initial period of a month, or six weeks, or two terms, or a specific number of lessons, during which time only the spoken language is to be taught and no written forms are to be introduced; this is a decision about *staging*. In order to carry out this scheme, the full range of phoneme-items and an outline of the patterns of word-stress have to be presented to the pupils within a very short period from the beginning of the course, and long before either grammar or lexis has progressed very far; this is a consequential decision about *sequencing*.

The interrelations between language skills and the main linguistic categories can be shown on a diagram, the names of these categories being accompanied in this case by the 'labels' commonly used in language teaching for approximately the same notions.

The relation between language skills and the introduction of items at different levels of language.

LANGUAGE SKILLS	CATEGORIES OF LANGUAGE				
	GRAMMAR 'Structures' 'Grammatical patterns'	LEXIS 'Vocabulary'	CONTEXT 'Situations'	PHON-OLOGY 'Patterns of sound'	GRAPHOLOGY 'System of writing and spelling'
I. UNDER-STANDING SPEECH	Some grammatical and lexical items are needed from the outset; they can be increased progressively		Dependent on what has been introduced in the preceding column; all items in grammar and lexis must be fully understood from the outset; new items must be introduced in meaningful ('contextual') ways	Full range essential from the outset	Not essential
II. SPEAKING					
III. READING				Not essential but often helpful	Full range essential from the outset
IV. WRITING					

Staging, then, is a task affected especially by two factors: first, by the number of lessons that constitute the course and the intensity of the teaching measured in classes per unit time, which in turn depends on the average length of the lessons and the frequency with which they are given; and secondly, by decisions about the skills which the course sets out to teach.

Sequencing is that section of the total task of grading in which the teacher decides to teach item x before item y. A great many practical examples of sequencing exist in the shape of syllabuses and textbooks which have been given their present internal sequence of teaching by deliberate and thoughful choice on the part of the compiling teacher, but there exist very few statements of principles for the guidance of others who wish to do likewise. In fact, for an intelligent approach to sequencing it is almost essential to have practical teaching experience with the pupils for whom a given course is intended, because here above all the teaching programme must be sensitive to the precise needs of the pupils, both in general terms and in close detail.

What criteria can we discover that will guide us in sequencing a list of teaching items? To begin with there are the same criteria that were considered in the discussion of *selection*. In general, teaching items that are in frequent use need to be taught before those that are more rare, whether we are talking of formal (grammatical and lexical) items (e.g. words like *he, is, the* before words like *nevertheless, impossibility, volcano*), or grammatical categories (e.g. verb forms like *he comes* before verb forms like *he might not have been coming*) or types of context (e.g. language suitable to the classroom before language appropriate to the parade ground). So the criterion of frequency not only helps to decide whether an item shall be selected for inclusion at all; it also helps to decide the sequence in which the items selected shall be taught. The same applies to the other criteria, *disponibilité*, teachability and classroom needs.

One might be tempted to think, if there were no more to sequencing than this, that the two processes of selecting a stock of teaching items according to certain criteria and using the same criteria as a guide in putting these items in sequence could well be run into one, and that the process of selection could at the same time give us the sequence. But in the question of sequence we are concerned with actually *teaching* the items in the inventory and not merely with *listing* them, and this brings into play a further vital and related feature, the experience of the teacher. This experience helps him to know the practical problems which accompany the teaching of various items, to be aware of the pieces of language which can be used for the purpose of leading up to others as opposed to those language items that lead directly to the edge of methodological precipices, and to be familiar with the sequences which make for more effective and rapid teaching.

Linguistics is a science, teaching is an art. Some of the benefits of objective criteria can be made available to the classroom teacher if his material is prepared in the ways suggested, and in a large number of places (taking a course as a whole) the teacher's intuition and experience will produce no special reasons for preferring one sequence rather than another. But in other places, some of them of strategic importance for the course as a whole, the experienced teacher will often feel that he prefers one particular sequence rather than another 'because it works better'. In these circumstances, when there is a firm professional judgment that the sequence x—z—y is preferable to a sequence x—y—z which might have been indicated purely on the basis of objective criteria, the teacher should have the final say. It happens that different individuals practise their art in different ways and that different preferred sequences may be set up by different teachers. Examples of this are especially copious in the opening lessons of English courses for beginners. Author X prefers to teach as the first item of all *This is a . . .*; Author Y prefers *I am the teacher;* Author Z relies on half a dozen isolated words, *book, table, chair, boy, girl, teacher.* The objective criteria we have discussed are not sufficiently clearcut to provide a strong indication in favour of one or the other of approaches such as these, although all of them would probably be indicated as coming somewhere in the early stages. There is every likelihood that in the hands of good teachers all these gambits would be more or less equally effective and that many others might also be possible. In other words, objective criteria can give a general idea of where in the total sequence a given item should appear, but for fine detail the teacher's classroom experience should be followed.

There are, however, several interesting examples of linguistic theory dictating in broad outline the sequence of linguistic items. Thus, teachers of English who make use of transformational grammar sometimes maintain that 'kernel sentences' should always be taught before sentences regarded as involving a grammatical

transformation: for example, attribution, passive (voice) and interrogative (mood) must in this view come later than predication,
active and affirmative respectively. The sequence of the stages
which are required, in the description of English, by this particular
theory is directly reflected in the sequence of items selected for
teaching.

8

So far we have considered two main divisions of the framework of
organization: *limitation* and *grading*. The path has led from techniques that are largely linguistic, in the case of limitation, towards
those of grading which are largely pedagogical. The next stage in
the process is one which we shall call *presentation*. This is chiefly a
matter of practical classroom teaching and corresponds closely to
what is meant by *methodology*. But the overlap between the two is
not by any means complete, and indeed if we have used the word
'methodology' sparingly it is because in our opinion much more is
involved in the classroom end of language teaching than just that
which is commonly referred to as methodology. Language teaching
is methodology plus a great deal more. Some people have declared
themselves 'opposed to' linguistics on the grounds that linguists
despise methodology and wish to see it replaced by linguistics. In
Britain, at least, this is not true. The professions of teaching
English overseas and of teaching modern languages in Britain have
evolved highly sophisticated classroom techniques and methods
which British linguists respect and value, and which lend themselves
easily and effectively to a marriage with applications of linguistic
theory. Methodology combined with applied linguistics is more
effective for teaching languages than either methodology without
linguistics or linguistics without methodology; and the development of just such a union, which is now taking place in a number of
different British universities, is especially to be welcomed. It is true
that an acquaintance with modern linguistics based solely on some
American writings during the period from 1940 to 1955 might lead
to the impression that linguistics is being offered as the successor
to and substitute for methodology and classroom techniques. There
was indeed a period when dissatisfaction with the effectiveness of
conventional methods of language teaching led some people, per-

haps especially in the United States, to believe that language teachers should be replaced in the classroom by practitioners of 'structural linguistics' in the sense of phonemic-morphemic analysis. That belief has never been held by linguists in Britain, and in the 1960s it is fast losing ground in the United States. Linguists in Britain have always regarded the aims and methods of general and descriptive linguistics as being different from those of language teaching, however much the two may be related.

Why, then, do we now propose to use the term *presentation* instead of the familiar *methodology*? The answer is partly that more is intended by *presentation* than is usually included in *methodology*, and partly that the term *methodology* is interpreted by different individuals in different ways. We mean by *presentation* the kernel of the teaching process, the confrontation of the pupil with the items being taught. More often than not this means classroom teaching of the conventional kind, but new and exciting ways of carrying out the task are continually being developed which also fall under the heading of *presentation*. As we write, audio-visual courses and language laboratories are becoming commonplace; teaching machines are being programmed for teaching languages; television is being developed as a vehicle for language instruction on a large scale; new methods of 'activity' teaching are being investigated. In all these approaches there exists a phase in which each teaching item is presented to the pupil.

In practice, a distinction needs to be made between *initial presentation*—'first-time teaching'—and *repeated presentation*. The first time any language item is aimed at the pupil he must be confronted with it in a manner that enables him to add it to his existing stock of items and to weld all the separate items into the exercise of those skills at which the teaching is aimed. On any given occasion the teaching may be successful or it may not be; a new word (let us say) may be learned, it may be partly learned, it may be learned but quickly forgotten, it may not be learned at all, or it may be actively *mis*-learned. Whatever may be the case, the next time that word is used in the teaching course it is no longer a new item and the techniques of presentation must take account of that fact.

The techniques governing repeated presentation must take account of two main purposes: *reinforcement* and *remedial teaching*. These terms are self-explanatory: reinforcement is the further presentation of an item (for instance, in drills and exercises) either as soon as possible after its initial presentation or as deliberate revision at a later point in the course; remedial teaching is the further presentation of an item that has been forgotten or mis-learned—the filling of gaps and the unlearning of bad habits.

Once again, in presentation as in grading, the contribution of linguistics to a process that is chiefly methodological in its nature is twofold. In the first place, and pervading the whole task, linguistics provides both the description of the L2 and an understanding on the part of the teacher of how the components make up the whole —of how the language works, in fact. Secondly, reference back to linguistic categories will ensure that, in the planning of a teaching programme, all aspects of language that need to be are included. This does not imply that phonology, graphology, lexis, grammar and context need to be taught as separate levels: these are linguistic categories, concepts for the description of language, not teaching procedures. Besides, there is strong evidence that the more closely the teaching items that fall within these categories are integrated and presented as total language behaviour in a real situation the more effective the teaching is. But integration is not always possible, and many teaching situations lead to a concentration on one level rather than another at any given point in a lesson. It is in conditions like these that the teacher, and more especially the constructor of syllabuses and textbooks, needs to be reminded that all the relevant levels of language must be covered.

9

The fourth main subdivision of the framework of organization is *testing*. It is not sufficient that a teacher should know precisely what items he is teaching and in what order, and that he should present them according to the best possible and most appropriate methods of teaching; he must also know how far his teaching is effective: that is to say, to what extent learning is taking place among his pupils. The individual class-teacher needs a feedback mechanism to monitor the effectiveness of his teaching; the school as a whole needs to know how classes are progressing; the educational system needs a way of measuring progress over the country in general. These different yet related tasks are all aspects of testing, which can most conveniently be discussed under three main headings: formal and informal testing, objective and subjective testing, and tests as distinct from examinations.

A good teacher develops a set of techniques for questioning, probing and observing his pupils, techniques which enable him to know when to slow down his teaching, when to speed it up, when to repeat an item, when to single out an individual for special attention, and so on. These are all informal testing techniques. Formal tests are an attempt to construct an instrument for measuring attainment, or progress, or ability in language skills. Clearly, each of these qualities can be assessed in terms of each of the four basic language skills; what is not so widely realized is that within each of these skills it is desirable to pay separate attention to each level of language. A test of attainment in understanding the spoken language, for instance, can be used to test the learner's command of the language at the *phonological* level and to discover how far he recognizes the sound contrasts of the language; it can also test his command of *grammar* and, to a greater or lesser extent, of *lexis*.

All this may seem obvious when it is read in cold print, yet very few tests have been devised for any language that exploit these obvious facts and deliberately seek to measure the learner's performance separately for each linguistic level. Indeed, the vast majority of tests at present in use for English do not even cover all the skills, still less the different branches or aspects of each skill. Nearly all *tests* in English are in fact *examinations*; they are subjective in their setting and marking; they cover only the skills of reading and writing; they measure the pupils' knowledge *about* the language rather than their performance in it; and they confuse the testing of language with the testing of literary and cultural attitudes and knowledge. This catalogue of the technical shortcomings of present tests applies to much of the testing both of English in Britain and overseas and of foreign languages in Britain.

By 'examinations' we mean 'institutionalized tests', tests which have an official or administrative function over and above their task of measuring performance. A test which is also a school-leaving certificate, or a university entrance qualification, or a matriculation equivalent, is in fact an examination. It is not necessarily a worse test because of its additional function, but there are three inescapable features of examinations which are not necessary features of tests and which may have serious consequences. The first is that examinations are conducted in terms of 'pass' or 'failure', terms which are *evaluations*, not *measurements*. What is more, as year succeeds year, any large-scale examination is bound to set up statistical notions to relate the numbers of candidates who are awarded a pass to the total size of the entry to the examination: to say, for instance, that 65% of all candidates will pass, the pass mark being established accordingly; and this in turn means that at the vital point around the pass mark the precise measurement of performance may be overruled (in either direction, upwards or downwards) by the external factor of the year's statistics. Of course such statistical questions are essential to the conduct of any large-scale examination system, and far from criticizing the fact of their existence we would welcome their extension and refinement. But examinations, which give a qualification, would need to be distinguished from tests, which give a measurement, for this reason alone, even if no other reasons existed.

The second feature of examinations is that they are by nature inflexible. Being related to an educational system they have an obligation to remain reasonably constant and to change only when accompanied by the necessary changes in school teaching methods and curricula. This means, in practice, that examinations tend not to change at all but simply maintain their existing shape and content regardless of professional developments and innovations elsewhere. Hence they readily serve as a protective barrier against change for those teachers who wish so to use them. There are, of course, many teachers of English and other languages, both in Britain and overseas, who criticize existing examinations; these usually maintain that no notice is taken of their objections. Examiners, on the other hand, can often be heard to say that they would like to experiment (some even support the notion that a change is essential) but cannot do so 'because the teaching profession would not accept it'. There are a number of possible solutions to this deadlock, but a prerequisite for any major change is a large-scale project for trying out new *tests* as the basis of future *examinations*.

The third inescapable feature of examinations is that they control the teaching. Whatever techniques and principles may be developed for evaluating and constructing language-teaching syllabuses, in practice it is the examination even more than the syllabus that determines the kind of teaching which is carried out in all but the best schools in a given area, and an improved syllabus can therefore only be effective if the examination permits it to be so. This kind of problem is well known to schools inspectors, who often have to decide where to put their weight in the first instance when a major reform in teaching is to be introduced. Can they concentrate their energies on the schools only, or will their efforts there be useless because of the antiquated nature of the examination? Should they rather begin by pressing for a new examination, so that schools can be led to improve their methods by working to its requirements? Enlightened teachers often talk of 'the bad effects of examinations upon teaching', and certainly where examinations are bad they usually lead to bad teaching. On the other hand a good examination can have good effects on teaching, and one way of bringing about improvements in language teaching is to introduce improved techniques of examination.

This is what has been done with great effect in West Africa. When the West African Examinations Council was set up to co-ordinate examination policy and to bring examinations more in line with the requirements of the English-speaking countries there, one of the first decisions taken was to introduce an oral examination in English. The examinations in English available at that time for secondary school children of about 16 years of age were identical in almost every respect with those set for and sat by equivalent children in Britain, in spite of the fact that the West African candidates had learned English as a second language. It was in recognition of at least part of this anomaly that it was decided to introduce an oral test in English.

There arose at once the question of what kind of test should be devised, and how it could possibly be administered in the physical, geographical and educational conditions of West Africa in the early 1950s. Very few schools at that time taught spoken English as such, or paid attention to practical ability in understanding and speaking English. Those few schools which did teach spoken English (almost invariably schools with 'expatriate' native speakers of English on their staff) welcomed the proposal: many of the others showed their dismay. But for several years while the oral test was being devised and developed only those few schools were involved in the test which had volunteered to put up candidates; a proviso was made that the results would not affect their final English mark in the School Certificate examination. Then, when examiners were available in larger numbers, more schools were brought into the scheme until now many thousands of candidates are examined each year. Side by side with the gradual spread of the test, there has been a parallel spread of oral teaching, so that now very few secondary schools do not make an attempt to provide teaching in spoken English that will help their pupils to pass the School Certificate Oral Test in English. Other areas of the world with similar problems can benefit from this experience.

It would be necessary to write a separate book to do justice to the subject of language examinations. The essential point here is merely that they are not the same as tests; and that although a new examination, if it is to be valuable, should be based on well-tried and fully developed tests, once it is established it is likely to operate in a way which makes its function quite different from the functions of a test.

Within the category of tests, there are further differences between the three kinds already referred to: tests of ability, of attainment and of progress. Tests of ability are generally predictive: that is, they attempt to measure features of performance which are known to correlate closely with effective and rapid language learning. Prognostic tests of this kind are still in a very early stage, but it seems likely that it will soon be possible to pick out from a group of pupils on the basis of a simple test the individuals who will learn languages most easily.

Tests of attainment are what they seem: measurements of practical performance. One great trouble with tests of attainment is that any learner of a foreign language quickly reaches a degree of competence, or part-competence, where he has learned, or partly learned, such a sheer quantity of linguistic material that testing all of it becomes a 'pseudo-procedure'; it just cannot be done. Consequently attainment tests have to be partial and selective, and they often pick out for testing just those points which a given batch of learners habitually makes mistakes with. In other words, they have to be based on a comparison of the learner's language and the language being learned, or on the experienced teacher's knowledge of common and persistent errors. This represents a parallel in pedagogical terms to the linguist's technique of bilingual comparison.

Tests of progress are simply tests of attainment per unit time, a measure of the difference in the attainment of an individual at one moment and at a later moment. If such tests are integrated with the teaching programme, they can be related to quantities of material

small enough to be tested in depth and in detail. And this gets round
the difficulty mentioned earlier, that of testing pupils whose total
potential ability is very extensive. The answer is an obvious one:
the more frequently formal tests of attainment are given, the more
likely it is that they can cover everything that has been dealt with
in a given section of a teaching programme.

Another distinction which was made above was that between
objective and subjective testing, a topic which tends to arouse
passionate feelings among teachers. It is highly unlikely that all
aspects of language performance can be tested objectively, whether
or not it is desirable that they should be; but it is certainly true that
in the early stages of a learner's progress tests of an objective nature
can be devised to measure performance in each of the levels and in
each of the basic skills, and in our view such tests should be used
much more widely than they are at present.

What is meant by subjective and objective tests? A subjective test
is one where the mark depends on the examiner's opinion, judgment
or evaluation. An objective test is one in which marks are gained
(or lost, as the case may be) solely by reference to the subject's
performance in such a way that all examiners would agree on the
apportioning of marks. It follows that objective tests generally test
only one item at a time, and that they often take the form of 'tick-
cross-underline' tests, or 'forced choice' tests, such as the following:

Ex. 1
Read each of the following sentences. If you think they are
acceptable, place a tick √ in the box. If not, place a cross:

I'm going to London   [√]
I'm going to bed   [√]
I'm going to home   [×]

Ex. 2
One of the following words does not rhyme with the others.
Underline it:
sheer, pier, clear, bear, fear

Such tests as these, if they are carefully linked with a teaching
programme, offer a simple, rapid and effective way of keeping a
close check on learning and teaching. In the final analysis teaching
proceeds by discrete steps, each step being deliberately introduced

and taught by the teacher. Each step can thus also be deliberately tested, at least once; and it is worth saying explicitly here that, if a point can be identified, a means can be devised for unambiguously testing it, no matter which linguistic level it belongs to. As a point of operational technique, moreover, once individual items are specified for testing, the person conducting the test can test one item at a time. This is the biggest single factor in moving away from the subjective 'overall assessment' method towards objective techniques: the latter are closely dependent on the ability to test discrete teaching items.

Many people believe that certain kinds of elementary language behaviour cannot be tested, or that they can be tested only by techniques which are either subjective or very cumbersome, or which demand specialist training on the part of the tester. The area most frequently mentioned in these criticisms is the spoken language. It is certainly true that the direct measurement of performance in connected speech is a task requiring special training and long experience. But if it happens that we are concerned with testing performance in pronunciation, many aspects of this can be done in other ways than by listening to connected speech. Precisely what techniques are appropriate will vary from one teaching situation to another; but other techniques than this are certainly available, and they can be presented to the classroom teacher in such a way that he can mark the phonetic performance of his pupils as objectively as he can mark their faults in spelling.

Let us take as an example the learning of French pronunciation by English-speaking pupils. French makes a distinction between the words *lui* and *Louis*, a distinction that is typical of many other pairs, and which constitutes a persistent difficulty for many English-speaking learners who do not have the sound [ɥ] in their language. How can we test whether a given pupil can make this distinction? One answer is to get him to read, or to converse, and to note whether he makes this sound accurately at all those points where a native speaker of French would make it; but to do this requires a great deal of experience and training on the part of the tester, and is both time-consuming and mentally exhausting when carried out for a long period. If there were some other way in which phonetic performance could be identified, some other manifestation of the ability to make the sound [ɥ] and the sound [w] at will, the task would be much easier.

It is well known to linguists and language teachers that the ability to make *productive* contrasts must always be preceded by the ability to make similar *receptive* contrasts. To take our example, no learner of French will *render* the distinction between *lui* and *Louis* until he can *hear* it. It is not necessarily true that if he can hear the difference he therefore both can and will reproduce it accurately; but at least it is certain that if he cannot hear a difference between these words he will not make one at all. One possible solution, then, is to construct some kind of spoken test in which these words are used in crucial contexts, to ask the pupil to listen, and then to ask questions of him. If this text is in the form of a recording on disc or tape, it can be used for any number of tests on different pupils. And if the accompanying questions are presented in writing, and the answers are asked for in written form, we have eliminated from the test any necessity for specialized training in phonetics on the part of the teacher.

Ex. 3
(Specimen text, recorded by native French speaker)
    A. Bonjour, François. Qu'est-ce que tu fais?
    B. Bonjour, Philippe. J'attends mon frère Jean. Tu l'as vu?
    A. Non, je ne l'ai pas vu. — Attends! Là-bas, c'est lui? C'est ton frère?
    B. Oui. C'est bien lui.

Question: What was the name of the brother they were waiting for? Underline the name you think is the correct one: *but Louis could be another brother not waited for.*

<u>Jean.</u>   Louis.

This example is based on the need to distinguish between *lui* and *Louis*. It is true that a single example could be right by chance alone; but objective tests are generally constructed with large numbers of examples, providing sufficient repetition for chance to be ruled out. It is also true that this is an artificial, constructed example that might not work in practice for reasons that would only emerge in practical trials of large numbers of questions. The construction of objective tests of language performance is a slow and painstaking business, but it *can* be done; and it represents a further example of the application of categories drawn from linguistic theory to procedures related to teaching.

A summary of the framework of organization of a list of teaching items, as supplied by the procedures of 'methodics'.

PROCEDURES OF METHODICS		LEVELS OF LANGUAGE AND THEIR EQUIVALENTS IN METHODOLOGY			
		PHONOLOGY 'sounds of speech'	GRAMMAR 'structures' 'grammatical patterns'	LEXIS 'vocabulary'	CONTEXT 'situations'
LIMITATION	Restriction				
	Selection				
GRADING	Staging				
	Sequencing				
PRESENTATION	Initial Teaching				
	Repeated Teaching				
TESTING	Formal/Informal				
	Objective/Subjective				
	Tests/Examinations				

BIBLIOGRAPHY

See items 2, 4, 6, 10, 11, 19, 28, 39, 68, 74, 91.

Chapter 8

Studying the native language

1

The place of English in the curriculum of our schools, and as a compulsory subject at all levels in the examination systems, is well established by tradition; its value is seldom called into question, and therefore seldom explicitly formulated. This is a pity, since such unquestioning acceptance may help to encourage the continued teaching of English by old-fashioned methods in pursuit of out-of-date aims. The teaching of English in English schools could, in our opinion, become every bit as valuable as some of its advocates claim it to be already. But it will become so only if its aims are examined thoroughly and objectively, and its methods revised in the light both of the aims as newly formulated and of recent advances in the relevant background subjects.

The starting point for any discussion of the role of native language teaching is an understanding of the nature of language and of the characteristics that define a native language in contradistinction to a foreign one. We have tried to fill in some of the background to these questions in the chapters on descriptive linguistics and phonetics and on institutional linguistics (Part 1). Language, defined by descriptive linguistics, is patterned, social activity of human beings, displaying patterns of substance (phonic and, at least potentially, graphic), form (grammar and lexis) and context. In other words it has certain properties which clearly exclude mathematics, traffic lights, knotted cords and the dances of bees from the category of language. A language, defined by institutional linguistics, is the set of such activities performed by the members of a community who regard themselves as speaking 'the same language'.

Any given individual may make use of more than one language

so defined, but the one that is defined by the community of which he himself is a member is his native language. In general, 'native language' equals 'L1'; that is, the majority of people have one native language which is, and remains throughout their lives, the one from which all their registers and restricted languages are drawn. A minority of people have more than one native language; and a minority—not the same minority—replace the native language by a foreign language as their L1. A few even acquire more than one language as L1: that is, they come to use more than one language for all the purposes for which they use any language.

The majority of the citizens of Britain have English as their unique native language, and retain it throughout their lives as their unique L1. When they learn a foreign language, it is with the intention of using the foreign language as an L2: as an alternative form of activity available to them in certain registers. It does not replace the native language, which retains its L1 status in the sense that it is always on call for all the types of purpose that language activity fulfils in their lives. In other words a British native speaker of English, like the majority of native speakers of English and many, but not all, other languages, requires that his language should be able to do for him all the work for which he needs language at all.

This language he learns from his elder siblings, parents, other children and other adults with whom he comes into contact. The way in which he learns it, and the order in which he acquires the patterns, are important questions both for general and for applied linguistics; up to the present rather little is known about them. These lie beyond our present scope; but one feature of the learning process is important to the discussion. In the course of learning the language the child makes 'mistakes': he deviates at one level or another from the patterns of the language. Anyone listening to small children can pick out examples at all levels, phonetic, phonological, grammatical and lexical: it is in fact a useful linguistic exercise to classify the errors as one hears them. The son of one of the present writers, at a certain stage, replaced all initial weak CV syllables of lexical items having strong second syllables by 'be-' (phonologically /ˌbɪ/): 'remember', 'forget', 'tomato', 'pyjama' were 'bemember', 'beget', 'bemato' and 'bejama'; 'believe' was, of course, correctly, 'believe'. This was a phonological error restricted to a certain place in the structure of certain lexical items.

Such errors are self-correcting. The child need not be taught that the past of 'catch' is 'caught', just as he need not be taught the phonetic distinction between alveolar and velar plosives; children often mix these latter up at an early stage, saying for example 'tat' for 'cat'. By the time the child goes to school most of such errors have already been eliminated, and the few that remain soon disappear. Once the necessary phonetic skills have been mastered, the elimination of self-correcting errors of any kind is a highly specific and limited aspect of the child's learning of his native language, and one that should not be over-emphasized. Of course the learning of any new form of activity is a process that is likely to involve mistakes of some kind; but it would be misleading to regard the learning process itself as being primarily the correction of errors. This is particularly true in the learning of language, where the addition of new patterns plays a far larger and more central part than the correction of errors in the use of patterns already acquired.

Primary school teachers are well aware that there is no need to concentrate in the classroom on the correction of the relatively few remaining errors of this type. In any case the teaching of the native language in the first years of school has to cope with a much greater and positive task, the teaching of reading and writing. This requires the extension of the child's native language habits into a totally new medium. The magnitude of the task of acquiring these new skills, including new manual skills, is so obvious as not to need labouring; but it is sometimes not realized that there is another side to the problem, namely that in acquiring the new medium the child is at the same time learning to use language for completely new purposes. And it is here that the main problem of native language teaching, that of the balance between prescriptive and proscriptive teaching on the one hand and descriptive teaching on the other, arises for the first time: because the conventions of written English are different from those of spoken English.

There is an important distinction to be made among the three types of, or approaches to, language teaching: the productive, the prescriptive and the descriptive. Productive language teaching is the teaching of new skills; this includes the greater part of foreign language teaching and certain aspects of native language teaching, of which the teaching of reading and writing is perhaps the most obvious. Prescriptive language teaching is the interference with existing skills for the purpose of replacing one pattern of activity, already successfully acquired, by another: it is thus restricted to the

8+L.S.L.T.

native language. 'Prescriptive' here includes 'proscriptive', since each 'do this' implies a 'don't do that', whichever of the two formulations is given the major emphasis. Descriptive language teaching is the demonstration of how language works: this involves talking about skills already acquired, without trying to alter them, but showing how they are used. There is a logical progression for descriptive language teaching through three stages corresponding to the age and experience of the child: first, how the native language works; second, how particular foreign languages work; third, how language in general works. Each stage can begin at an appropriate point in the school career and, once embarked upon, can usefully continue throughout.

Certain specific criticisms can be made of the approach to native language teaching still followed in many of our schools. Prescriptive teaching is overemphasized at the expense of productive teaching; the spoken language is largely neglected; too little attention is paid to non-literary registers; and both the linguistic theory and the description of English that underlie the teaching are lacking in interest and explanatory power.

2

In this and the next two sections we shall consider the three types of language teaching in turn, in the order prescriptive, descriptive and productive. They are not of course mutually exclusive, and all may have a place in the native language class, provided they are reasonably balanced and their different purposes are understood. Each of the three implies a different answer to the question: 'what do we teach the native language for?'. In the case of prescriptive teaching, the answer is: 'to teach the children to replace those of their own patterns of language activity which are unacceptable by other, acceptable patterns.'

The desire to replace existing patterns by others implies that something is wrong with the existing ones. The nature of this 'something wrong' has been examined above, in Chapter 4. The judgment is always, it cannot be too strongly emphasized, an institutional and not a descriptive one: any native language patterns which the normal child has mastered, in the sense that he is using them in the way they are used by those he learnt them from, are 'just as good', *quâ* language, as those he is expected to substitute for them. This applies whatever level of language is involved: grammar, lexis, phonology or phonetics.

Prescriptive teaching therefore means selecting those patterns, at any level, which are favoured by some, including some of the more influential, members of the language community; and using standard teaching practices to persuade the children to conform to them. The teacher may give no reason, the wrong reason or the right reason; but the main point in favour of giving the right reason is that this is the only way in which the child can be persuaded that he has enlarged his control over the external world by learning them. Otherwise, prescribed patterns in language remain unique among what is taught in the classroom, in that they impinge on the child's experience and yet run counter to it. Telling the child that he must say 'between you and me' and not 'between you and I', or vice versa, because the one is 'better' or 'clearer' than the other corresponds to nothing in his experience of language. Such instructions carry more weight if they are grouped together with other social conventions where they belong. You say 'different from', and learn those curious B.B.C. diphthongs, for the same reason as you may put your fork or spoon in your mouth but not your knife: because certain adults prefer it that way.

Prescriptive teaching takes a number of different forms. Some prescriptions cover both speech and writing; most, however, are specifically directed either at spoken language or at written language. Within the latter comes the special case of prescriptions concerning the transference of spoken language patterns into the written language, particularly in the early stages of the teaching of reading and writing. The teaching of reading and writing is itself productive, not prescriptive; it may entail some prescriptive teaching if children are taught that some patterns which are acceptable in speech must not be transferred into writing. This is a consequence of the divergence between written and spoken language, and opinions differ as to how far this divergence should be a matter for prescriptive teaching. Some teachers feel that children are best assisted in learning to write by being allowed to write down what they say as they would say it; others hold the view that, since the written language has its own conventions, these should be taught from the start.

Freedom in *orthographic* conventions, such as spelling, punctuation and the use of capitals, is a totally different matter. These
things are taught productively, since there are no existing patterns
to be altered, and the case for not correcting *orthographic* errors at a
certain stage could only rest on general educational theory. This is
governed by the same considerations as lead some teachers in the
arithmetic class, for example, not to penalize a child who has written
some of the figures backwards provided he has got the sums right,
on the grounds that the incentive should be clearly tied to the
arithmetical skill. There is of course a linguistic implication: if this
view is put forward in favour of some orthographic tolerance, it
means that the teaching of orthography is regarded as the teaching
of a technique, a means to an end, and that the true purpose of the
teaching lies in the use of written language. Linguists would of
course support the latter view, but would not feel competent
to say that *therefore* orthographic freedom should be allowed;
such a conclusion can only be assessed by reference to pedagogical
theory.

Correcting formal features of the child's written language, not
allowing him to transfer to the written language patterns acceptable
in the spoken, is, whether or not pedagogically desirable, a type of
prescriptive language teaching that has certain dangers. Children
who are made too aware of a difference between spoken and written
language, by having acceptable spoken forms penalized when used
in writing, may come to feel uncertain of the 'correctness' of anything they write, since no general criteria are offered to them. They
may feel they are being asked to learn a completely new form of
activity, one which bears little relation to language as they know it.

Is there any reason why our teaching should strive to maintain
the dichotomy between spoken and written English at its present
breadth? Certain differences there always will be, since they follow
from the nature of the medium. Writing is normally situationally
self-sufficient, in the sense that it represents (together with its
'opposite number' reading) the whole of the activity that is taking
place in the given situation: it therefore has to supply all contextual
information explicitly, a task that is made no easier by the general
absence of intonation symbols in our orthography. Speech on the
other hand may make up anything from almost the whole to only
a tiny fragment of the total activity in the situation in which it is
operating. But these differences determined by use arise naturally

and, if taught at all, can best be taught productively: they are a necessary *consequence* of the different functions performed by speech and writing. It is worth distinguishing these from the arbitrary conventions which require the replacement of one pattern in speech by another one in writing, which put a brake on children's self-expression and lead ultimately to the listlessness of some classroom essays.

In later years prescriptive teaching in the written language is usually concentrated on the various do's and don't's of traditional grammar; in time these merge, via restrictions on the use of 'get' and the like, into rules of composition such as the prohibition on the use of the first personal pronoun and on too close a repetition of the same lexical item. Many of the prescriptive 'rules' rest on false notions of English grammar; but since they represent social attitudes and have no significance as statements about the nature of the language this does not matter. For example, 'it is I' is incongruent with the normal structure of English clauses, which would give 'it is me'. There is no reason to insist that 'it is I' is 'bad grammar', since languages tolerate plenty of incongruences; but they do tend to iron them out by analogy, which may explain why no one naturally says 'it is I'. The attempt to justify 'it is I' on linguistic grounds rests on a straightforward misunderstanding of English clause structure. In the spoken language, on the other hand, prescriptive alteration of the children's phonetic habits tends to be achieved rather by example and by social pressure, including ridicule, than by classroom teaching, though the elocution lesson is a notable exception.

There is no point in engaging in polemics against prescriptive teaching as such. The justification for it lies, as has been said, not in the English language, but in the attitude to the English language of some of those who use it. The danger of self-deception, and of deceiving others, has already been stressed. We have wished merely to insist on the entirely arbitrary nature of the prescriptions, all of which could be turned upside down without any change in validity: those who hold prescriptive views would still hold them and those who reject them would still reject them. At the same time there are, in our view, two ways in which positive harm may be done by prescriptive language teaching. One is that it too easily becomes proscriptive, with all attention focused on what must not be done. The other is that it may come to occupy, and there is no doubt that it still often does, a central place in the teaching of the native language.

If prescriptive teaching occupies more than a small fraction of the total native language teaching time, a completely false picture of the nature of language is built up in the pupils' minds. This not only creates in the pupils a misunderstanding of the nature of language which will hinder both their use and their appreciation of the native language, but makes it much more difficult for them ever to learn a foreign one. If in addition to this the teaching is proscriptive, then we have only ourselves to blame if we create generations of illiteracy and inarticulacy. Is our language so poor and uninteresting a thing that we put it in the school curriculum only in order to fight for its lost causes, to pass pathetic judgments on some of its marginal features? We should be ashamed to let anyone leave our secondary schools knowing so little of how their language works and of the part it plays in their lives. This is not their fault, if their salient image of 'English language' is : 'state what is wrong with the following sentences'.

As long as questions of this kind are asked in the examinations, for so long will teachers have to teach children how to answer them. Such questions already figure very much less prominently than they used to, but they still appear, with the result that the emphasis has by no means entirely swung away from prescriptive teaching. A recent G.C.E. paper contained the question: 'In each of the following sentences, one word is wrongly used. Choose *seven* of them and (a) explain *very briefly* why you think that the word is wrong, and (b) suggest a word or phrase which you consider would be correct.' The sentences included various malapropisms and spelling mistakes, but also the following:

(i) The girl literally flew down the road.
(iv) Due to his illness, he was unable to sit the examination.

(Universities of Manchester, Liverpool, Leeds, Sheffield and Birmingham Joint Matriculation Board: G.C.E. English Language Paper A, Ordinary, June 1960). Even foreign students are expected to be familiar with our linguistic scale of values: 'The following sentences are grammatically incorrect. Write the sentences correctly.' Two of the sentences were:

(i) If I was you, I should not go.
(iii) He is the youngest of the two and always in the trouble.

Throughout, errors—that is, non-native forms such as 'in the trouble'—were interspersed with arbitrarily proscribed native forms such as 'if I was you'. (Scottish Universities Entrance Board Preliminary Examinations, Special Paper for Foreign Students: English, March 1960.)

It is likely that many teachers of English language would welcome a change of emphasis away from prescriptive teaching, provided that there was something more useful to put in its place. What could take its place is descriptive and productive teaching. It is indeed often not those who teach English language but teachers of other subjects who are most fierce in their prescriptive attitudes. In the universities the most diehard self-appointed protectors of the language are often found among the natural scientists, some of whom comment on the language of their students' essays, misapplying the precepts of some former school English teacher with all the authority of the French Academy. Possibly they are feeling a justifiable resentment at the uselessness of prescriptive English teaching to themselves as scientists. Certainly if English language teaching cannot be made relevant to the interests of those who are going to be electronics engineers it has no place as a compulsory subject in our schools. In fact, the study of the native language is not only relevant; it is central. But it has not yet been shown to be so.

3

The second type, or component, of language teaching is description. The aim of descriptive language teaching is clear once it is pointed out that here 'descriptive' is used as in 'descriptive linguistics': what is being taught is how language works and how a given language works. In descriptive language teaching, the native language must play the central role, for the very simple reason that it is the language the pupils know best. Far too often, children in our schools acquire what understanding they have of the nature of language only through the study of foreign languages, as a by-product of the difficult process of learning them. Since traditionally it is Latin rather than the modern foreign languages from which they derive their ideas, at least about grammar, their task is made doubly difficult: not only is Latin new to them, but also, being a dead language, it is taught only as a written language. This means that Latin as it impinges on the pupil is performing only half the functions of a language, and it does not help him to understand the part played by spoken language in our lives.

This is not the fault of the teachers of Latin. It is impossible to describe Latin fully as a spoken language, since it is no longer anybody's native language. However much it may still be used in some countries as a spoken L2, its use in speech is confined to certain registers only; there is no one for whom it performs the full range of operations of a native language. Besides, it is not the task of the teacher of Latin to use his class hours for general instruction in the nature of language. It would indeed be a pity if it was, since Latin is probably of all languages learnt at school the one most different from English. This latter point might be considered a third reason why it is unsatisfactory for English children to learn about the nature of language solely through the study of Latin. Not only is Latin as we have it an incomplete language and one which they know only very imperfectly; it also differs markedly from their native language.

It is perhaps somewhat revolutionary to suggest that children should be taught anything about the nature of language at all. The view is often taken, certainly implicitly if more seldom explicitly, that the purpose of the study of languages, native and foreign, in the school curriculum is to enable the children to make use of these languages, without there being any necessity for them to understand why and how these languages can perform the functions expected of them, or indeed what these functions are. It is assumed perhaps that in the course of learning the foreign language, and of having his attention directed towards the native one, the child will inevitably absorb and form for himself some notions about what language does and how it does it. This he will certainly do. But we are not content to let the child get his ideas about the British constitution from his general experience, into which goes everything from the whole childhood mythology about the nature of authority to his own family's attitude to industrial strikes, and from a few history lessons on Boadicea and King John. Yet we allow his understanding of language to rest on foundations no less shaky than these would be: general experience in the use of his native language, together with a few descriptive statements of doubtful value about languages he does not know and has no experience of in use. It is surely a general pedagogical principle to relate the teaching wherever possible to the child's own experience: conclusions drawn by the child from his experience alone are fallible, but instruction bearing no relation to it is much less useful than teaching which systematizes it, adds to it and draws valid conclusions from it.

If it is part of a child's education to learn about his environment, both social and natural (in the sense in which these words are used when one speaks of the social and natural sciences); if, in other words, he should know something of how society, and in particular his native society, functions, about how the television works and where the water in the taps comes from; then under the same heading it is part of his education to know how language works. And this has to be taught to him primarily in reference to his native language; not only because this language is, and will almost certainly remain, the most important to him, but because it is the only one he knows. For him it *is* language, just as half-crowns and sixpences and pennies *are* money, and we would not initiate English children into the nature of money by talking about roubles. But he knows it so well, even by the time he first goes to school, that there is in his vast and expanding store of native-language experience material enough and a thousand times over for him to be given informative and exciting descriptive language teaching at any stage in his school career.

What we mean by descriptive language teaching therefore is showing the child how language works by displaying, ordering and adding to his use of his native language. If it is objected that this means linguistics in the classroom, the answer is that it does: in the same sense and to the same extent that teaching how money works, for example while young children 'play shops' under guidance, means economics in the classroom. There are indeed methods of descriptive language teaching appropriate to any age at which the teacher wishes to introduce it. These can be related to the general concept of 'strata' of linguistics, or more specifically 'strata' of grammar, of lexis and so on, as the links which together make up the chain from academic 'back-room' linguistics at one end to class-room practice at the other.

The first stratum is work on general linguistic theory by linguists and phoneticians, work such as is published in the main academic journals of linguistics in this country and elsewhere. The second stratum is the use of this theory to describe actual languages: for example, comprehensive statements of the grammatical categories

8*

required in the description of English, or a detailed account of the phonology and phonetics of English intonation showing its total range of contrastive patterns and the phonetic properties of each. This is still back-room work, but it is getting nearer the classroom. The university student who takes linguistics or phonetics as an undergraduate learns to interpret, evaluate and use writings of this second stratum; those who go on to specialize in linguistics or phonetics, usually at present in postgraduate courses, take up the study of general linguistic theory and learn to *make* such descriptions of languages.

The third stratum is the description of a language for the use of those who teach it. This work should be published in the form of separate books or monographs; it should be the subject of extensive discussion and criticism in particular at training colleges and in university language departments. Fourth comes the textbook, the work that is placed in the hands of the pupils themselves who are learning the language. It is at this stratum that the age of the learner enters in as a variable determining the choice of material and the method of treatment. The fifth stratum, which could perhaps be subsumed under the previous one, is the actual content of the classroom teaching: the methods by which the teacher displays the language at work, the features he selects to illustrate and the type of language he himself uses to talk about them.

It should not be necessary to stress the essential unity and interdependence of all these strata; there are many aspects to it. In the first place, the theoretical work of what we have called the first stratum is itself the outcome of countless observations on language, made from a very wide range of different standpoints. In the second place there should be constant feedback to the theory from the other strata, since the experience gained in the classroom by a teacher of native English to seven-year-olds could include much that was crucial to our detailed understanding of how English works. What is wrong here is that we do not get this feedback, because the approach to language is so dominated by notions long disproved and due to be discarded that at present the results of this native language classroom experience are largely useless, except in confirming the invalidity of the view of language presented. In the third place, while in general any individual participating somewhere in the 'language from back-room to classroom' process is likely to specialize at one stratum, or (preferably and more probably) at two adjacent strata, simply because life is short, the more people there are who know something about all strata the better educated our children will be.

One of the most important recent moves in this direction is the establishment, already referred to, at certain universities of new courses designed precisely to give those taking them some knowledge of all strata. Some variation in emphasis has been allowed for and has, in fact, been built into these schemes as deliberate policy on a national scale: those wishing to take such courses should find out which kind of emphasis best suits their own purposes and interests. Similarly, the training required will be somewhat different according to whether the main emphasis is on English as a native language, English as a foreign language or on some foreign language or languages in England. But whether the emphasis is directed more towards the underlying theory or more towards classroom practice, what is stressed is the unity of the process as a whole. Even those who think of themselves as being primarily involved only at one stratum, whether because they prefer to do so or have no opportunity to do otherwise, might well like to look a little way to left and right if they were encouraged to do so. We should like to encourage them. The language teacher wanting to find out more about general linguistic theory will have to work hard, since language, not surprisingly if one considers the complex and varied uses to which we put it, is a highly complex form of activity; general linguistics, as we have said, is no more and no less 'just common sense' than pure mathematics or nuclear physics. But he may be consoled by the fact that the academic linguist starts with no less ignorance about how to put language over in the classroom.

While saying, therefore, that the main emphasis in native language teaching should be on productive and descriptive as against prescriptive teaching, we stress once again that the role of the linguist and phonetician is to provide good descriptions. He comes in at strata one and two, and desirably, in collaboration with teachers and training college staff, also at stratum three. If the linguist is able to say anything about the materials and methods used in the classroom, this is because, and to the extent that, he has taken the trouble to learn a new discipline, that of pedagogical theory and practice. Our aim here is to encourage descriptive language teaching; we are not trying to tell the teacher how to teach. What follows, therefore, is merely a hint of how it seems to us that time spent on English in school might be used to make children aware of the working of their language, and through that of the place of language in life.

Much can be done with a minimum of terminology: there is no need to name linguistic categories in order to show them at work. Guided play provides opportunities for encouraging linguistic awareness. Any play situation, such as the shop, can be used to illustrate not only well-known grammatical contrasts like singular and plural, positive and negative or active and passive, but also other systems, basic to modern English, that have been recognized only by modern linguistic methods of description. The children do not need to be told what to say; what counts is that they should observe the result of what they say, and be shown, by the introduction of variations, what it is that led to that result.

When the child says 'I want two loaves of bread, please', something happens. The whole utterance led to a certain result; certain features of the utterance led specifically to certain features of the result. If the utterance is varied to 'she wants', 'I don't want', 'two slices' or 'one loaf', something different happens. In each case: who did what, and why? The answer to that is part of the meaning of the utterance.

Let the children supply the language activity in a situation that is enacted without words: how did they know what utterances were appropriate? In situations like 'the shop', in which the language activity plays a small but crucial part, each utterance can be accompanied by some non-language activity that is determined by it. In other situations the language activity is more self-sufficient: in explaining the rules of a game, for example. This is a linguistic exercise at which some children excel, and one can pinpoint the linguistic features crucial to the exposition: not by finding fault with the child's use of language—still less with the language itself!—but by following the instructions the child has given. (Since this chapter was first written, we have seen an American language-teaching film showing children at shop-play using exactly the sort of language activity referred to above. Although the film was for older students, the events were being used to demonstrate linguistic contrasts in precisely the way suggested.)

Clearly the language the child normally uses when he speaks is not the easiest material through which to teach him to read and write: quite apart from the inconsistencies and omissions of our orthography, no one has yet recorded and analysed enough of the speech of children to be able to simulate it in writing. But it is an advantage if the child's introduction to the written language can be more closely linked to a demonstration of his own use of the spoken language. This does not exclude the narrative register, which after all is also part of most children's experience of spoken language; but it shows the written language in use in non-narrative registers, such as shopping lists and the rules of games. The more that writing and speech can be made to appear as operating with the same *forms* of language, and differing only in substance, the more relevant will writing seem to be.

When linguistic terminology is eventually introduced, the purpose of it is still to display the resources of the language. The question can be posed: what does English do with the 'clause'? The major contrasts that are made at this rank in English, such as dependence, mood, transitivity and theme, can be outlined and shown as meaningful selections linked to actual situations in which spoken language is used. Once a system has been displayed at work in the spoken language, and it has been shown that the choice of one term rather than another determines, or is determined by, other observable factors in the situation, it becomes easier to understand the operation of the system in the written language, where there is usually no comparable external situation to which to relate the forms of language used.

For example, the pupil reports a motor accident: 'The driver was injured; his hand was cut by broken glass'. One point for discussion is why this is passive, and what the effect would be of replacing passive by active. The answer is different in the two clauses. If the verbal group in the first clause is replaced by an active form, a new element of clause structure is then added: why? All English affirmative and interrogative clauses, except those of some particular sub-classes, have a subject. What then is the role of the category of 'subject' in the language, and how is a subject identified? Any single utterance of pupil or teacher can be used to show the magic of a living language. No matter at what point one plunges into the grammar, there is a path to start the careful observer on his journey of exploration.

Lexis no less than grammar can be linked to observable features in the situations chosen to display the language in use. It is easy, and not unrewarding, to commute lexical items: to ask which could replace a given item, with greater or less likelihood, if everything else is unchanged. In 'a loaf of . . .', what can occur other than bread? In 'a slice of . . .', what can occur other than bread? In 'a slice of . . .', it might be cake. If I say 'I want to buy a puppy', there is nothing improbable unless the situation happens to be, let us say, a chemist's shop. But 'I want a loaf of cake' is highly unlikely even at the baker's. This is a formal restriction: the collocation does not occur.

Lexical items can be grouped into situational 'sets', and instances noted where the choice is doubtful. There is the 'set' of items used to name containers, including 'jar' and 'bottle'; there may be uncertainty over 'bottle of sauce' or 'jar of sauce'. What then seems to determine the choice: shape, perhaps, or material, or contents? Whichever it is will be reflected in collocation: if it is called a bottle because it contains sauce, then the collocation of 'sauce' and 'jar' is presumably unlikely. Other instances of doubt may arise in referring to actions: if I kneel on the floor and sit back on my heels, am I kneeling or sitting? It is interesting to observe what instructions have to be given if a person is required to perform specific movements of this kind. The question of criteria is often a complex one: what, for example, is the difference between a door and a window? The class can compile its own dictionary, not forgetting the citations.

Phonology is seen in operation through grammar and lexis; it cannot be linked directly to situations, except for the feature known as the 'phonaesthetic series'. These are marginal to language, though English has more than its share: for example, if I hear an unfamiliar lexical item beginning with /sl/ it probably means either something thin (slim, slit, slot, slip, sliver, slice, slender) or something slippery (slide, slime, slip, slush, slither, sleet, slick); if it ends in /əmp/ it will probably be lumpy (bump, hump, mumps, rump, clump, stump, plump). Apart from instances such as these, phonological contrasts are illustrated by showing that if we replace one phonological item by another the result is either a different formal item or else nonsense. Nonsense utterances, incidentally, are extremely useful in demonstrating the different levels of language; there is much to be learnt from a piece like this:

> 'Haven't you got a glozier prine to snarp with? This one's
> too capsimated; it won't wendle.'

In the variety of English represented by many speakers of RP, twenty-one distinct vowels occur in strong syllables, leaving aside

items like 'freer' and 'doing' which could be regarded as mono-
syllables but consist of two morphemes. The twenty-one include
six simple and fifteen complex, the latter falling into different types
according to the direction in which the tongue and lips are tending
at the end of the vowel: four tend towards the 'i' position, three
towards the 'u' position and six towards the 'ə' (called 'schwa')
position, the remaining two having a 'curved' tendency i+ə and
u+ə. These can be represented phonologically as follows:

	SIMPLE		COMPLEX $+i$		$+u$	
SIMPLE	i	tin	i^i	tea		
	e	ten	e^i	tay		
	a	tan	a^i	tie	a^u	town
	ə	ton			$ə^u$	toe
	o	toss	o^i	toy		
	u	took			u^u	two
COMPLEX $+ə$	$i^ə$	tier				
	$e^ə$	tare				
	$a^ə$	tar	$a^{iə}$	tire	$a^{uə}$	tower
	$ə^ə$	turn				
	$o^ə$	tore				
	$u^ə$	tour				

There are no environments in which all twenty-one are in contrast,
and in any given environment there may be only a small number
which occur. The lavishness of English with at least this part of its
phonological resources is easily demonstrated. If for example we take
the syllable /bred/ 'bread' and replace /e/ with other vowels, only
these occur: i^i (breed), e^i (braid, brayed), a^i (bride), a^u (browed),
u^u (brood, brewed) and $o^ə$ (broad), unless perhaps a hillside can be
'briared'.

It can then be shown that items which are in contrast under
certain circumstances are not necessarily so under all circumstances.
/d/ and /t/ are normally in contrast, but after initial /s/ they are not:
the sound represented by the 't' in 'star' is some way between the

two. At the end of a syllable they are in contrast unless they are the exponent of the grammatical morpheme of past tense: 'wand' differs from 'want', but in the past tense the choice is determined by the preceding phoneme, except in a few cases like 'learnt' and 'learned' where both occur although with no contrast between them.

Intonation, which forms an important part of the phonological resources of English, can be described in such a way as to interest any native speaker. Here one can show it 'at work', so to speak, in that it is a direct carrier of grammatical systems which can in turn be related to situations. One cannot link 'the phoneme /n/' as such to situations in which language operates, because it enters into thousands of different grammatical and lexical items and has no independent job of its own in the language: it does its work through its participation in the phonological make-up of the items concerned. But in the two utterances //1 where are you / **go**ing // and //2 **where** are you / going //, the contrast of intonation carries the grammatical distinction between primary and secondary or 'echo' questions, and this can be linked to the situation: the secondary or 'echo' question shows that the person spoken to did not hear, had forgotten or was incredulous. The whole of the intonation system operates in this way, as the carrier of a number of grammatical contrasts.

If we can display the grammar and lexis of English, and at least a part of the phonology, by direct appeal to the situations in which language is used, we are exploiting the contextual meaning of language to throw light on its formal meaning. This probably has its uses at any stage in the pupils' learning about their language; later, however, the formal patterns themselves can be systematically presented and the phonology related to them. In this way one builds up a general picture of what happens in English. Even if this never proceeded beyond a few basic patterns and most general categories it would have the merit of being accurate and giving some idea of the nature of language. With the inclusion of a sound description of English phonetics, which we have not illustrated here but which is no less important and no less practicable, the descriptive teaching of the native language could be of the highest educational value. Moreover teachers of foreign languages might find their task much lightened if their pupils had first learnt something of the linguistics and phonetics of English.

4

The third type of language teaching is what we have called its 'productive' component. Descriptive language teaching aims to show the pupil how English works; this includes making him aware of his own use of English. Productive language teaching is concerned to help him extend the use of his native language in the most effective way. Unlike prescriptive teaching, productive teaching is designed not to alter patterns he has already acquired but to add to his resources; and to do so in such a way that he has the greatest possible range of the potentialities of his language available to him for appropriate use, in all the varied situations in which he needs them.

Only a very small part, if indeed any part at all, of productive teaching in the native language consists in actually teaching the child new formal patterns. Apart from technical terminology, which is a special case, the child learns the grammar and lexis of his native language, just as he learns its phonology and phonetics, outside the English class. He has learnt a large part of the whole apparatus before he goes to school; once at school he continues to learn much new lexis and some grammar, but still as a result of the enlarging of his general experience. Much of what is new to him comes through instruction in different subjects at school; the remainder from the development of his interests in new directions outside the school. He does not need the English period in the school curriculum for the purpose of 'learning English' in the narrow sense. It is fortunate that he does not, because there are so many other things that he can *only* learn in the English period. Whatever objections may be raised against descriptive and productive language teaching as we envisage it, it is unlikely to be criticized on the grounds that there would not be enough work to keep teacher and pupils occupied.

The child does, however, need to be taught the varieties of the language appropriate to different situations: the range and use of its registers and restricted languages. Part of this material, of course, will be presented descriptively: in discussing the use and meaning of a particular pattern or item, the teacher at the same time draws attention to the tendency for different patterns and items to be associated with different situation types. This tendency for the language to assume different varieties already intrudes itself, as we have seen, in the teaching of reading and writing: sooner or later the child learns that certain patterns found in speech are not generally found in the written language.

It was suggested earlier that the teaching of such register distinctions may be better dissociated from the teaching of reading and writing as such, for the reason that it is difficult enough to learn to read and write without having one's enthusiasm diminished by being forbidden to write the very things it seemed writing was going to be useful for. We can now add a second reason: that the choice of register is in fact more complicated than the mere distinction between spoken and written English. If we consider four accounts of the same event, let us say an exciting swimming match, recorded in a schoolgirl's diary, told by the girl to her parents, reported in the local newspaper and recounted by the headmistress on speech day, there is no reason to think that there would be fewer grammatical and lexical differences between the two spoken accounts, or between the two written accounts, than between one spoken and one written account.

It is the range and use of different varieties of the native language, then, rather than the actual introduction of new patterns and items, which is the focus of productive language teaching. Of course it is not suggested that there is a sharp line to be drawn between teaching the pupil how to use what he already knows and adding new items and patterns. Although he is likely to learn most of what is new to him in his native language either in the other classes or in his own extracurricular use of spoken and written English, there are always some features which he may meet for the first time in the English class; and a number which, though already met with, he may only learn to use and understand there. The line we do wish to draw is that distinguishing the productive from the prescriptive, between his learning of what is new on the one hand, whether it is the items and patterns themselves that are new or merely their distribution and use in different registers, and on the other hand the replacement of what he already knows by something else supposedly superior to it.

In maintaining as we do that traditional native language teaching in Britain has greatly overemphasized prescription (while almost totally neglecting description), we are not suggesting that it has had no productive side. This it always has had. But productive teaching has tended to be rather unevenly balanced: it has been very largely concentrated on the teaching of composition. There is perhaps no need to argue about whether learning to write literary essays is an essential part of a child's education. But this does not help the child to use the spoken language, and it is not the only, or even the most obviously necessary, written language skill; moreover the relative value to different children of training in composition is extremely variable. We cannot afford in any way to neglect the language requirements of whose who are going to become nurses, engineers, technicians, draughtsmen, transport workers, private secretaries, shorthand typists or members of any other of the thousand and one occupations that by some miracle feed, clothe and house us.

Each of us has to learn to manipulate English in a range of varieties, some of which are developing very rapidly. How does our English teaching help an electronics engineer learn and carry out his job? What can we tell the compiler of a computer programming manual about the use of English in that restricted language? Surprisingly, perhaps, we *could* tell him a great deal, now that many linguists are coming to use computers in their own study of language. But how much will he have learnt, at school, about the way his language works and about the properties a restricted language of this sort is likely to have? Has the English class helped the citizen to write dressmaking instructions, compile official forms, describe symptoms to the doctor or teach an apprentice about circuitry and the repair of cathode ray tubes? Has it even helped him to understand the instructions or to fill up the forms?

These, we may be told, are practical, everyday uses of language; they do not need to be taught. But it seems to us that most people could be better trained than they are in the use of English for such purposes; and that this training in the classroom could be not only effective and interesting but also of positive educational value. A rather different objection is that such uses of English have no aesthetic value and therefore lie outside the scope of the teaching of English, the alleged purpose of which is to teach the appreciation and the production of a type of English with some literary merit. But if the English teacher does not teach the non-literary uses of English, there is no one else to do so. It is not enough to identify one or two highly formulaic restricted languages, and to spend a few hours teaching the pupils how to write letters applying for jobs, as if the operation had nothing to do with the English language. Moreover the pupil is more likely to appreciate English literature if he can also understand and get the most out of English in its non-literary uses. Literature is only literature against the background of the language as a whole.

All the uses and varieties of a language are part of that language. Rather than trying to draw a line between those which are worthy of study and those which are not, we should perhaps look a little more closely at life in twentieth-century Britain, or wherever we may live and work, to see what its citizens use their language for. We have no right to say that the understanding of a car insurance policy is less important than the understanding of Shakespeare. If we do say this we shall simply lose Shakespeare, because we shall have divorced one use of the language, which the citizen can do without, from all the others which he cannot do without. If we regard non-literary language as hardly language at all, as a formless array of habits picked up throughout life, instead of realizing that in the language of the supermarket as in the language of Shakespeare, whatever the respective *merit* of the two, there is just as much *pattern* at every level, then we run the risk of stifling all interest in language as a medium of literature. And meanwhile the science teacher has to take over a part of the task of the English teacher because his pupils' ability to use language as a scientific medium has always, quite mistakenly, been taken for granted.

In the study of language, the opposition of art and science has no place: language neutralizes it. Human experience may be the object of scientific analysis, or aesthetic appreciation, or it may be left unprocessed as mere simple observation. Whichever it is it can be, and often has to be, organized in language. The native language has all such purposes to serve, and it is the task of all those responsible for the organization of English teaching to see that it does. Above all, perhaps, we should stop treating English as a more or less exclusively arts subject.

Productive teaching is a familiar feature of the native language class; enough has perhaps been said to suggest in what ways it might be broadened in coverage and application. The aim is the most effective use of English. We have tried to make clear the distinction between value judgments on language itself, on particular patterns or varieties, and assessment of the effectiveness of the use of language in relation to specific purposes. There is no such thing as 'good English' in the abstract. But there is such a thing as 'appropriate and effective English for the given purpose', and it is the ability to speak and write such English that productive teaching seeks to develop.

We may sum up by saying that at present, in our English language teaching, there is excessive emphasis on prescription; what description there is is out of date; and productive teaching is too much focused on literary composition. At its worst, such an approach can hinder rather than help the child in developing his native language skills. But the answer is not to abandon the teaching of English language, as some teachers have done out of dissatisfaction with its aims and achievements. The answer is to reduce prescriptive teaching to a minimum, to introduce valid scientific description and to broaden the horizons of productive teaching. If it is to retain its place in the syllabus, the teaching of the native language must relate, and must be seen to relate, to 'how we use language to live'.

We could perhaps enumerate what seem to us to be the four principal aims of native language teaching. The first is educational: everyone should know something of how his own language works. The second is pragmatic: everyone needs to learn to use his language most effectively. The third and fourth are indirect, in that their value lies in application: to know about the native language is to be well equipped both for learning a foreign language and for understanding and appreciating the native literature. To justify the last point, a few words are needed concerning the place of statements about language in the teaching of literature.

5

Literature is language for its own sake: the only use of language, perhaps, where the aim is to use language. This is not offered either as a definition of literature or as a contribution to a discussion of its nature and purpose: it leaves entirely open the question whether a work of literature excites, exhorts, edifies, entertains or merely exists. It is an aphoristic label serving to distinguish the language of literature from other uses of language. We have noted earlier that there are other types of event in which virtually the whole of the relevant activity is language, including many uses of written language and some of spoken: a discussion on politics, for example. But any non-literary use of language presupposes some situation, some wider framework of events and activities in which the participants in the language activity are also participating, even if only indirectly. A work of literature on the other hand creates its own situation, its own framework of events. Whatever the role attempted or achieved by literature in society, as language it is self-sufficient and self-contextualizing.

In order to analyse a work of literature, one must be able among other things to talk about the language of it. What proportion of the whole analysis will be taken up by statements about the language of the text is one of the questions which the specialist in literature has to decide. It is he who integrates the textual analysis, which represents the findings of linguistics and phonetics, with the findings of other disciplines such as psychology and social history as well as with biographical and other evidence that is not subsumed under any specialist study. If he finds psychology relevant to the understanding of a particular text, he will probably prefer to base his observations on the most recent and well-founded theories and methods of that subject. Similarly in order to discuss the language of the text he needs the most recent and well-founded theories and methods of the linguistic sciences. This applies to the teacher of literature as much as to the academic literary specialist; and the curious statements about language that continue to be made by some writers on literature only make it more urgent that there should be more such valid linguistic studies of literary texts.

These do not contribute directly to the *evaluation* of a work of literature. Linguistics and phonetics contribute to literary analysis, not to literary criticism. It is of course important to study the language of works of different genres that are considered to have literary merit in order to try and find out how they differ from those that are not. It may in time be possible to show a correlation between linguistic features and consensus of literary opinion. This would not explain anything; but it would make it possible to say that if a work of a particular genre displays certain features there is a strong chance that it will be generally regarded as good, or if others then as bad, literature.

What is said about the language of literary texts must, if it is to be of any value, be related to a general description of the language. A writer, however original, is using the resources of the language; he is selecting from its total repository of items and patterns, and it is in the selection and combination that originality lies. The reader, in turn, is recognizing the selected items and patterns from his general experience of the language. There is no use in setting up *ad hoc* categories to talk about the language of a particular poem as if it bore no relation to the rest of the English language; as if the arrangement of features in the poem had some inner significance totally divorced from the place of those features in the language as a whole.

Such 'unattached' observations are common in discussions of literature. They contribute nothing to literary analysis and do not help to explain the impact of the work on the reader, who has, we trust, been making fairly extensive use of the English language for some time before being expected to appreciate its literature. Moreover they make all comparative description impossible. Accurate linguistic comparison of one text with another, especially if the two are likely to have features in common (being written for example by different writers but of the same period and genre), is no less valuable than other comparative studies in literature. But linguistic comparison is almost impossible if two works have been described in terms of different sets of categories, and completely so if, instead of anything we could properly term description, we have nothing more than the undocumented intuitive observations of a particular critic or teacher.

The linguistic analysis of a literary text begins as 'pure' description, in the sense that a literary text is described in the same way as any other text. It can be described at one or more of various levels, with the same categories that are required to account for English in any of its uses; in this way the teacher can show what selection the writer has made from the resources of the language. The description need not of course be exhaustive: any feature can be picked out for focus of attention. But there are three respects in which the analysis of a literary text may depart from or supplement a 'pure' description. These arise from the fact that the linguistic study of literature is an application of linguistics; they are comparable to the special statements made in applying linguistics to foreign language teaching (see Chapter 5 above), statements which would not form part of a description made simply for the purpose of displaying the language at work.

First of all, it may be necessary to realign linguistic categories so as to bring together features which, in a general description, would turn up at different places in the statement. For example, all languages display certain features which can be regarded as cohesive; such features are of different types and belong to different levels, but all contribute to the internal binding of the text. The fundamental type of cohesion is of course the relation of structure itself: two or more items entering into a structure always cohere. But there are other, non-structural features exerting a similar force. In English these include grammatical anaphora, grammatical substitution and lexical anaphora; the first is reference back by personal pronouns and by deictics such as 'the', 'this' and 'his'; the second is the use of 'do' and 'one' in the verbal and nominal groups, as in 'I might do' and 'a big one'; the third is the repetition of a lexical item, or occurrence of a second item from one lexical set. All such features, including those which extend across sentence boundaries, will figure somewhere in a description of English; but for literary analysis they need to be brought together, since together they constitute an important feature in which one text may differ strikingly from another.

Second, the literary text is as it were the product of linguistic form and literary form. The latter can be regarded as imposing restrictions, either statistical or absolute, on the selection made within the former. The linguistic and phonetic properties of particular literary forms must therefore be taken into account. For example, the actual rhythm of a couplet in iambic pentameter is the product of two factors, one literary and one linguistic: the line of five metric feet, each of two syllables arranged weak-strong, plus silent foot at the end; and the rhythm of spoken English based on the foot as a unit of phonology, having any number of syllables of which only the first is strong. As another example, all grammatical structures in non-literary English are assigned to one or other of the grammatical units. But in some verse forms the units of literary form may be used to carry grammatical structures. In analysing eighteenth-century heroic couplets, it is revealing to describe not only the grammar of the sentence, clause, group and so on, but also the grammar of the couplet, line and half-line, a study for which the term 'grammetrics' has recently come into use. In prose also literary form affects linguistic patterning: not only in obvious ways, such as the linguistic differences between narrative and dialogue in fiction, but also in less obvious ones. There may for example be a tendency for a different density (repetition rate) of lexical items, and different degrees of cohesion, in the short story and in the novel.

Third, we have to examine and take into account the relation between the linguistic patterning that is specific to literary usage, whether or not referable to particular literary forms, and the normal patterns of language at the various levels. A literary text, like any other, is *selecting* from the total patterns available; it is also *arranging* the selected patterns into further patterns. But within this concept of arrangement there is a distinction to be made. On the one hand there are regular features of arrangement: repetition of certain clause or group structures, for example, or of phonemes or classes of phonemes in alliteration, or vowel patterning in strong syllables. These we may call 'regularities'. On the other hand there are the variations in arrangements and deviations from the general, non-literary distributions: no repetition where repetition would be predicted, or the use of infrequent structures and collocations. These we may call 'irregularities'.

These regularities and irregularities, superimposed on the normal patterns of the language, together make up the originality of a literary text. This originality could in the last resort be quantified and stated statistically, since it consists not in the creation of new language but in the new use of existing resources. But it can be clearly displayed even in quite short texts by a teacher starting from a descriptive knowledge of the language. He can show for example an unusual distribution of adverbial groups in the clauses of one particular poem; or that the lexis of another may be characterized by the interplay of high probability and low probability collocations. The general picture that emerges is often one of controlled originality: new but not too new, and with a firm anchor in the familiar.

Much, then, of what the linguist has to say about the language of a literary text is no different in scope from what he has to say about any text. The remainder is an extension of it, required by the specific end in view, the analysis and understanding of literature, but still using the same theories and methods. If one did not use the same theory and method for describing literary texts as for describing language in other uses, linguistics would be of no value in the study of literature, since it would not show what were the special features of a particular work of literature, nor what on the other hand it had in common with other texts in the language in which it was written. By the use of the same theory and method it becomes possible both to analyse a literary text and to compare it with other literary and non-literary texts in the language.

The result of this process is to bring more closely together the study of language and the study of literature. These two are not the same thing. The study of literature involves other disciplines which are not within the linguistic sciences; it may, though it does not necessarily, include the evaluation and criticism of literary texts. In the study of language, on the other hand, we are interested in all uses of language, non-literary as well as literary. But the two subjects come together in the study of the text. The more that can be said in the literature class, rigorously and meaningfully, about the language of the texts being studied, the easier it will be to bridge this cleft, artificially widened and deepened as it has been, between language and literature in the English teaching programme.

We have made the point earlier (in Chapter 1) that there is no paradox in the assertion that it is modern scientific and even statistical linguistics that can throw most light on a work of literature. There are precedents and analogies for this: the singer is no less appreciated because we can now produce singing voices on speech synthesizers. The qualified language teacher does not make the literature teacher unnecessary; nor does the linguist put the literature specialist out of a job, although some literary critics engage in polemics against linguistics with a vehemence which suggests they fear he might. On the contrary, precisely because linguistics provides tools for making more observations and making them more accurately, it yields much more evidence for the literary analyst to take note of. He is the only specialist who can draw together all the domains of experience, organized and unorganized, that lie behind a work of literature. Just as the more research is done in social history the more powerfully he can illuminate the social background of a work, so also each new advance in linguistics and phonetics enables him to ask more revealing questions of the language of the text, and to help to find the answers to them.

What is presented in the classroom, at least until a fairly advanced stage, will be the *result* of the linguistic analysis of a text. As with descriptive language teaching in general, it is not necessary to impose a terminological load before talking about the language of works of literature. Phonological features of rhythm and intonation, and collocations in lexis, can be shown at work in poetry without the use of any technical terms. It is difficult to discuss grammar without naming some categories; but provided such categories, and the names given to them, are those used in the language class, they will be familiar enough to be safely applied to the literary texts. For example, if the pupil knows the difference between the three main uses of 'the' in the nominal group, whether or not he has learnt names for them, he can appreciate the very particular way in which 'the' is used in Yeats's poem *Leda and the Swan*.

It will probably be readily admitted that what we have called the 'traditional' approach to the description of English has yielded relatively few useful results in application to the study of literature. This is no doubt the main reason why there has been so little serious linguistic analysis of literary texts. Many teachers who would like to look more closely at the language of literature, however, find somewhat forbidding the threefold requirement involving some understanding of up-to-date linguistic theory, a knowledge of English grammar and phonology, and skill in the linguistic analysis of texts; especially in view of the paucity of published material to guide them. Linguists and phoneticians have a great deal to learn from the textual application of linguistic descriptions. It is not unreasonable that they should be expected to produce the material required to make such application possible.

BIBLIOGRAPHY

See items 23, 56, 57, 58, 67, 84, 89.

Chapter 9

Learning foreign languages

1

This chapter will be concerned with some general problems of foreign language learning, and thus also, since the double-sided nature of the learning and teaching process is nowhere more obvious than here, with broad issues of policy and practice in foreign language teaching. Some of the examples are drawn from the field of English as a foreign language, and some from that of foreign languages in Britain; the two are complementary, and experience and progress in either area can contribute to developments in the other.

Foreign languages are learned and taught in a wide variety of ways, some more effective than others; it is hardly possible to classify them in simple terms, at least by reference to the classroom approaches which they illustrate. But within the total range of operations which merit the label of 'teaching a foreign language', two subdivisions must be singled out. The first is the teaching of a language by teaching *in* that language; the second is the teaching of a language by teaching *about* that language.

It can be assumed that the tasks and aims of foreign language teaching include the imparting to the student of some or all of the basic language skills—understanding speech, speaking, reading and writing—which he did not previously possess, or which were present only in a limited form. One way of acquiring these skills is by 'experiencing' them: by encountering them in use in real situations and coming to associate certain activities, persons or topics with the foreign language. This is what happens when the foreign language is also the medium of instruction, as English is in Nigeria and other countries. It is also what has been deliberately attempted and achieved in several experiments in foreign language teaching in primary schools in Britain. The language is taught, at least in part, by the device of teaching *in* the language, by lessons in geography perhaps, or history, or arithmetic.

There is of course a danger here. The undoubted effectiveness of teaching in a foreign language as a means of teaching the language does not mean that the language teacher supersedes the teacher of geography or history or mathematics; as any language teacher well knows, this is neither possible nor desirable. What it does mean is that a way has been found of avoiding the unwelcome gap in classroom operations which teacher and pupils face when the interest and variety of 'teaching the language' have begun to ebb. Teaching in a language is partly the provision of interesting further practice material for the exercise of the skills being acquired, partly the reinforcement of learning by enabling the pupils to experience the language in new contexts and combinations, and partly (but only partly) the introduction of new grammatical patterns and new vocabulary items. At the same time it is a step in the direction of syllabus integration, which in primary schools especially is regarded as a desirable aim.

The implications of teaching in a language can be clearly seen from the situation in countries such as Nigeria where English is the medium of instruction for almost all the teaching in secondary schools. This has two important consequences. In the first place, the sheer quantity of classroom experience of English that each pupil receives is much greater outside the English lesson than within it. It has even been suggested that if the lesson labelled 'English' were removed from the timetable of all secondary schools in Nigeria, little or no effect would be noticed on the ability of the pupils in English when they came to leave school, simply because these classes provide only a minority of their total exposure to English. But in the second place, the children are influenced by class teachers other than those who specialize in English, so that the ultimate performance of the pupils in the language relates to the average standard of English of the teaching staff as a whole rather than simply to the standard of the specialized teacher of English. Teaching *in* a language is a remarkably effective means of teaching a language; but it carries with it the implication, sometimes overlooked, that all those who teach subjects in the foreign language need to be able to perform adequately in it themselves.

At the opposite end of the scale from learning a language through being taught some other subject in that language is the use for language teaching purposes of descriptive statements *about* the language. To say that German has three genders, masculine, feminine and neuter; that in French the pronoun as complement occurs in the verbal group preceding the verb; that the RP accent of English has six simple vowel phonemes: these are observations *about* the languages concerned. They have an essential place in the *total* scheme of teaching these languages. But frequently these and similar statements about languages are offered as if they represented the obvious and most effective means of imparting the language skills.

It is true that there is one category of pupil who can make effective use of statements about a language: this is the sophisticated adult learner, especially one with experience of using and learning about several languages. He can interpret statements about another language in the light of his existing skill, and can control his performance accordingly. But such learners are relatively rare, perhaps extremely rare. It is true also that advanced pupils, even those at a younger age, may be guided towards greater sophistication and understanding by being taught about the mechanism of the language they are learning, by learning *about* its grammar and its phonology. But their new understanding comes from being shown the patterns inherent in the skills which they already possess; the skills themselves can only very rarely be imparted in the first instance by teaching the learner *about* them.

Teaching about a language has the seductive merit of being relatively easy to carry out. The use of a grammar book turns a 'skill' subject into a 'content' subject, one in which the teacher can teach facts instead of imparting skills. But an hour spent in teaching the facts of grammar, of phonology or of lexis, is not an hour of teaching the language. Teaching a language involves conjoining two essential features: first, the learner must 'experience' the language being used in meaningful ways, either in its spoken or in its written form; and secondly, the learner must himself have the opportunity of performing, of trying out his own skills, of making mistakes and being corrected. These are the essence of language learning; and teaching about a language does not contribute directly to either of them.

We are not of course suggesting that no learner need ever know anything about the language he is learning; far from it. Nor should it be thought that, because we emphasize the need for the learner to experience the language in use, and to have the chance of trying it out himself, we are advocating some rigidly defined version of the old Direct Method. But in far too many instances teaching about the language is allowed to take the place of teaching the language, thereby consuming valuable syllabus time without producing adequate results. This seems to be symptomatic of a twofold confusion which often afflicts the teaching of foreign languages.

In the first place, there is confusion about whether the particular pupils should be learning *about* the language at all, and if so to what extent and for what purposes. Knowledge about a language may be beneficial in its own right as providing an intellectual exercise; this does not necessarily determine its place, or even determine that it has a place, in a language course. Some teachers impart knowledge about the language they are teaching because such knowledge is necessary for passing examinations; this is merely evidence that the examinations should be reviewed. Others teach about a language because the textbook they are using teaches about the language, and familiar teaching aids tend to perpetuate themselves. All these might be considered non-linguistic reasons for teaching about a language: they are extraneous to the language-teaching task.

In the second place there is a more fundamental confusion, about how language skills are actually acquired. Some teachers maintain that learning to perform in a foreign language presupposes knowing about that language, and that therefore some degree of (for example) overt grammar teaching, whether or not desirable for its own sake as intellectual exercise, is essential if the job of teaching is to be carried out properly. There is, as we have said, a potential role in the total educational process for learning about a language; but it is not true that practical performance necessarily depends upon it. Indeed, the audio-visual courses in French and in English for adult beginners devised by the École Normale Supérieure at St. Cloud demonstrate that extremely rapid and effective foreign language teaching can take place, at least up to a certain level, without any teaching about the language. Knowledge about a language is valuable for advanced learners, and especially for sophisticated adults and adolescents who already have a wide and firm command of the language concerned, and perhaps before that have learnt about other languages in the same way. But in the initial stages, and especially in large classes, it rarely helps and can often hinder the attainment of practical language skills by the learner.

2

This immediately raises the question of what the aims of teaching foreign languages really are. There has been a good deal of criticism in Britain in recent years of the level of attainment reached in foreign languages by the average pupil leaving the grammar school. Some people point to the fact that most grammar school leavers cannot adequately understand or make themselves understood in any foreign language, even when they may have been supposedly learning one or more languages for six years; this state of affairs has been described by such observers as a national disaster. Others maintain that the majority of these same school leavers have shown the ability to read a play by Racine or Schiller and to write a comprehensible essay in the language, and this ability is put forward as evidence that an important educational job has in fact been done.

But the teaching of practical ability in a language, at least in certain directions, is a task quite different from that of teaching the understanding and appreciation of literature in that written language. Not only are the two different in kind, but also practical ability must inevitably precede literary appreciation of works in a foreign language. The attempt to introduce foreign literature to a learner before he has sufficient command of the language in which it is written frequently leads to frustration, boredom and antipathy on his part, so that there is much to be lost and little to be gained by bringing the cultural task too far forward in time.

The discussion of the relation between language and literature in foreign language teaching is frequently obscured by terms which are imprecise or variable in usage and by highly charged slogans that cannot be realized in practice. To say for example that it is both impossible and undesirable to divorce language from literature in foreign language teaching is rather like saying that it is both impossible and undesirable to divorce arithmetic from algebra in mathematics teaching, or physics from chemistry in the teaching of science. It is certainly worth making a plea for retaining, within the wider educational orbit, the study of cultural and literary achievements as represented in works of the language being learned; but the plea would be better formulated if it did not imply an identity between a language on the one hand and literary works in that language on the other, or between the acquisition of language skills on the one hand and the appreciation of literature on the other.

The essence of the matter is that there are two separate and distinct tasks here, and that different people take the one or the other as an index of the effectiveness of the language-teaching effort. In our view the primary task of language teaching is to impart practical command of the four basic skills of language, for use in the widest possible range of different situations; and therefore we cannot help regarding the average product of a school language learning career as being sadly and grossly deficient. Whether or not he can read a play or a novel in the foreign language and write an essay about it is a very different question; such abilities must not be allowed to conceal grave defects in other directions. The criterion for labelling as 'deficient' the average grammar school leaver is that he can often neither understand the language he has been learning as spoken by a native speaker in a 'real life' situation, nor make himself understood in it, nor read material of everyday importance, such as a newspaper or a customs declaration form, nor write acceptably on subjects relevant to life outside the classroom.

3

No matter what precise degree of pessimism one may habitually express about the results of current foreign language teaching methods as they are organized in schools in Britain and abroad, a more important question is how quickly these results can be improved. Already a number of radical changes are taking place, and the improvements to which they are leading can and, we think, will be extended and accelerated once a fairly small number of crucial features of language teaching have been grasped by public opinion and incorporated into the system.

One of these features has been touched on already, namely the clear recognition of the difference of objective which separates the teaching of practical ability in language skills from literary and cultural studies. Second only to this in importance is the need to pay much more attention to the spoken language. Very often the procedures and techniques used in teaching Latin are transferred wholesale into teaching French, German or English as a foreign language. There are several reasons why the teaching of Latin is an unsuitable model, not the least being the fact that Latin as it has come down to us is only part of a language; moreover it is always a secondary language to those who use it, unlike the others, which are spoken by millions of people as their primary language.

What does 'paying more attention to the spoken language' mean? It does not mean simply including spoken language where previously this was neglected. It means basing all instruction, during the early stages, upon the spoken language, and delaying the introduction of reading and writing until the onset of that special kind of reading-readiness, different from the one we associate with infants learning to read in their mother tongue, which indicates that the time is appropriate for the change. Objective evidence on this subject is difficult to come by, but it is increasingly widely held that the total process of L2 learning is more rapid and effective if a command of the phonological system, and a good range of grammatical patterns and some basic lexical items all in the spoken medium, are taught *before* the learner is introduced to written forms.

It is sometimes contended that people learning foreign languages only rarely need to speak them, and that it is far more important to acquire a 'reading knowledge' of a foreign language. The reply to this falls into two parts. First, outside a few specialist groups, such as engineers or scientists or journalists, the number of people who genuinely need to be able to read a foreign language without also having the need, or at least the opportunity, to speak it is just as small as the number of those who need to be able to understand and speak it without being able to read and write it. The discrepancy in numbers which is popularly held to exist between the 'reading only' group and the 'speaking only' group is hard to substantiate. For those few whose needs are genuinely of the 'reading only' type, such as scientists who find themselves wishing to learn Russian solely in order to read scientific journals, specialized courses can be devised, and indeed many such courses exist; but these courses generally take account of the fact that the learners are sophisticated adults. Such courses are not to be confused with the kind of language instruction given in schools; here, the eventual career of any individual pupil cannot be predicted and it would be contrary to educational practice to give as the standard course something that related to an unusual and highly restricted objective. Tuition in the normal case has to provide for the widest communicational needs of the average citizen who successfully completes the educational ladder to the top of the school. Those 'early leavers' whose requirements, in the event, are reckoned to be less far-reaching have then at least been given the same initial opportunities as the others.

The second and more cogent reply to the 'reading only' argument is that, for children at least (but also for some adults), it is easier to acquire an effective reading knowledge of a foreign language *after* gaining some command of the spoken language. Seen from the standpoint of linguistics this is not at all surprising, since, although as we have pointed out written *language* is not merely a visual representation of spoken language, the *items* of the written language have their linguistic referents in the spoken medium. The written form 'house' represents in writing the same formal item *house* as is known and identified in the spoken language as /ha^{u}s/. This pattern of representation is well established for the native language, and explains why in the learning of a foreign language a reading knowledge most readily follows a speaking knowledge; it does not easily replace it, especially with children.

Other arguments are sometimes put forward by those who find it difficult to accept a preliminary stage of language teaching which is oral only, preceding the stage where the oral and the visual combine. One is that the pupils demand written texts and reading material, and if they are denied access to writing this creates psychological difficulties. The extent to which this is true depends largely on the linguistic sophistication of the pupil; but such a demand is in any case learned behaviour. If the language concerned is the pupil's first foreign language, and if nobody persuades him that he *ought* to want to see written representations of the language he is hearing and speaking, it is generally true that the pupil finds no difficulty at all for a considerable period in learning without the use of written forms. The only doubtful question is how long this period should last, and here each teaching situation will require a different decision.

If the pupil has previously learned other languages, especially any classical language, he will be predisposed to regard as normal teaching procedure those methods which make use of written material from the outset, and in order to bring him to forgo written forms a certain amount of persuasion may be necessary. The more sophisticated the learner, the stronger the expectation of using written forms is likely to be. Nevertheless, even in fairly extreme cases it is still advisable to begin with an 'oral only' stage, and not to introduce written forms before the phonological system is firmly established. One effect of this is likely to be that the learner's pronunciation will be better than it would normally be as a result of the more usual process, and spelling pronunciations are likely to be greatly reduced.

Among the various unacceptable reasons which are sometimes advanced against beginning with an oral stage, perhaps the worst is that no homework can be set; and yet this is seriously raised by some teachers as a practical justification for introducing written forms from the outset. It is commonly claimed that homework is necessary for schoolchildren because the number of teaching hours in class time alone is insufficient for the educational task; this is an argument based on views about teaching that one may or may not accept. But to reject one of the chief tenets of modern methodology in the teaching of language on the grounds that homework cannot be set is to put the cart before the horse. In any case, a little ingenuity could suggest various forms of out-of-school activity that could be set on the basis of a purely oral beginning in a foreign language. This 'no homework' argument ought not to need refuting, but it has to be mentioned because it all too often appears as the last ditch defence against oral teaching in the early stages.

4

Just as English is taught overseas mainly in secondary schools (with a few exceptions, most of them in Africa) so also in Britain it is chiefly in secondary schools, and above all in grammar schools, that foreign languages have been taught. Yet this is not the only possible educational pattern, and indeed there is already a growing stream of interest in experiments with the teaching of foreign languages in secondary modern and primary schools in Britain. It is beginning to look as if a radically different treatment of foreign languages may be expected within the next few years.

Once it is admitted that practical ability in a language can be separated as a teaching aim from any wider cultural or literary objective, and that the younger a child is the more readily he acquires a command of foreign languages, then the inference is obvious: language ability is not only a possible aim for the primary school, it is actually rather more appropriate there than in the secondary school. One could go further than this. It is commonly observed that success in foreign language learning among primary school children is within wide limits unrelated to the 'intelligence' of the individual. There seems to be a quite separate ability in language behaviour which does not correlate closely with IQ. Yet the 'streaming' of children which takes place in British schools after the age of eleven in effect decides, on the basis of an intelligence test, whether an individual child will have the opportunity of learning a foreign language at all by allocating him to a grammar school, where he will, or to another kind of school, where he will not. The teaching of languages in the primary school would avoid this unhappy consequence of the selection methods at present in use. *Almost all children*, not simply the small minority who go on to the grammar schools, would be taught languages, and they would be taught with a purpose and in a manner that could enable them to understand and speak in these languages, and to read and perhaps to write a little also. This appears to be one of the remarkable effects of language teaching in primary schools: a high degree of success is normal, if one looks at the class as a whole, regardless of intelligence and social background. It is true that relatively little experimental evidence has yet been presented to support this view. But many of the teachers engaged in foreign language teaching in British primary schools have reported this as a personal observation.

We need to reconsider, in the light of modern knowledge and conditions, not only the conventional patterns of language teaching in the British educational system but also the choice of languages to be taught. Both adolescents and adults frequently hold the view (which, even if it has not been deliberately taught to them at school, is nevertheless a learnt attitude) that some languages are very difficult or even impossible for native speakers of English to learn. For adults, there is a modicum of truth in these views, since the older one grows the more deeply embedded are the patterns of one's native language, and the more likely it is that one has been taught one or more other languages from the same language family as one's mother tongue. The primary school child is free of both these drawbacks (which are in any case much exaggerated), and can be taught Russian as easily as French, Chinese as easily as Italian.

Thus it is not unrealistic, from the pupil's point of view at least,

to envisage primary school children acquiring as a normal matter of
course a basic command of one or even two foreign languages, one
perhaps drawn from a familiar list and one from an unfamiliar list:
for instance, one from either French or German and one from either
Russian or Arabic or Chinese. The teacher's point of view, and that
of the national educational pattern, may make it necessary to
restrict the range of choice open to any given child and to retain the
present numerical preponderance of French; nevertheless a great
increase in foreign language teaching in the primary schools is both
inevitable and desirable, and we should not unthinkingly accept as
immutable the same restricted list of languages that has become
established in the secondary schools.

Before going on to consider the implications for secondary schools
of language teaching in primary schools, we should stress that we
visualize as the end-product of a primary school foreign language
course something vastly different from the average performance at
the 'pass' standard in examinations such as Ordinary Level in
English General Certificates of Education. The primary school
leaver would know nothing about grammar, would not be able to
conjugate a verb or to name exceptions to rules; he would not in fact
be able to talk about his languages at all. But he would be able to
use them in everyday talk about the situations common to eleven-
year-old children: 'My father has gone away for three months.'
'Her little brother is seven tomorrow.' 'If we do woodwork
tomorrow, please will you show me how to sharpen a chisel?'
'Please may I leave the room?'

Languages in the primary schools would make the existing
secondary school pattern quite irrelevant. Instead of being presented with an intake of linguistic virgins, some of whom at present
never entirely lose their innocence even after six years of teaching,
all secondary schools—not just the grammar schools—would
receive in their lowest classes a full complement of pupils already
able to perform to a limited extent in at least one foreign language.
And so all schools, technical, modern and grammar alike, would
have as one of their tasks the totally new one of arranging to maintain this practical ability and to prevent it from evaporating through
lack of practice and reinforcement. Apart from this, each different
type of school would be likely to assume a language teaching function of its own.

The grammar schools would be able to extend and deepen the

practical ability in foreign languages already present in their pupils, and to add to it the cultural, literary and general educational content which they already impart in their present-day teaching; this task would be the easier in that it would not be impeded by the necessity of teaching a basic command of the language at the same time. The grammar schools should also be able to offer the chance of acquiring one or two additional languages. Either these would be taught fairly rapidly as 'practical performance' languages only, or else they would be taught in the first place as practical subjects and later accompanied by studies in literature and general culture. These languages might be chosen from the two lists of languages, familiar and exotic, suggested earlier. Such an arrangement could make two languages the minimum attainment for any secondary school pupil at school-leaving age. The four-language pupil, with two languages in which he had acquired practical ability in the spoken language only and two in which he had this ability backed by literary and cultural knowledge, might become the norm among grammar school leavers on the modern and classical side. Four languages, all for practical purposes but with some study of scientific registers, might be the normal attainment for the grammar school specialist in science.

The secondary modern school would have a new task in keeping up and consolidating the existing languages of its pupils, and it might make one or even two additional languages available on a 'practical performance' basis. The upper limit of these language studies might take in the registers of industry and commerce, into which a large number of secondary modern school pupils may eventually pass.

The technical secondary schools, too, would face the problem of keeping up and extending existing language ability. They might make one extra language available as an option, and both this and the existing languages of the pupils would be extended to take in the usage in those technical registers, such as draughtsmanship, motor car fitting, cookery and farming, which main groups of school leavers would be likely to need. The notion of a *commis chef* able to discuss French cuisine in French, or of an apprentice mechanic being able to read the maker's workshop handbook of a Mercedes-Benz in the original German, or of a junior business clerk being able to understand correspondence received from Italy or Russia, will not seem so far-fetched if the nation's foreign language studies can be reorganized around practical language teaching from the primary school upwards.

These are simply some of the consequences of modern views on language teaching which we believe to be within the bounds of possibility, and indeed to be on the way to realization. But a number of very great practical difficulties stand in the way. There is for instance the problem of teaching materials for use in primary schools. The first teachers to embark on French or German or Italian in the primary schools would find practically no suitable materials for use in class. Not that very much exists even for the purpose of teaching practical language ability by modern methods at an older age; but the needs of the primary school can in any case not be equated with the kinds of textbooks and readers commonly used in conventional secondary grammar school language courses.

The primary school task is almost totally different from the G.C.E.-oriented requirements of present-day secondary school language teaching, and the materials needed are different in consequence. What the primary school teacher needs is, first, a handbook for his own use; he also needs pictures and objects from the foreign country; gramophone records and tape recordings; audio-visual materials; films and film strips; puppets and models, and radio and television programmes. And in order to be able to make the best possible use of these he needs an appropriate training in his new task, either during his initial period of training as a teacher or by means of in-service training.

It may seem fairly obvious that primary school language teaching, being a completely new task, needs unusual and unorthodox teaching materials. It is perhaps less obvious, but it is equally true, that teaching materials of similar kinds are needed for the secondary schools also. In fact, these are the modern tools for teaching practical language skills to beginners, whether we are considering English as a foreign language or foreign-language teaching in Britain, and whether we are thinking of young children, adolescents or adults. The grammar-and-dictionary approach to language teaching has no place in modern methods: it has been replaced by an approach that links the utterance with the experience of seeing and hearing the situation in which that utterance takes place. In this new approach, the classroom tools are also of a new kind. Yet the 'grammar-translation method', as it is labelled, remains even in the 1960s the most usual form of language teaching that is to be found, both in Britain and elsewhere. The response of many teachers who use this method to those who propose new ways is often: 'Well, what is wrong with the grammar-translation approach?' The reply to this question deserves a section to itself.

5

The grammar-translation method of language teaching, as its name implies, leans heavily upon the formal description of the language being taught and upon the exercise of translation into and out of the mother tongue. The method would be somewhat more effective (but not greatly so) if the grammar used were linguistically more valid and were more directly relevant than it usually is to some current variety of the language being taught, preferably a spoken variety. Much of the grammar taught within this method is pedantic, or archaic, or even erroneous; this holds for English as well as for French and German.

But suppose the grammar were both well described and relevant: although as we have said grammar has an important place in the total operation of language teaching, it would still not be an adequate substitute for the teaching of practical skills in the language, since it is simply a form of statement *about* the language. Certain highly selected learners may be able to convert grammatical description into practical operation; but grammar is commonly presented as the main form of instruction to younger, inexperienced and unsophisticated learners, for whom this is not the most effective approach. In other words the grammar taught is often poor grammar; it is used for a purpose which it is inherently unable to fulfil and presented to pupils before they are able to benefit from it.

The role of translation in language teaching is of course a separate matter; its use is neither presupposed by, nor does it presuppose, the teaching of grammar. In the conventional pattern of foreign language teaching, however, translation alternates with formal grammar as the main activity in class and homework: hence the linking of the two in the term 'grammar-translation method'. In the extreme form of this approach, from the very beginning the learners are presented with sentences in their mother tongue and required to translate them into whichever L2 they are learning: that is, to replace them by sentences in the second language. This is sometimes

9*

defended on the grounds that, in the very earliest stages, the English sentences act as stimuli for the recall to memory of the total language teaching event: that they can elicit a complete sentence in the target language by recalling the situation in which that sentence was used. But there are counter-objections to this defence. We have already expressed the opinion that so early in the process of learning a language the pupil should not be confronted with written forms at all. Whether or not this is granted, it remains true that to face him at this stage with an ungraded mixture of problems in grammar, lexis and orthography is pedagogically unsound: translation is an exercise which entails and indeed entangles all these levels. Moreover the pupil has to learn the rules of a whole new technique of question answering at the same time as he is trying to learn the language.

These objections are of course additional to the equally valid but more familiar arguments against the use of translation at this stage. The use of isolated sentences lacking any linguistic or situational context, other than the artificial situation of the translation exercise, renders the translation process meaningless as linguistic activity and leads to a concentration on formal equivalence at the expense of contextual equivalence. No attention is paid to appropriateness of register, since there is no clue to what use of language is involved by which such appropriateness can be judged. The answers are marked 'right' or 'wrong' with no indication that translation equivalence is a matter of 'more or less': that a version could be 'more probable' or 'less probable', or right in some circumstances and wrong in others. These and other such shortcomings have long been known to teachers of foreign languages.

Later in the course, translation as a teaching technique, instead of becoming easier, becomes more difficult to set and to mark, as well as more difficult to perform. There are many reasons why this is so, but two reasons dominate all others: first, the learner has to select *the* single appropriate equivalent from among all the various possibilities, whose number he finds to increase very greatly as his own experience of the language grows; secondly he has to decide what to do with a stretch of language, of whatever length, which is patently untranslatable. We give below an example of each of these kinds of difficulty:

Example (a)
Q. Translate into French: Did you sleep well?

A. Est-ce que vous avez bien dormi?
   Avez-vous bien dormi?
   Vous avez bien dormi?
   As-tu bien dormi?
   Tu as bien dormi?
   Dis donc, t'as bien dormi, toi?

                          etc. etc.

In specific situations, any one of these, as well as others not
included in this list, represents a possible and acceptable translation.
As the learner's experience of different situations, of grammatical
patterns, and of stylistic and registral variations continues to develop,
so he finds himself needing to guess which alternative the teacher
(or examiner) is looking for; the teacher, in turn, cannot give a
complete model answer to a translation question without at least
touching upon the differences between these various possibilities.
One of the present authors vividly recalls returning from his first
visit to France and, on being asked to translate *is it yours?* into
French, proudly writing *c'est à toi, ça?* Needless to say, what was
required was *est-ce que c'est le vôtre?* Having discovered this, the
schoolboy concerned joined the disillusioned ranks of thousands
before and since who have learned to distinguish between the
foreign language used in the classroom and the foreign language
used in the foreign country. The point about translation in general
is that it requires the selection of one response out of the very many
which might be possible, depending on factors of context which the
learner does not know.

Example (b)
Q. Translate into English: Mon joli philosophe, vous me
   serez à jamais un témoignage précieux de l'amitié d'un
   artiste, excellent artiste, plus excellent homme;
                          (DIDEROT, Correspondance.)
A. My pretty philosopher, . . .

We do not suggest that no translation could be made of this passage
(which occurs in at least one school exercise book of 'passages for
translation'), but simply that the first nominal group *mon joli
philosophe* is *to the schoolboy learner* untranslatable. The task of
translation here requires a degree of literary and historical sensi-
bility, to say nothing of stylistic feelings for English, that few schoolchildren possess.

Translation is, in fact, an extremely complicated and difficult task. It is far from being the simple, obvious exercise it is sometimes described to be. In its usual form it is appropriate more to the advanced stages of a university special degree course, when literary and historical styles are being studied, than to the early stages of acquiring practical skills in a foreign language.

6

The grammar-translation method is being replaced by other teaching procedures, all of which concentrate more on practical performance, especially in the spoken language in the early stages, and many of which use electro-mechanical aids. These aids range from the gramophone and tape recorder at one end of the scale of complexity and cost to language laboratories, audio-visual techniques and teaching machines at the other. It is not widely realized that in the exploitation of teaching aids foreign language teaching in Britain has lagged behind that in the United States, France and the Soviet Union. This is partly due to lack of money, which has prevented even those who wished to be adventurous from buying these expensive pieces of equipment and trying them out; but it was also due, in the past, to a reluctance on the part of some people in the language-teaching profession to experiment with new methods. The 1960s have brought a fresh and more adventurous outlook which is reflected in the sudden and widespread acceptance of new aids and techniques.

Language laboratory and audio-visual techniques can make the teaching of languages more successful, more rapid and more interesting than it is without them; moreover they carry no threat to the teacher. It is not true that the language laboratory can or should take the place of the teacher; nor is it a means whereby pupil or teacher can achieve their aims without physical and mental effort. But it can make the teacher's work more effective and rewarding, especially in those areas of routine drills and practice where the task is most mechanical and makes the least demand on his qualifications and skill. At the same time the teacher does need some special training if he is to make the most efficient use of audio-visual language courses.

These new techniques of presentation are a challenge to the

teacher, and there is no doubt that for some time their introduction will tax the individual classroom teacher to the utmost. Unlike the preparation of conventional textbooks, which is in the hands of a small number of writers, some of them no longer practising class-room teachers, the preparation of materials for use in language laboratories is not yet the responsibility of anyone in particular and there is no recognized source from which authors may be drawn.

The necessity falls on the teacher operating each language laboratory to construct his own materials. No doubt this is wasteful of effort, and no doubt it often means that teachers have more responsibility of authorship thrust upon them than they realized when they pressed for the installation of language teaching equip-ment. In the long run this may be beneficial to the teaching pro-fession: a greater diversity of materials will emerge than might otherwise have been expected, and a large number of teachers will have extended and tested their abilities in a field where they have had no previous training or introduction to the equipment. But the writing of such courses is a specialized and lengthy task, not one to be thrust upon a full-time teacher in his spare moments. Even com-petence in the *use* of audio-visual techniques takes time to acquire; ideally it should be included in the training of every teacher of foreign languages as part of his professional course, but when this is not possible special provision should be made to enable those already in service to acquire it.

7

There remains the perennial problem of the way in which teaching is influenced, generally for the worse, by the examination syllabus. If the teaching of English as a foreign language is affected by inappropriate examinations, foreign language teaching in Britain suffers much more so because it is part of a system in which French, German, Russian and other foreign languages are generally thought of as 'examination subjects' rather than as necessary components in the education of citizens. All the main disadvantages referred to above—concentration on grammar and on translation, confusion of purpose between practical language ability and literary or general cultural aims, neglect of the spoken language—are enshrined in the make-up of the G.C.E. examinations, and since schools value the reputation gained from a record of examination successes it is almost always in the direction of passing these examinations that the teaching is oriented.

It is sad and disturbing that any forward-looking language teacher should be prevented from introducing better methods by the fear that his pupils might as a result be jeopardized in the hunt for 'O' Level examination successes. Every effort needs to be made to devise improved examinations, and the Modern Language Association is to be congratulated on making a start in this matter. Meanwhile it is noteworthy that some at least of the present experiments in language teaching in primary schools have stemmed from the conflict between the desire to experiment on the one hand and the fear of disturbing the examination candidate on the other. For years the argument has been used that, however good certain new lines might appear to be, it was not fair to try these out on schoolchildren who, if the experiments failed (or even if they succeeded), might have less of a chance in the 'O' Level scramble. Down in the primary schools the child is safe for a year or two: he can always be retaught later and given a dose of examination cramming. This is a pathetic state of affairs, which needs urgent attention so that examinations may be introduced that bear a closer relation to modern views on the nature and aims of foreign language teaching.

Just as the introduction of new methods and aims in teaching is dependent on changes in the examination system, so also any change in the examination system can come about only in the context of the wider dissemination of new ideas, both those that are the result of modern research into the nature and operation of language and those that stem from new developments in pedagogical theory and practice. Such new ideas are still far from being fully incorporated within the training given to language teachers; indeed professional and vocational *training* for the teaching of languages in Britain has not kept pace with developments within the profession itself. In the case of English as a foreign language, much of the time-lag has been made up in the past three or four years, so that training facilities are now available which take account of the latest developments in teaching aids and techniques. But in the teaching of foreign languages in Britain the pace is being set more by the inspectorate and by a small but growing number of forward-looking teachers and training college staff, rather than by the professional teacher-training bodies as such, although this situation may well change in the coming years and there are already honourable exceptions to the general rule. This point is an important one. The rate at which new ideas spread within the teaching profession is affected very closely by the extent to which the new recruits to the profession are familiar with these ideas and regard them as normal. It cannot be said that a happy position yet exists in foreign language teaching in Britain, although with the growth in recent years of university facilities in phonetics, linguistics and applied linguistics the outlook is hopeful.

The teaching of foreign languages in Britain is going through a period of change. It may be some time before the change is complete: before the practising teacher, and behind him the teacher-training institution which represents traditional professional expertise in education and methodology, come to terms with the new techniques and equipment; before they both accept the help which they can get from linguistics but which linguistics cannot force upon them; and before the profession hammers out and reorganizes the whole structure of its aims, courses, methods and materials, examinations and teacher-training facilities.

BIBLIOGRAPHY

See items 4, 6, 11, 21, 28, 38, 39, 58, 91.

Chapter 10

English at home and abroad

1

In this final chapter we bring together a number of features specifically relevant to the teaching of English. Some of those are shared in
common by the two kinds of English teaching, the teaching of
English as a native language and as a second or foreign language;
others apply only to one or other of the two. A suitable point of
departure may be found in those cases where English is taught to
pupils for whom it is a foreign language by the same means and
along the same lines as it is taught in Britain to native speakers of
the language. There are two issues in this matter: first, whether the
aims and methods of teaching English in Britain are suitable and
relevant in countries overseas; and second, whether and to what
extent these aims and methods are appropriate in Britain itself.

There are teaching situations abroad where it can be argued that
it is right and appropriate for British practice in teaching English
to be transferred without modification. One may think in particular
of some of the 'English medium' boarding schools established during
the past fifty years in many countries in the world and designed to
be faithful copies of a typical British public boarding school. If one
accepts the school framework (and this is a separate argument in
itself) then British English-teaching methods may perhaps be justifiable. But even if this is accepted in these cases—and one may
doubt the wisdom of teaching English solely along British lines even
here—such institutions are, relatively speaking, extremely rare. The
vast majority of those who learn English as a second or foreign
language do so for purposes that are very different from the purposes of an English schoolboy; they come to the subject with a
linguistic, cultural and social background that makes their task very

different from that of their British counterparts; and they are taught by teachers whose preparation and approach to the subject are different in important ways from those of the British teacher of English. Under these circumstances, how can the aims, syllabuses and textbooks of the English class in British schools be relevant or appropriate to the overseas learner? The answer is that they cannot and are not. The sooner those teachers overseas who are expected to follow normal British practice persuade their authorities to analyse the nature of the English teaching problem, the sooner will improvements in English teaching become possible.

The question of the suitability of the aims and methods of teaching English in Britain is much less clearcut. There are many devoted and brilliant teachers of English who lift their subject to the high level it should always occupy and provide vital, exciting instruction that illuminates language and literature for their pupils in a deep and lasting way. Such teachers command the greatest admiration. But few people are unaware of the fact that English is also sometimes taught as a dull, purposeless grind relevant to no kind of life that the pupils will ever lead. There is more to this than the statistical observation that there will always be a proportion of teachers whose misfortune it is to make their subject dull and boring; the quantity of lifeless teaching in English seems to be greater than would be expected from the more random distribution of less inspiring teachers among subjects as a whole. The chief reasons, in our view, are those implied in the diagnosis given above (Chapter 8): the aims of English teaching are often weak and undefined, the content is restricted and irrelevant, and the syllabus and teaching materials are unimaginative and ill chosen.

A large part of the blame for this state of affairs lies with the syllabuses for public examination in English language and literature in the schools. But there is another possible reason for matters being as they are. What machinery exists, it must be asked, for injecting new methods and ideas? Teachers teach as they do, and use the material they use, at least partly because of the professional training they have received, and in 'professional training' is included their degree course as well as any postgraduate teacher-training qualification they may acquire. This total period of training is now firmly established along a small number of different lines and it allows very little scope for change. The conventional lines of an honours degree in English almost always include the study of literature and

literary criticism, although still often excluding the literature of
present-day writers; and the study of historical philology is the only
main alternative or accompaniment. There is no need to cast doubts
on the value of such courses. The study of literature written in
English, and of the historical development of the language which is
the vehicle of this literature, are time-honoured fields of intellectual
activity whose position and importance are not being called into
question. In their academic forms, however, they are not very
closely related to the teaching of English language *in schools*; and
yet they form, in the undergraduate degree course, the major portion of a teacher's professional training. It is common for students
of English to be told that 'of course' what they learn at the university will not be suitable for direct application to the task of teaching
their subject; in consequence many of them arrive in the classroom
well educated in terms of academic standards, well trained in terms
of educational theory, but largely unprepared for teaching English
in ways or for purposes that are relevant to the average schoolchild.

A partial solution to this problem is fairly easy to suggest and has
already been inaugurated in a small number of universities. The
simple addition to existing degree syllabuses of a section concerned
with the study and description of present-day English would provide students with an understanding of English which they should
receive in any case as part of a degree in English, and which for
those who become teachers would be of direct practical relevance
to their profession. This trend has been visible in growing measure
since 1960; probably not many years will elapse before the study of
the present-day language has a place in every English syllabus in
British universities. When that comes about, and quite apart from
any additional changes or improvements in degree or teacher-
training syllabuses, we can expect in consequence an upsurge of
enthusiasm and an increase of effectiveness in the teaching of English
in Britain.

In making the distinction between the teaching of English in
Britain and the teaching of English overseas, we have already
deplored the uncritical transfer to the overseas situation of English
teaching as it is carried out in Britain. Curiously, however, the link
in the opposite direction is suddenly proving to be useful. Many
teachers of English in Britain, searching for ways of enlivening and
enriching the subject for their pupils, have come across titles in
publishers' booklists that seem to offer the kind of help they need,

have bought copies of the books and have been surprised to discover both that they are in fact useful and at the same time that they
were written for foreign learners. In the years since 1959 there has
been a sudden and unexpected rise in the sale to teachers of English
in British schools of textbooks designed for use abroad. Some of
these books are of a kind that we have criticized, in detail or in
principle, but the point remains valid: the experience from the
teaching of English to foreign learners is feeding back, through
specialized teaching courses and descriptions of English, to the
teaching profession in Britain.

The teaching of English as a foreign language, as has been shown,
can be and is being improved and made more effective through the
intelligent application of linguistics and of theoretical principles of
foreign language teaching. Nor of course is the teaching of English
to foreign learners the only L2 teaching operation being carried on
in Britain, or based on Britain while carried on at a distance; the
many teachers of French, German, Russian, Italian, Spanish,
Chinese and other modern languages are all occupied in a task that
in theory at least is closely parallel to the teaching of English as
a foreign language. Moreover the relevance of linguistics to large
areas of their total field, already fully accepted in the United States,
is suddenly becoming widely realized in Britain also. The methods
and approaches described in some sections of this book form the
basis of new attitudes towards modern language teaching in Britain,
just as they underlie the teaching of English as a foreign language;
and it is the linguistic sciences that form the theoretical basis for
the new methods and procedures.

The 1960s have thus already seen the formation of a new nexus
of interests created from familiar components of the British educational scene. The teaching of English in Britain now finds itself
linked with the teaching of English as a foreign language, and both
of them find affinities with the teaching of foreign languages in
Britain. All three can be helped, though in different ways, by the
intelligent application of modern linguistic theory and techniques.

2

Language teaching, viewed in this light, contains three major
interacting components: first, a linguistic component; second, a

pedagogical component; and third, an organizational component. The first two supply the attitudes, the facts, the theories, the techniques and the methods, by which teachers guide their professional activities. The third supplies the 'glue' which binds together the first two, as well as fitting the language-teaching activity of a country into the appropriate slots in policy, administration, and society as a whole.

In the linguistic component, 'linguistic' means both 'of language' and 'of linguistics'. The teacher must obviously have a command of the language under instruction such that his pupils can use him as a suitable model to be emulated and copied in their own efforts. But 'the teacher' includes the specialists behind and beyond the classroom, those who write textbooks, prepare audio-visual courses, write radio and television scripts, and generally support the class teacher from a distance; they, too, provide a knowledge of and a guide to performance in the language concerned.

But this component presupposes in addition a framework of linguistic categories, a comprehensive description of the appropriate variety of the language, and an awareness of the nature of language and of its function in society. People can certainly learn languages without benefit of systematic instruction. But when systematic instruction *is* involved the value and effectiveness of such instruction will be determined in large measure by these two aspects—the practical and what one might call the immanent—of the linguistic component.

The pedagogical component of language teaching is as indispensable as the linguistic one; being a language teacher means *being a teacher*, just as it means being a performer in a language and knowing something about language in general. Indeed 'education' in its vocational teacher-training guise is a branch of activity which is well suited to take from linguistics its specialized skills and knowledge and to incorporate them into sound teacher-training methods. There should be much greater interpenetration than occurs at present between the linguistic sciences and those who train teachers. The training of a teacher lies partly in his study of pedagogical theory and of the psychology and sociology of education; and partly in gaining practice in a range of classroom techniques and familiarity with aural, visual and other teaching aids. But all these must be illuminated by an understanding of the precise points at which each is relevant; the language teacher must know what are the different areas of language skills where each can be most effective, and the limitations and potentialities of each kind of teaching aid. All this is neither linguistics alone nor educational theory alone, but the product of welding the two closely together.

This welding process is brought about by the third component of language teaching, organization. The most immediate and obvious function is in 'methodics', that area where linguistics and educational method meet in the preparation of syllabuses, courses, textbooks and other teaching materials. Teaching method provides for the task to be broken down into a basic inventory of items to be taught, and for the most effective techniques of presentation to be employed at each point. Linguistics provides a set of attitudes towards language and an understanding of how it works, an array of categories for talking about and describing languages, and a suitable description of the particular language to be taught. Methodics supplies a framework of organization within which these two prior components may be matched to each other and blended into the acceptable, economical and effective tool for language teaching that we know can result from these procedures.

There are two other organizational functions that need to be carried out. The first concerns the language-teaching profession of any given country. The process of ensuring that teachers receive in their training the maximum professional knowledge and expertise is obviously a matter of organization, but it is one where the extent to which the organization is centrally created varies greatly from one country to another. In a country such as Britain, where centralized authority exercises little direct control over teacher-training courses, it should become somebody's responsibility (which at present it is not) at least to make available to members of the profession information about modern developments and the results of research in language teaching and linguistics, as well as to encourage the profession to incorporate these as quickly as possible into teacher-training courses.

The second function parallels this on the international plane. Countries whose language-teaching technology, so to speak, has reached a high stage of development should organize in such a way as to meet the most pressing needs of those in a less advanced state. France is an example of a country which spends great sums of money on the organization of specialized technical assistance to countries wanting help with the teaching of French. The United

States does the same for English, by sending abroad teachers and teaching materials, by training teachers from overseas in America, and by supporting overseas training centres.

Britain cannot yet match the scale of financial assistance given by France and the United States for language teaching, even though it is from Britain that the greatest number of individual language teachers has gone as part of a long-standing tradition of educational service overseas. But the British Council, for all its comparatively tiny budget, has been a most effective centre of organization for language teaching. British universities, too, are beginning to increase the scale of their contacts with language-teaching problems overseas. Two new and hopeful trends can be seen: one is the increase in links between universities in Britain, America, France, Australia and New Zealand for the purpose of collaborating in meeting the demands from other countries for language-teaching assistance; the second is the growth of sponsorship by universities in these 'base' countries of language-teaching centres and teacher-training programmes in other countries that have extensive problems of this kind.

Linguistics, education, organization: these three pillars of language teaching are as important and as relevant for teaching one language as another, though perhaps they are more firmly established for English than for almost any other language.

3

We have outlined above (Chapter 8) what seems to us to be, from the standpoint of the linguistic sciences, a possible view of the aims and content of native language teaching. What was said there applies to the teaching of any language within the community that speaks and writes that language, including the teaching of English in Britain. Although for obvious reasons the illustrations were drawn from English, it may be useful to bear in mind that the teaching of English in Britain is merely one instance of native language teaching, which includes in addition not only the teaching of English in Australia, the United States and other English-speaking countries but also the teaching of French in France, Russian in the Russian-speaking areas of the U.S.S.R. and so on.

Nevertheless although there are likely to be features in common to the methods and problems of native language teaching any-where in the world, at the same time each community is likely to have its own special problems arising out of its own history and the history of its use of its own language. The different types of script used with different languages provide a clear instance of the varia-bility of problems of native language teaching: the task of teaching Japanese children to read and write Japanese is very different from that of teaching Russian children to read and write Russian, and the methods most appropriate in the two instances will be at least partially different.

In discussing the teaching of English in Britain therefore it is important to ask not only the general question 'what are the problems of teaching a native language?', but also the specific question 'what are the special problems of the teaching of English in Britain?' It is not within our scope here to attempt anything like the general survey required to yield an answer to this second question. A great deal has been written on this subject, some of it very good indeed; and while we feel that there is still a need for a systematic and up-to-date review of the problem, based on current findings not only of linguistics and phonetics but also of other relevant disciplines, we would emphasize that the writing of such a review would be a highly specialized task calling for collaboration among a number of different experts. We would strongly recommend that a scholarly study should be made of 'problems of the teaching of English in Britain'; with the proviso that, while we would not for a moment suggest that this should be carried out exclusively by linguists and phoneticians, it is unlikely to be very effective unless linguists and phoneticians are among those taking part.

Meanwhile in this final chapter we should like to bring together one or two points concerning English teaching in Britain which seem to us to emerge when one as it were thinks linguistically about the problem. From the very start we face the difficulty that not nearly enough is yet known about the early stages of native-language learning. We must know in what order children of English-speaking parents in an English environment tend to learn the patterns of their native language, at the various levels, and what is the range of variation in the order in which they learn them.

Unfortunately some of what has been written about the language development in young children is much less useful than it might have been. In some instances the investigators knew little about language and how it works; consequently they were looking for and recording the wrong things, or stating the facts in a way which made them incapable of being interpreted. Moreover the sort of material needed is very difficult to collect, because many of the situations in which children use language are almost impossible to cover with a tape recorder: even though the language activity may be recorded it is all too often drowned by the various non-linguistic noises.

However, recording techniques are improving, and we do now know what to look for. We can make reasonable predictions about the ways in which patterns of English are acquired and the likely order of progress: at least we know what information we should try to collect and what questions we should try to answer. Much of this information could be supplied by studies of the language activity of large numbers of children of different ages, starting it might be with children of about twelve years old and working backwards; coupled with studies of the language development of a small number of children followed right through almost from birth. Quite apart from its language-teaching applications, such material is badly needed in medical research: the diagnosis and treatment of speech disorders of all kinds in children depends on an understanding of the language activity of the normal child. Pediatricians and linguists are now working together in research projects to study the attainment in grammar, lexis, phonology and phonetics of children of different ages; but the scale of these studies is still far too small.

The result is that, although when he starts primary school the English child has learnt much more of his native language than often seems to be assumed, there is so far no measure of his probable linguistic attainment. The range of variation in this attainment that can be regarded as 'normal' in young children is as great as it is in any other aspect of their development; primary school teachers learn from their experience to predict what the child of five is likely to be able to do with his language, his ability both in speaking and in listening. But observations made by one individual, however wide his experience, cannot replace an assessment based on descriptive studies of the English language as used by people of all ages and incorporating the actual sequence in which different features are normally learnt.

When, in the absence of such studies, it is desired to measure the attainment of English children in their native language, undue reliance tends to be placed on the one readily applicable yardstick:

the concept of literacy. This, however, is not at all an easy concept. In the first place literacy, however widely or narrowly defined, relates to the child's *ability in the written language only*, and has nothing to do with his ability to operate the spoken language. The latter is often either ignored altogether or, alternatively, assumed to correlate with ability in the written language—which it certainly does not.

In the second place, again whatever factors are subsumed under it, literacy is a matter of degree: we should talk about 'more' and 'less' literate, not 'literate' and 'illiterate' as a simple polarity. But the question arises of what is being measured. The Chinese in their native-language teaching measure degrees of literacy by reference to the number of 'characters' (the symbols of the Chinese script) in *active* use: that is, the number that the child can write correctly at the same time as identifying correctly the formal item represented by each. This criterion is of no use to us, since the symbols of our scripts represent phonological and not formal items; we do not ask how many letters of the alphabet the child knows, except in the sense that we cannot start measuring literacy until he can produce them all, and identify them correctly according to how he has been learning: by name, by phonic label or embedded in the representation of formal items. One could, at least with some of the methods that are used for teaching reading and writing, take advantage of the partly Chinese nature of the English script—its tendency to distinguish between formal items that are pronounced alike—and count the different (orthographic) words that the child can write. But there seems little point in this: after all the English script is still *mainly* phonological, so that once the child has grasped its phonemic principle he can make intelligent guesses at writing words he has never seen before with a fair probability of being right.

In the third place, we feel that somehow comprehension should enter into criteria of literacy, and this is a further complication when it comes to measurement. We are not simply looking for the ability to make the correct match, actively and passively, between graphological and phonological item. In other words, it is not enough (a) that the child should be able to form the letters *h o u s* and *e*; nor even (b) that he should be able to connect this sequence in both directions (both in reading and in writing) with the phonological item /ha^{u}s/. He must also be able to identify both *house* and /ha^{u}s/ as the lexical item 'house'. The concept of 'spelling' indeed depends

on this identification: one cannot ask in English how to spell a
phonological item, since only a formal item can be 'spelt'. Not, for
example, 'how do you spell /reɪn/?': the answer could be *rain, rein*
or *reign*; but 'how do you spell "reign" as in "the reign of Queen
Victoria"?'

With single formal items there is no real comprehension problem:
or rather, the problem is solved by the child once and for all when
he grasps the essential nature of English writing, though he gets
there by different routes according to the method by which he has
been taught. Once this has been grasped, *house* is identified both as
/haᵘs/ and as 'house' at the same time. But the comprehension
requirement may be carried higher, to the understanding of written
sentences and longer passages. To extend the example, the child
must know when to read *house* as /haᵘs/ and when as /haᵘz/. It is at
this point that criteria of rather a different nature tend to creep in.
The literacy test tends to become a measure of general language
ability; the child is asked comprehension questions on passages of
English prose, and his ability to answer them depends not on his
control of the script but on his total linguistic resources.

It is useful to make a distinction here between 'literacy' and
'articulacy'. The recognition of this distinction not only facilitates
the measurement of linguistic attainment but may also make it
easier for the child to learn about his native language and extend
his control over its use. Articulacy is the measure of a person's total
control of his native language. Since his resources in the written
language will in practice never outstrip his resources in the spoken
language, for purposes of assessment this can be equated with his
control of the spoken language; but articulacy is the ability to use
the *language*, not the medium, and is therefore as relevant to the
visual as to the auditory skills. Sometimes in fact it is more easily
observed through the medium of the written language. Literacy can
then be restricted to the sense of 'control of the written medium',
the control of the medium itself being something that it is necessary
to be able to observe and refer to quite separately. If articulacy and
literacy are kept apart the search for valid criteria of standards of
attainment becomes more profitable.

There are two aspects to articulacy: the 'formal' or purely linguistic, and the institutional, corresponding roughly to the division
into descriptive and institutional linguistics. The use of language
is most easily observed through the active skills, speaking and

writing. Moreover, although the converse is not true, we can assume
that if a person uses a certain pattern meaningfully in speech he
can understand that pattern when spoken. We can define articulacy therefore by reference to the active skills. Formal articulacy
is control of the formal features of the language; the ability to
operate its grammatical and lexical patterns and items in their
contextual meanings. Institutional articulacy is control over the
uses of language: the ability to use the formal patterns and items
in the appropriate registers and restricted languages. The two can be
separately assessed. If a girl writes an account of how she made a
dress for herself in imitation of one she had seen in a shop window
and liked, her account will display a range of formal features
selected from those at her command and organized in a particular
register. The formal patterns themselves give an indication of her
total resources; the appropriateness and consistency of their use in
this register give an indication of her ability to match her language
activity effectively to the type of situation.

A high degree of 'formal' articulacy is, as we have pointed out,
achieved early in life: even in Britain, where children start school
relatively young, they have mastered much of the grammar and a
large part of the general vocabulary of their native language before
they get there. Even after they have started school it is largely
outside the class that they extend their control over the language:
at least outside the English class. This does not mean, however, that
the English class has no part to play in the development of their
articulacy. Too often in the past English teaching, while developing
literacy, has neglected and even stifled articulacy by excessive
proscription. One contribution of the English class therefore is that
of developing articulacy by the use of productive language teaching.
Besides this, it is only in the English class that articulacy can be
observed and measured, and the children's progress tested and
recorded.

4

Many of the grammatical patterns of English, as well as features at
other levels, offer scope for observing children's use of the language
and measuring their attainment and progress. In place of the old
prescriptive exercises, of the 'correct what is wrong with the

following sentences' type, the teacher of English can elicit from his pupils, by a variety of methods and to different degrees of complexity according to their age and the aim he has in view, instances of every aspect of the resources of the English language. Moreover he can use spoken as well as written English for the purpose, an important factor with children who are at an age when the written medium may cause difficulties which are irrelevant to the exercise or test in question.

With such an approach it is possible to avoid two false notions about the nature of English, or perhaps about language in general, which prevail in the minds of many pupils after they leave school. One is that 'correct' grammar, in the prescriptive sense, is an indication of clear thinking. In fact 'correct' grammar is neither a sufficient nor a necessary condition of clear thinking; but if prescriptive rules such as the ban on 'due to' as a preposition, or that on formulations of the type 'the reason is because . . .', are defended on such grounds the pupil may be left with the impression that conformity with these rules is a prerequisite, or even worse that it is a guarantee, of clarity of thought. This misconception need never arise if the teaching is focused on the English language instead of on that tiny fraction of the language to which such rules happen to relate. The second false notion is that speech is 'less grammatical' than writing; that the spoken language is somehow less regular in its patterns, or even that it is not patterned at all. It might be thought that this fallacy would now be seldom met with; but it seems that in some schools native language teaching is still so exclusively oriented towards the written language that the pupil is led to regard speech as nothing more than an untidy procession of featureless fragments, incapable of analysis. Naturally, conversation looks quaint when transcribed into the written medium, just as written language sounds odd if introduced into conversation; but only the most superficial observer would be misled, by the frequency in speech of the various signals, such as 'well' and 'I mean', that keep open the channel of communication, into doubting the grammatical and lexical orderliness of the spoken language.

Many excellent productive exercises in spoken as well as in written English are in regular use by teachers of English up and down the country; but they are more often devised by the teachers themselves than supplied in the school textbooks, which still tend to concentrate mainly on literary composition and linguistic proscription. As always, however, the basic material required is a good description of the language. It is impossible to give in a short space examples that are fully self-explanatory, precisely because this can only be done in the framework of the total description of English grammar; but the following may perhaps be adequate for the purpose of illustrating the present point.

TRANSITIVITY

UNIT: *clause*
SYSTEM: *transitivity*

	TERMS	SYMBOL	EXAMPLES
(a)	Intransitive	P	he called; he left
	Transitive:		
	Single:	PC	
(b)	Extensive	PC^E	he called her; he left a note
(c)	Intensive	PC^I	he sounded a foreigner; he felt a fool.
	Double:	PCC	
(d)	Extensive	PCC^E	he called her a taxi; he left her a fortune
(e)	Intensive	PCC^I	he called her a beauty; he left her an orphan

(P stands for 'predicator', C for 'complement'. An *intransitive* clause has no complement, a *single transitive* clause one and a *double transitive* two. Intensive clauses are those having a complement but allowing no choice between active and passive in the verbal group (or only one such choice if there are two complements); intensive complements have the same referent as the preceding nominal group.)

Basic operations on this material include the following:

(1) Supply an item (finite verbal group) which can occur at P in clauses of more than one class.

e.g. (a) and (b)   Verbal group with verb 'know'
     (a) and (e)   ,,   ,,   ,,   ,, 'think'
     (a), (b) and (d) ,,   ,,   ,,   ,, 'tell'

(2) Construct classes of more than one transitivity class using the same item at P.

e.g.   'gave'   (a) the roof gave;   (b) he gave a talk;
                (d) he gave me lunch.

(3) Explain and construct ambiguities arising out of this system.

e.g.   call him a porter
       they made them free gifts

Which of such items are in fact normally ambiguous in spoken
English (e.g. 'call him a porter' would probably be Tone 1 if
extensive, Tone 2 if intensive)? Construct linguistic contexts to
'resolve' the ambiguity.

TONICITY

> UNIT (phonological): *tone group*
> UNIT (grammatical): variable; here exemplified by *clause*
> SYSTEM: *tonicity*

TERMS	EXAMPLES

(a) Neutral (tonic on final lexical item)	//ˬ I've / been / **think**ing //
	 //ˬ I / posted them / **yes**terday /
	 //ˬ I / haven't / **met** them /
	 //ˬ I / wasn't ex/**pect**ing it / though //

(b) Marked (tonic anywhere else)	// **Mary** / showed them how to / do it //
	 //ˬ they're / **al**ways / asking / questions //
	 //ˬ I / didn't / see / **him** //

Operations include:

(1) Identify the *neutral* tonic in a given clause, and find out how
many different clauses could be produced by keeping the same
formal items in the same sequence and changing to marked
tonicity (i.e. by placing the tonic elsewhere than in the most usual
place) (a) without changing the rhythm and (b) allowing changes of
rhythm.

e.g.   // Peter / told me the / whole / **story** //
       (a) without change of rhythm: marked tonic could fall on
           Peter, **told, whole**
       (b) with change of rhythm: marked tonic could fall on
           me (// Peter / told / **me** the / whole / story //)
Suggest contexts for all possibilities.

(2) Construct different questions that can be answered by clauses having the same formal items in the same sequence and varying the tonicity.

e.g. (a) //ₐ there's a / cat in the / **gar**den // (where can I find a cat?)
//ₐ there's a / **cat** in the / garden // (what are you looking out of the window at?)

(b) // John / lives / **here** //　　　(where does John live?)
// John / **lives** / here //　　　(what's John doing here?)
// **John** / lives / here //　　　(who lives here?)

(3) Resolve ambiguities by changing tonicity.

e.g. // take that / chair out/**side** // (the chair may be inside, clause structure PCA (A stands for 'adjunct'); or outside, structure PC)

// take that / **chair** out/side // (the chair is almost certainly inside, structure PCA; it is seldom that the tonic falls on the head of a nominal group when this is followed by a qualifier)

All examples here are suitable for Tone 1, but the system of tonicity can of course be demonstrated on any tone.

It is not suggested that the 'operations' are ready-made exercises and tests: they are offered as the raw material out of which exercises and tests are built. The principle is a familiar one; productive exercises are commonly used in the teaching of some patterns such as those of sentence structure. The pupil is given a string of unconnected 'free' clauses that could cohere into a passage of narrative or description, and asked to link them together; then restrictions are added: he must not use the same item twice; he must not use 'and', 'but' or 'or'; he may make controlled changes, such as finite to nonfinite in the verbal group; and so on. But the number of patterns treated in this way tends to be very limited; main attention is often concentrated on marginal features, and the operations based on a rather unreal or at best unintegrated picture of English grammar. Instead, productive tests and exercises could embrace the whole of the language, spoken and written, in one way or another; they could be based on a powerful description and focused on patterns that are central to all or to any particular use of the language. And those who do not wish to use technical terms would find it possible to operate entirely without them.

In its institutional aspect articulacy can be assessed by reference to the range of registers in which the child can operate. Instances

The great misconception — *F. CS Lewis*

have already been cited above. Can he, for example, give clear spoken instructions to a friend on how to mend a bicycle tyre? Can he write to the headmaster asking for a day off because his father is going overseas for six months? Can he persuade a reluctant customer to buy a second-hand car? Can he write an election address to the voters of his ward? In addition to such questions, the pupil can be asked to shift from one register to another on the same topic: to change the style of discourse keeping the field of discourse constant, as in the different accounts of a swimming match referred to earlier.

In developing and in measuring the ability of English children to put their native language to effective use, we have stressed the importance of the spoken medium. It may be that it is unrealistic to hope that much more use could be made of this medium in the English language class than is generally attempted. Certainly the range of registers available in written English is quite wide enough to allow useful assessments of the pupil's overall articulacy. But it is important to remember that the written medium gives an incomplete picture of a person's language ability. One of the greatest changes that has taken place in the use of English in the twentieth century has been the advance of the spoken medium; a number of new modes of discourse have developed, in which this medium has taken over functions previously confined to writing. It would be a pity if in the struggle to teach the mastery of the written medium we neglected to develop our children's skills in the use of their language as a whole.

5

If, then, articulacy is defined as competence in the whole range of uses of English that are needed by a citizen of our language community—and a citizen is by definition an educated citizen—'literacy' can be restricted to mean the ability to handle the written medium as such. Literacy is probably best measured in relation to articulacy in the spoken medium. That is to say, it is not very helpful to discover that a child cannot perform a certain operation in writing if he cannot perform the corresponding operation in speech: we are no wiser with regard to the extent of his literacy. Instead of asking: 'Can he read this passage, never mind whether or not he could understand it read aloud?', we should ask: 'I know

he could understand this passage read aloud; can he read it?'
Literacy is then being regarded as the ratio of written to spoken
language control, and 'full' literacy as the ability to perform with
the written language all the operations that one performs with the
spoken language, *mutatis mutandis*.

Of course 'mutatis mutandis' here covers a great deal, since, as
we have noted, the two media are used for different sets of purposes,
with no exact correspondence between them; and different formal
features are often associated with each. Nevertheless it is meaningful
to ask whether a pupil who, for example, does not fully understand
a news item in print would have understood the same news item if
it had been read aloud. If not, it is not his literacy that is deficient
but his articulacy. If he does understand the passage when listening
to it, his performance in reading was a fair measure of his literacy
(Once he had heard the passage, of course, he could probably read
it; but for test purposes the reading could be done first; or a
different passage of comparable difficulty chosen.)

The complexity of the English script (in the technical sense of
the graphological system) means that literacy is not only more
difficult to achieve; it is also more difficult to measure, since it is
often impossible to say whether the failure to understand a passage
of written English is due to lack of control of the language or lack
of control of the medium. Estimates of 'illiteracy' among adults and
teenagers generally fail to distinguish the two, and are thus not easy
to interpret; but then the distinction is less easy to observe in
English than, say, in Italian. The same reasons that make it more
difficult to observe, however, also make it more important that we
should observe it: the more difficult the script is to learn, the more
careful we should be to distinguish failure to master the script from
failure to operate the language.

A more serious aspect of the same problem is that failure to cope
with the script may inhibit the child in his efforts to extend his
control over the language. It has become fashionable to decry those
who warn against 'inhibiting' the development of children; and no
doubt the term, and the concept, have been overplayed and sometimes sentimentalized. But this is no reason for ignoring a very real
instance of such inhibition, which commonly occurs as a result of
over-insistence on performance in *written* English. A child is made
to feel that if he cannot use the written language he cannot use
language at all; and this makes him ashamed and inarticulate. We

10+L.S.L.T.

have referred above (Chapter 8) to the desirability, in general, of keeping the teaching of writing as a medium separate from the teaching of 'the written language'—that is, of the forms of the language that are considered appropriate to its written uses; and of not insisting in the early stages that children should reject 'colloquialisms' and compose only texts acceptable in writing. In the special case of English, where the script is more than usually difficult, we should add that in both descriptive and productive language teaching there is much to be said for devoting time specifically to the development of the pupils' spoken language skills. The use of language is then not confused with, or restricted to, the ability to read and write; and the latter problem can be singled out for special treatment.

In this connection experiments with simplified scripts in the teaching of literacy are especially to be welcomed; such as for example the current use of the Initial Teaching Alphabet at primary schools in various parts of the country. It is sometimes asserted that, as long as we continue to write English as we do now, the use of any other script, however simplified by phonological and phonetic regularization, as a bridge to literacy is merely postponing the problem and in the long run adding to the children's burden. But no evidence has yet been brought forward in support of this view, and the preliminary results of the I.T.A. trials seem encouraging. Furthermore Chinese experience in recent years suggests that the average time taken by both adults and primary school children to reach a given standard of literacy *in Chinese characters* is considerably reduced when they learn to read and write in a phonological script first—and the transition from this to the normal script is much more formidable in Chinese than in English. Anything which may lessen the difficulty of learning to read English should be put to the test; one cannot be certain in advance, but a group of consultants including a specialist in education, a psychologist, a linguist and a phonetician could assess whether or not a new method had a reasonable probability of succeeding. Most of us have forgotten the effort we put into learning to read; but this does not justify our accepting the view that 'the good ones will learn anyway, and the others never will'.

Just as in teaching children their native language, so also in measuring their native language abilities, we depend on a good description of the language, covering the formal properties of its

principal registers as well as the features at every level which are
common to all its uses. We also depend on an understanding of the
normal child's pattern of native language learning. The theories and
methods of linguistics and phonetics are available for—indeed exist
for the purpose of—carrying out such studies; their value has been
proved in the work already done on English and other languages.
We have stressed throughout that a vast quantity of research is
needed, even into the best-described languages, of which English is
one, before those who teach children to become fully articulate and
literate can be supplied with all the information they really need.
Some of this work can be done by groups of investigators without
electronic or mechanical resources; some need a phonetic laboratory, computer or other ancillary equipment. One does not need,
however, to be a laboratory linguist or full-time research worker to
contribute to these studies. Anyone who learns to recognize basic
clause structures in an English text, for example, or to record and
transcribe conversations accurately, can find out new and interesting
things about the language. But he must learn some linguistics and
phonetics first; not because linguists or phoneticians form a club
with conditions for entry, but because otherwise months and years
of hard and careful work may be utterly wasted. This has happened
in the past; and neither the individuals concerned, nor the community to which they belong, can afford such a squandering of their
efforts and abilities.

6

The procedures involved in organizing the linguistic content of a
foreign language syllabus or course have been discussed above
(Chapter 7); all that was said there applies to the teaching of English
as a foreign language. But there is another sense in which the content
of English teaching is a matter for decision, in the answers given to
such questions as these: What kind of English should be taught?
Should teachers try to get their pupils to speak English like Englishmen? Should the teacher aim at perfection on the part of his
pupils?

The answers to these and similar questions are bound up with the
political and social history of many of the countries where the
teaching of English has become of first importance. These are

questions relating to the 'model' of English that is accepted by the teaching profession generally, and behind them by public opinion, as the most appropriate kind of English for educational purposes; and they are questions to which in some countries the answer in 1964 may not be the same as it was in 1944 nor as it will be in 1984, since certain revolutionary changes are taking place, in countries where English is used, in the attitudes towards some of the main varieties of the language.

Before 1945 it was quite common for the children of wealthy families in India or Africa to be sent to Britain for their education, to attend one of the major public schools and one of the older universities, and then to return home to become a barrister, a doctor, or a senior civil servant. In addition many of those who received their basic education in the home country were able to complete their studies at a British university, returning thereafter to take up a professional post of some kind. Apart from the relatively few local people who were products of this system of education, most members of the English-teaching profession were native speakers of English, so-called 'expatriates' who had chosen to work abroad.

One consequence of this system was that virtually the only variety of English to be recognized as a model in the Commonwealth countries was Standard English grammar and lexis, spoken with RP or, sometimes, with an educated Scottish accent. American English was considered fit for the inhabitants of the Philippines and the non-British islands of the Caribbean, but elsewhere, whether in Japan, Siam or the Argentine, whether in Europe, Africa or the Middle East, in the West Indies or in Australia and New Zealand, British English was what was thought of whenever 'English' was mentioned. It is not surprising, perhaps, that during the period of colonial rule it seemed totally obvious and immutable that the form of English used by professional people in England was the only conceivable model for use in education overseas; and that to the extent that pupils fell short of this model, so far was the English language in danger of deterioration, decadence and divergence. There are many expatriate teachers and administrators who still hold these views even in circumstances where they are no longer acceptable to the local community.

In the 1960s, matters are vastly different. Where the choice used to be between American (in a few marginal cases) and British

English, now it is between American, British, Australian or other regional variants. English is no longer the possession of the British, or even of the British and the Americans, but an international language which increasingly large numbers of people adopt for at least some of their purposes, without thereby denying (at least in intention) the value of their own languages; and this one language, English, exists in an increasingly large number of different varieties. Standard English as used by the English, spoken with the accent of RP, remains the automatic and obvious choice for most Europeans and perhaps for the remaining colonies. There appears to be sufficient reason, either of geographical propinquity or of political dependence, for the situation to remain as it has for so long been in these countries. But even here we must note the increasing acceptance of American varieties of English, at any rate for adult learners. This doubtless reflects the increased stature of the United States in the post-war world; but it also reflects the very much greater and more widespread activity of English teaching that American agencies have carried on, in Europe and overseas, compared with the British effort. To say this is in no way to belittle the achievements of the valuable but still insufficient teaching programmes of the British Council.

American forms of English are now accepted, either side by side with British forms or even in preference to them, in a number of new countries where before 1945 'English' meant 'British English'. This is especially true in Japan, largely because of the military occupation of that country; it is also true in South-east Asia generally, in South America, and to a smaller but growing extent in India, Pakistan and West Africa. The Peace Corps is likely to extend this process even further, since very many of its members are being employed to teach English even though they have not been professionally trained for the work.

A new feature is the emergence of Australian English, or rather Standard English with an Australian accent, as a model for teaching English in parts of South-east Asia, especially New Guinea and parts of Indonesia. As the programmes of English teaching develop in Australia and New Zealand it is likely that we shall see an increase in their influence; indeed, it is probable that Australia and New Zealand will assume a large part of the sponsorship of English language teaching in South-east Asia and the Indian subcontinent, since Britain is unable to meet the total need and Americans have found some difficulty in gaining full acceptance for educational projects in these areas.

But the most important development of all is seen in the emergence of varieties of English that are identified with and specific to particular countries from among the former British colonies. In West Africa, in the West Indies, and in Pakistan and India (though with reservations to be mentioned below) it is no longer accepted by the majority that the English of England, with RP as its accent, are the only possible models of English to be set before the young. These countries are now independent yet retain English as an administrative and official language. Many of the new professional and political leaders, however, speak English very differently from the way Englishmen speak it. Their grammar remains that of Standard English, with few important variations; their lexis, too, differs little from the normal usage; but the accent is noticeably and identifiably local.

One need be neither surprised nor upset by such developments, which are part of a normal pattern of sociological and political evolution. They provide these countries with their own 'model' of English and permit the school generation to orient their learning towards a home-grown product rather than an imported one. It seems to be in general true that, if the people of these countries identified the English language with colonial rule and lack of independence, this was very largely through the social and educational accent-markers of the professional and governmental Englishmen they were accustomed to meeting; English without these markers, and *a fortiori* English with local markers, is quite neutral and can the more readily become a tool for communication, to be used or discarded according to practical considerations.

This is a general picture; the actual situation of course varies considerably from one area to another. A typical example is West Africa, where the process of independence is well advanced; here an 'educated West African English' is emerging to replace 'British English with RP' as a model. It is still 'English as a foreign language', and the teaching of English is still an L2 teaching operation. English is an important instrument for the task of becoming fully integrated in the modern world; the instrument is imported, but it bears superficial markings which distinguish it from the original article.

There are dangers inherent in this process, as already mentioned

(Chapter 4): one is that the status of the native language or languages may suffer; the other is that English may come to be regarded as an L1 and the teaching of it may thereby be rendered less effective. Even in an area like the West Indies, where it is commonly said that nearly everyone has some form of English as their primary language, for speakers of Jamaican Creole the learning of 'educated West Indian English' would probably be better treated as an L2 teaching problem; and the status of Jamaican Creole as a language is not even brought up for discussion, though it certainly should be. This is not to say of course that the extensive use of English in different regions of the globe should in any way be deplored; on the contrary it is an inevitable and, potentially, an entirely beneficial development, one that meets an obvious need both nationally, where there are a number of different primary languages, and internationally. Where English clearly retains the status of an L2, as in West Africa, the danger that the primary languages will come to be regarded as inferior can be avoided, even if a regional variety of English emerges as a model. It need not be suggested either that this English is a native language of the country or that it is in any way superior to the languages that are. But it is desirable that, whether or not a local variety of English is accepted as a teaching model, intelligent public attitudes towards the language should be formed, and if necessary re-formed, as part of the total educational policy, so that no linguistic snobbery is allowed to complicate the issue.

Perhaps the most difficult of all such problems is posed by the status of English in India and Pakistan. The complexity of the language situation in these countries removes it far beyond the scope of the present discussion; let it suffice here to say that it needs a geat deal more serious study and that no generally acceptable solution has yet been found. One point, however, does need to be made about 'Indian English', which hardly yet applies to the West African and West Indian varieties of the language: that the single label 'Indian English' is used to cover a very great number of different varieties of English. The label has been used to refer, at one extreme, to various semi-pidgins that are at first encounter quite unintelligible to speakers of American or British English and almost certainly also to each other; and at the other extreme, to Standard English of the most acceptable and consistent kind, accompanied by an RP accent with only a single variation, namely the use of retroflex consonants (made with the tip of the tongue curled back) for /t/, /d/, /n/, /l/. It is quite clear that not all the kinds of variant English denoted by 'Indian English' are acceptable alternative models.

It is possible to suggest two basic criteria to determine whether a variety of English is acceptable for use as an educational model. First, it must be a variety actually used by a reasonably large body of the population, in particular by a proportion of those whose level of education makes them in other respects desirable models. This means that we would exclude forms of English which have been invented or imported and bear no relation to the professional and educational standards of the country. Second, it must be mutually intelligible with other varieties of English used by similar professional and educated groups in other countries. This establishes a necessary link between, let us say, 'educated West African English', 'educated Indian English' and educated British or Australian, on the practical plane of intelligibility; and it follows from this that the extent of deviation from Standard English grammar and lexis must be small. It also follows, as far as phonology is concerned, that while the actual quality of vowels and consonants may vary a great deal between one accent and another, the number of contrasts, the number of phonological units, and the number of systems being operated must also remain fairly close to those of other 'educated accents', since otherwise speakers of one would have great difficulty in understanding speakers of another. The only kind or kinds of 'Indian English', or of any other variety of English, which we should regard as acceptable and appropriate for use as a model in teaching (that is to say as a target for the school generation) are those which meet these two basic requirements: prior use among educated people in the country, and mutual intelligibility with comparable varieties from other countries. Given these constraints, to 'speak like an Englishman' is by no means the only or obvious target for the foreign learner.

7

There remain a few considerations that do not fall appropriately in the preceding sections, yet which need to be mentioned in view of their great and growing importance. These considerations are largely in the area of the methodology of teaching as applied specifically to the teaching of English as a secondary language.

As is well known, the younger the pupil is when he starts to learn a language, the easier the task is for him; he has a greater ability to 'pick up' a language, to acquire it simply by hearing and seeing it used in a normal way. But against this the young child has much more difficulty in learning *about* a language, where the kinds of abstraction and reasoning involved cannot be handled until a later stage of maturation. These two apparently opposing factors can be made to pull in the same direction, as experiments in teaching foreign languages in English primary schools, notably in and around Leeds, have shown. Children below the age of about 10, in the care of a good primary school teacher who can *use* the language, for example in teaching arithmetic, will learn a foreign language with little difficulty and without needing to be taught *about* the language at all. Since primary school teachers have only rarely received training in how to teach a language as a school subject, which normally includes the requirement of teaching *about* a language, and since one of the greatest problems is to train enough teachers of languages even for the higher forms, it may be that one way to relieve the strain on secondary schools is to teach *practical* language ability in the lowest forms of primary schools, with teachers who simply use the language and do not 'teach' it as a 'subject'.

This applies equally to English overseas. Just as a greatly extended use of foreign languages in primary schools in Britain seems to us to be inevitable if standards of language ability are to be drastically improved, so also one of the biggest single contributions to the teaching of English as a foreign language in many countries would be to lower the starting age and let the pupils learn by experiencing the language in use. In countries abroad where the study of English *is* begun in primary school, the approach is all too often formal and 'academic', a diluted version of the same 'teaching about the language' that tends to be excused in secondary schools on the grounds that the aims of foreign language learning are educational rather than pragmatic.

Of course, no national programme of English language teaching can be carried out without the majority of teachers becoming involved in the hard daily grind of 'the English class'. This is inevitable. Yet at the same time those responsible for administering large-scale English teaching programmes should be encouraged to look into the exciting range of modern teaching aids and materials that already exist and are being added to every day. In particular, teachers should have the opportunity of using gramophones and tape recorders, of seeing (not once, but several times) suitable films, and of participating in English lessons on sound radio. The use of television for teaching English is a most promising development which teachers should welcome and support. For adult learners especially, new audio-visual techniques and the use of language laboratories offer great improvements over conventional methods. Finally in this catalogue of new methods of teaching languages two further trends are prominent: first, the emergence of 'activity' teaching, the teaching of language by teaching some other subject in it; and second, 'programmed instruction', not only in the shape of teaching machines but also in the form of carefully sequenced teaching programmes in which each item is tested as soon as it has been taught.

Such new forms of instruction and new attitudes to language teaching as are embodied in this final section dovetail easily into the total framework which, together with the outlook that lies behind it, we have tried to expound in this book. It would require a separate volume to deal adequately with them; here we must be content with a simple mention which will perhaps encourage those unfamiliar with them to pursue their own enquiries beyond the point where we have left off.

BIBLIOGRAPHY

See items 1, 2, 10, 15, 50, 58, 59, 60, 61, 74, 82, 88, 90.

Appendix

In Part I we tried to give a brief account of language from the stand-point of contemporary linguistics, stressing that against the common background of the subject there are different approaches, or 'models', representing the different aims of linguistic theory, and areas of disagreement within or between these approaches where linguists hold divergent views. It seemed desirable to present a single, integrated approach, the one which we consider to be most appropriate to language-teaching application at the same time as resting on sound theory, rather than to attempt a survey of the major current trends. Even as it is we have had to confine ourselves to the broad outlines of the subjects; to have discussed, without loss of cohesion, other approaches where these diverge from our own, unless we were merely to have skimmed the surface, would have demanded many times more space. The purpose of this brief appendix is to mention the principal alternatives to parts of the present account.

The best known and, in some ways, most important of other contemporary models is that known as 'transformation' theory, which in fact embraces the levels of grammar and phonology. This is primarily the work of Chomsky (9), of the Massachusetts Institute of Technology, who in turn owed much to Harris (25); and of Halle, Lees, Stockwell and others; it has many points of contact with the relevant parts of the theory discussed in this book. It differs in that, instead of relating language events to a defined set of categories (e.g. 'unit') and controlling the description by requiring that all statements about a language refer in specific ways to particular instances of these categories in the language concerned (e.g. 'clause' in English), it assumes only 'sentence' as a (theoretical) category, other terms like 'clause' being used as *ad hoc* descriptive labels, and controls the description by deriving all exponents from this initial 'sentence' by a set of rules of two specified kinds to be applied in a given sequence. In the grammar (our sense of grammar; in transformation theory 'grammar' is used to include both grammar and phonology), the first set of rules, known as 'constituent-structure' rules, produces structures and some formal items, those regarded as basic or 'kernel' types in the language concerned; the second set, the 'transformation' rules, produces the remainder of the formal items, deriving them by transformation from the products of the first set. *After* the grammatical rules have been applied, further rules of a basically similar type but repetitive in their operation turn the items produced by the grammatical rules into their phonological exponents.

The method is extremely powerful for handling very delicate distinctions in language. Furthermore, by taking this two-stage derivational procedure as a model of how language works, it is enabled to achieve a very simple form of statement and one which can be tested. The cost of this is that the rules must be applied in a definite order, and this imposes a unidirectionality in the description: grammar must precede phonology, and within each level each rule has a more or less fixed place, since no rule can presuppose the result of one that follows it. Transformation grammar has thus taken over, but reversed, the hierarchical relation among the levels that is characteristic of phonemic-morphemic theory (26): the progression from sound to sentence has been replaced by one from sentence to sound. This unidirectionality has drawbacks, by contrast with the (still theoretically determined but non-hierarchical) relation between grammar and phonology that we have postulated: for example, it is difficult to incorporate systems carried by intonation in their appropriate places in the grammar. Similarly the fixed sequence of rules within the grammar makes it less easy to handle contrasts where the criteria for selection cut across each other, as often happens; and to introduce variable degrees of delicacy, as is frequently desirable in a description used for language teaching purposes.

Of course the shift of direction from 'from sound to sentence' to 'from sentence to sound' is a crucial one; it enables the description to be 'generative' in the sense that it can in principle account for all events that are regarded as possible in the language and exclude all others. Those who use transformation theory rightly insist on the power of generative linguistic descriptions. Some linguists have even denied the validity of anything but generative description; but this depends on a particular philosophical stand-point, and implies a more clearcut distinction between generative and other models than we would accept. In our view the value of a theory depends on what use is to be made of it, and a model is tested by its effectiveness for specific purposes. A generative description cannot easily be used in textual work, in the study and comparison of literary or other texts. Moreover, it requires a sharp distinction to be drawn between 'grammatical' and 'ungram-matical' sentences, a distinction which we do not want to draw in this way, since not only is acceptability a matter of degree but it also depends on the use of language: what is acceptable in one register may not be so in another.

An important aspect of linguistic description is the study of the relations between sentences, extending across sentence boundaries; this is difficult to integrate into a model which takes the sentence as its point of departure. While no linguistic model can yet account adequately for all levels (we have referred above to the gaps in our understanding of context), transformation theory neglects both context and lexis, and has not yet at any rate begun to take account of registers. In phonology, transformation theory works with 'distinctive feature' analysis (see below), and this permits its integration with phonetics; but although there have been suggestions for incor-porating the lexical category of 'collocation' into transformational grammar it is not yet clear whether this can be done without con-siderable modification of the theory, and attempts at semantic analysis are far from being integrated into its framework. Finally, transformation theory does not easily lend itself to the statistical study of language events, which is important for a wide range of applications of linguistics as well as contributing to our general understanding of grammatical and lexical patterns where partial dependences or large samples are involved.

Transformation theory developed out of, and partly in reaction against, the earlier structural linguistics of the 'phonemic-mor-phemic' type. Whereas the earlier model had been *procedural*—that is, had specified the steps to be taken to arrive at the description of a language, transformation theory resembles our own approach in being *theoretical*—that is, it specifies the form the description must

take, regardless of how it is arrived at. The apparatus that transformation theory inherited from structural linguistics, that of
'phonemics', 'morphemics' and 'immediate constituent' analysis,
has thus been considerably modified; but some essential features
remain which differentiate the picture of language presented in a
transformational description from our own account, quite apart
from the difference in the form of the description imposed by the
models themselves. For example, 'constituent-structure' in transformational grammar resembles immediate constituent analysis in
having no scale of rank, so that one cannot ask questions such as
'what are the contrasts carried by the clause in English?' in order
to distinguish these from, say, the patterns carried by the group in
English, or by the clause in French. Similarly there remains, as in
conventional morphemics and phonemics, an orientation towards
the minimal segment, the morpheme in grammar and the phoneme
in phonology: these are assigned, in both models, a less 'abstract'
status than the larger units, in the sense that only via these smallest
segments does the description make contact with phonic substance.
In the account that we have presented the linguistic *items* (formal
items, in grammar and lexis; phonological items, or 'expressions',
in phonology) are defined by place in exponence, which has nothing
to do with their size or extent; a formal item which is (the exponent
of) a sentence stands in exactly the same relation to its (own
exponent in) phonic substance as does an item which is a morpheme,
and the same applies *mutatis mutandis* to tone group and phoneme.
These different views of the very complex multiple type-token
relations in language, abstract and philosophical as they may seem,
have certain consequences for applications of linguistics.

While transformation theory partly resembles the present
approach in the view taken of the nature of theories in general and
of linguistic theory as a particular case of a scientific theory, the
work of Pike (53) and his colleagues, mainly also American linguists,
is closer in other ways, such as in the overall view of the patterns of
language and the integration of the description, with the levels
related horizontally. Lexis receives less attention, but the approach
to grammar, known specifically as 'tagmemic' theory, is extremely
illuminating, as is Pike's work on language in relation to other
human activities. Whereas transformation theory has been associated with very detailed studies of English and, more recently, a
small number of other languages, tagmemics is based on a wide

range of different languages observed with very great phonetic accuracy though with less detailed study of their formal patterns. Among the recent contributions of this model has been the development of methods of dimensional analysis by the use of matrices, to handle the multiple relations into which linguistic categories and items can be shown to enter.

An interesting issue in present-day linguistics is raised by the work of Roman Jakobson (29), formerly of the famous Prague Linguistic Circle and now working at Harvard and the Massachusetts Institute of Technology. According to Jakobson, all contrasts in grammar and phonology are inherently binary: that is, all choices are between two possibilities, and wherever there appear to be more, as in a system of past/present/future or of six cases in the noun, these are in fact made up out of combinations of binary choices. We do not adopt this view; but it is important to notice that its implications in grammar are very different from its implications in phonology. In grammar it is not related to any one particular kind of duality: a fresh set of oppositions is postulated for each system, and there are no general criteria whereby one can decide, for example, both (a) that first/second/third person are to be analysed as a choice between (i) first and second versus third followed by (ii) first versus second, and (b) singular/dual/plural are to be analysed as a choice between (i) singular versus dual and plural followed by (ii) dual versus plural. In phonology on the other hand all contrasts (other than prosodic ones, which have not so far been fully incorporated) are reduced to a set of (up to now) twelve pairs of opposed phonetic features, such as voiced/voiceless and acute (palatal, dental)/grave (velar, labial). Phonemes are regarded as complexes of such features-in-opposition. This 'distinctive feature' analysis is incorporated into the phonological level of the transformational model.

This view of binarity in language has nothing to do with the fact that all finite sets of *discrete* choices (as opposed to continuous variables or 'clines'), linguistic or otherwise, can be arbitrarily reduced to successive binary choices if the need arises, as it does for example in any work in which digital computers are involved. The letters of the roman alphabet can be encoded as a set of binary numerals each containing five digits; but there is no suggestion that each time we write, say, the letter *n* we are in fact making five separate choices, first between *a-m* and *n-z*, then between *n-s* and *t-z* and so on. Some communication engineers and others working with language under conditions demanding operational binarity have been misled into assuming that the fact that language (actually only some levels of language) can be represented by a binary code is evidence for its inherent binarity; but it is not. The angles *a, b, c* of an equilateral triangle can be represented in binary code; all this tells us is that they make up a finite set.

There is, however, a more serious fallacy about language that is sometimes found or implied in the work of communication engineers, psychologists, specialists in information retrieval and others interested in the statistical properties of language events. This is the failure to recognize the multi-level nature of linguistic patterning; or, less naïvely but still erroneously, the assumption that patterns at different levels can be conflated without loss of efficiency. The argument runs something like this. Written language is a string of letters, spaces and punctuation marks; sequences of these symbols show certain statistical properties. All the patterns of language can therefore be stated in terms of the patterning of such sequences. So of course they can. But the resulting loss of generality is so prohibitive that as a model of language this is quite worthless for all purposes except the straightforward transmission of messages. Rather less weak, but still totally inadequate for anything like information retrieval, machine translation or the study of human psychology, is the model of language as a statistically determined sequence of orthographic words. To describe language using such models is like describing the game of bridge by observing the sequence in which each card is played, *and nothing else*, in a large number of games and calculating the sequential probabilities. Bridge could be described in this way; and if the progress of an important bridge tournament was being transmitted over a wide communication network this information might lead to a considerable saving in the cost of transmission. But it would not be of much help to a psychologist interested in bridge as material for the study of human behaviour; nor would it be effective as the only data on which to programme a computer to play the game.

This view of language, which ignores structural patterns and recognizes only linear sequences because the latter are easier to identify, is not of course to be rejected for the limited purposes to which it is appropriate. It is a useful way of describing one property of the written medium. But it must be recognized to be quite inadequate for many of the purposes for which it is often invoked, specifically those mentioned above. Still more must it be rejected as a model of language as a whole, which it is sometimes claimed to be. We would draw a clear distinction between the various versions of linguistic theory discussed earlier, all of which represent valid and illuminating ways of describing language, and the 'ordered string of beads' view that passes for linguistics among some people who use statistics. This is not to deny that language can be described statistically; but the statistical methods must be those severally appropriate to each level, based on an understanding of the kind of pattern by which each level is characterized and indeed defined.

It is unlikely that this last approach, which comes from outside linguistics, could exert any influence on language teaching, to which it certainly has nothing to contribute. But the various approaches to language from within linguistics could all be applied to language teaching, and some of them have been so applied. Much more has been done in the application of linguistics to language teaching in the United States than in Britain. The linguist who has played the greatest part in this movement is undoubtedly C. C. Fries, whose work on English grammar (16), whatever its shortcomings when seen from today, was original, stimulating and highly influential. Other linguists have followed Fries in taking a major interest in problems of language teaching; prominent among them are Lado (38), Sledd (69), Gleason and Paul Roberts. Gleason is well known for his textbooks of linguistics (18); in a forthcoming book entitled *Linguistics and English Grammar* he surveys the whole background of English language teaching in the United States. Roberts has experimented with various approaches, and produced textbooks and teaching material accordingly; at present he is working on the teaching of English as a foreign language through transformational methods (61). Much of this work in the United States is focused on the teaching of English either as L1 or as L2, but it is well worth the attention of all teachers of languages.

The purpose of this short appendix has been to bring some of the trends and issues in present-day linguistics, with which those interested in the subject from the point of view of language teaching may be or become familiar, into relation with each other and with the viewpoint adopted in this book. It is not intended as a survey of world linguistics or of the world's leading linguists. We have not

10**

considered here historical or institutional linguistics, or the important new field of computational linguistics; nor the recent advances
in acoustic and physiological phonetics, and in automatic speech
recognition and synthesis. We have not referred to work in which
versions of the phonemics-morphemics model continue to be
developed and refined, or to generative models other than the
transformational one. We have not discussed the place of leading
linguists in Britain and elsewhere whose contribution is not
associated specifically with any one approach, but who concentrate
rather on those regions of the subject which are common to all
approaches. Nor finally have we mentioned those linguists, mainly
in Britain, whose work we consider to represent the approach to
language studies which is most widely applicable, and from whom
our own ideas are largely derived. We devote the concluding paragraphs to the background of our own viewpoint and its relation to
their work.

We have already indicated that the account of language presented
in this book derives mainly from two traditions in British scholarship: in linguistics, that associated with the name of J. R. Firth, the
late Professor of General Linguistics at the School of Oriental and
African Studies, University of London; and in phonetics, that
associated with the name of Daniel Jones, Professor (now Emeritus)
of Phonetics at University College London. Both these men in turn
owed much to one of the founders of modern linguistic science, the
great Oxford linguist and phonetician Henry Sweet: in a sense they
thus represent two complementary aspects of the same tradition.
To Daniel Jones and J. R. Firth above all is due the present active
state of descriptive linguistic studies in this country; and most of
the leading scholars today were pupils of one or the other of the
two. We must, however, make it clear that we are not claiming the
authority of these men, or that of our present colleagues who have
carried forward their work by adding to it their own originality and
insight, for the views we have expressed. These represent our own
assessment of which aspects and versions of linguistic and phonetic
theory are most useful and relevant to language teaching (without
prejudice to whether or not we consider them most useful and
relevant to other purposes); we do not suggest that what we have
written is either a complete statement of, or a faithful account of,
the views of all or indeed of any one of our colleagues. What we have
tried to do is to present a coherent account of language that is in

line with modern research in linguistics and phonetics; where we have represented a particular approach, one in which ideas developed in Britain play a prominent part, this is not because there is any virtue in their being British but because this approach seems to us to combine, better than any other, the requirements both of theory and of application.

In so doing we have in certain places presented our own ideas knowing them to be controversial; and we have omitted important aspects of descriptive studies in language which either are too complex to be treated in the present framework or seem less central to problems of language teaching. An example of an omission is prosodic phonology: while in our discussion of phonology we have drawn attention to prosodic features and shown how some of them may be accounted for in description (for example by recognizing the units 'foot' and 'tone group' in English), we have given no indication of the total range and power of a fully prosodic analysis; nor does our phonological transcription, oriented as it is towards language teaching, exploit the theoretical possibilities of a prosodic transcription. Likewise many aspects of grammatical description have been left untouched; and numerous other omissions could be cited. Our intention has been to show the range of what is to be accounted for in the study of language, and to suggest some of the principles underlying the linguist's pursuit of his task.

Select Bibliography

Items listed in the bibliography are numbered to correspond with the references at the end of each chapter. The main bibliography includes only works which had already been published at the time when this book was completed in typescript. A short supplementary list, of works appearing in print since the beginning of 1963, is added at the end.

Only books and independent monographs are entered in the bibliography. In addition to these, a large amount of published material in the linguistic sciences and in the field of language teaching is to be found in the relevant professional journals. In certain subjects in particular, such as the learning and teaching of foreign languages, comparative linguistics and general linguistic theory, much important recent work is in the form of articles contributed to these journals. The following are some of the leading periodicals in which such material can be found.

Archivum Linguisticum (Glasgow)
Bulletin of the School of Oriental and African Studies (London)
English Language Teaching (London)
Études de Linguistique Appliquée (Besançon)
International Journal of American Linguistics (Baltimore)
International Review of Applied Linguistics (Heidelberg)
Journal of the Acoustical Society of America (Lancaster, Pennsylvania and New York)
Journal of Speech and Hearing Research (Washington, D.C.)
Language (Baltimore)
Language Learning (Ann Arbor, Michigan)
Language and Speech (Teddington, Middlesex)

Lingua (Amsterdam)
Le Maître Phonétique (London)
Modern Language Journal (Ann Arbor, Michigan)
The Modern Language Review (Cambridge)
Orbis (Louvain)
Phonetica (Basel and New York)
Publications of the Modern Language Association of America (New
   York)
Transactions of the Philological Society (Oxford)
Word (New York)

1   ABERCROMBIE, David. *Problems and Principles*, vi, 97 pp.
    London: Longmans, 1956.

2   ALLEN, Harold B. *Readings in Applied English Linguistics*, xiii,
    428 pp. New York: Appleton-Century-Crofts, 1958.

3   ALLEN, W. Sidney. *On the Linguistic Study of Languages*, 30 pp.
    Cambridge: U.P., 1957.

4   BILLOWS, F. L. *The Techniques of Language Teaching*, xi,
    259 pp. London: Longmans, 1961.

5   BLOOMFIELD, Leonard. *Language*, ix, 564 pp. New York: Holt,
    1933.

6   BROOKS, Nelson. *Language and Language Learning*, xii, 238 pp.
    New York: Harcourt Brace, 1960.

7   CARROLL, John B. *The Study of Language*, xi, 289 pp. Cam-
    bridge, Mass.: Harvard U.P. (London: Oxford U.P.), 1953.

8   CHERRY, Colin. *On Human Communication*, xiii, 333 pp. New
    York: Science Editions, 1961.

9   CHOMSKY, Noam. *Syntactic Structures*, 116 pp. The Hague:
    Mouton (Janua Linguarum 4), 1957.

10 CORDER, S. Pit. *English Language Teaching and Television*, iv,
    107 pp. London: Longmans, 1960.

11 CORNELIUS, Edwin T., Jr. *Language Teaching*, vii, 168 pp. New
    York: Crowell, 1953.

12 FERGUSON, Charles A., and GUMPERZ, John J. (ed.). *Linguistic
    Diversity in South Asia*, vii, 118 pp. Bloomington, Indiana:
    Indiana University Research Center in Anthropology, Folklore
    and Linguistics (Publication 13), 1960.

13 FIRTH, J. R. *Papers in Linguistics* 1934–1951, xii, 233 pp. London: Oxford U.P., 1957.

14 FIRTH, J. R., and others. *Studies in Linguistic Analysis*, vii, 205 pp. Oxford: Blackwell, 1957.

15 FRANCIS, W. Nelson. *The Structure of American English*, v, 614 pp. New York: Ronald Press, 1958.

16 FRIES, Charles C. *The Structure of English*, xi, 304 pp. New York: Harcourt Brace, 1952; London: Longmans, 1957.

17 GIMSON, A. C. *An Introduction to the Pronunciation of English.* London: Edward Arnold, 1962.

18 GLEASON, H. A., Jr. *Introduction to Descriptive Linguistics*, ix, 389 pp. New York: Holt, 1955.

19 GOUGENHEIM, G., MICHEA, R., RIVENC, P., and SAUVAGEOT, A. *L'Élaboration du Français Élémentaire*, 256 pp. Paris: Didier, 1956.

20 GRAY, G. W., and WISE, C. M. *The Bases of Speech*, xiii, 562 pp. New York and London: Harper, 1958.

21 GUBERINA, P., and RIVENC, P. *Voix et images de France: cours audio-visuel*, xl, 195 pp. Paris: Didier, 1961.

22 GURREY, P. *Teaching English as a Foreign Language*, vii, 200 pp. London: Longmans, 1955.

23 GURREY, P. *Teaching the Mother Tongue in Secondary Schools*, x, 219 pp. London: Longmans, 1958.

24 HALL, Robert A., Jr. *Linguistics and Your Language*, xi, 265 pp. (formerly *Leave Your Language Alone!*). New York: Anchor Books, 1960.

25 HARRIS, Zellig S. *Structural Linguistics*, xvi, 384 pp. (formerly *Methods in Structural Linguistics*). Chicago: Phoenix Books, 1960.

26 HILL, Archibald A. *Introduction to Linguistic Structures*, xi, 496 pp. New York: Harcourt Brace, 1958.

27 HOCKETT, Charles F. *A Course in Modern Linguistics*, xi, 621 pp. New York: Macmillan, 1958.

28 HUTCHINSON, Joseph C. *The Language Laboratory*, vi, 85 pp. Washington: U.S. Department of Health, Education and Welfare (Bulletin 23), 1961.

29 JAKOBSON, Roman, and HALLE, Morris. *Fundamentals of Language*, ix, 87 pp. The Hague: Mouton (Janua Linguarum 1), 1956.

30 JONES, Daniel. *The Phoneme: Its Nature and Use*, xvi, 267 pp. Cambridge: Heffer, 1950.

31 JONES, Daniel. *An English Pronouncing Dictionary*, xlv, 538 pp. London: Dent (11th ed.), 1956.

32 JONES, Daniel. *Outline of English Phonetics*, xx, 378 pp. Cambridge: Heffer (8th ed.), 1956.

33 JONES, Daniel. *The History and Meaning of the Term 'Phoneme'*, 20 pp. London: International Phonetic Association (University College London), 1957.

34 JOOS, Martin. *Acoustic Phonetics*, 136 pp. Baltimore: Linguistic Society of America (Language monograph 23), 1948.

35 JOOS, Martin (ed.). *Readings in Linguistics*, viii, 421 pp. Washington: American Council of Learned Societies, 1957.

36 KAISER, L. (ed.). *Manual of Phonetics*, xv, 460 pp. Amsterdam: North Holland, 1957.

37 LADEFOGED, Peter. *Elements of Acoustic Phonetics*, vi, 118 pp. Edinburgh: Oliver & Boyd, 1962.

38 LADO, Robert. *Linguistics Across Cultures*, viii, 141 pp. Ann Arbor: Michigan U.P., 1957.

39 LADO, Robert. *Language Testing*, xiii, 389 pp. London: Longmans, 1961.

40 LEE, W. R. *English Intonation: A New Approach*. Amsterdam: North Holland, 1958.

41 LEES, Robert B. *The Grammar of English Nominalizations*, xxvi, 206 pp. Bloomington, Indiana: Indiana University Research Center in Anthropology, Folklore and Linguistics (Publication 12), 1960.

42 LONG, Ralph B. *The Sentence and Its Parts*, 528 pp. Chicago: U.P., 1961.

43 MALMBERG, Bertil. *La Phonétique*, 136 pp. Paris: Presses Universitaires de France (Que sais-je? 637), 1960.

44 MACCARTHY, P. A. D. *English Pronunciation*, viii, 179 pp. Cambridge: Heffer, 1944.

45 MCINTOSH, Angus. *Introduction to a Survey of Scottish Dialects*, xii, 122 pp. Edinburgh: Nelson (for University of Edinburgh), 1952.

46 MILLER, George A. *Language and Communication*, xiii, 298 pp. New York: McGraw-Hill, 1951.

47 NIDA, Eugene. *A Synopsis of English Syntax*, lxviii, 133 pp. Norman, Oklahoma: Summer Institute of Linguistics, 1960.

48 O'CONNOR, D. J., and ARNOLD, G. F. *Intonation of Colloquial English*, viii, 270 pp. London: Longmans, 1961.

49 ORTON, Harold, and DIETH, Eugen. *Survey of English Dialects: Introduction*, 112 pp. Leeds: E. J. Arnold, 1962.

50 PALMER, Harold E., and BLANDFORD, F. G. *A Grammar of Spoken English*, xxxviii, 298 pp. Cambridge: Heffer (Tokyo: Maruzen), 1951.

51 PENFIELD, Wilder, and ROBERTS, Lamar. *Speech and Brain Mechanisms*, xiii, 286 pp. Princeton: U.P. (London: Oxford U.P.), 1959.

52 PIKE, Kenneth L. *Phonetics*, ix, 182 pp. Ann Arbor: Michigan U.P., 1943.

53 PIKE, Kenneth L. *Language in Relation to a Unified Theory of the Structure of Human Behaviour*, x, 170; v, 85; vii, 146 pp. Glendale, California: Summer Institute of Linguistics, 3 vols. 1954–60.

54 POTTER, Simeon. *Language in the Modern World*, 221 pp. Harmondsworth, Middlesex: Penguin Books, 1960.

55 *Principles of the International Phonetic Association*, 53 pp. London: International Phonetic Association (University College London), 1949.

56 QUIRK, Randolph. *The Study of the Mother Tongue*, 23 pp. London: Lewis (for University College London), 1961.

57 QUIRK, Randolph. *The Use of English*, viii, 333 pp. London: Longmans, 1962.

58 QUIRK, Randolph, and SMITH, A. H. (ed.). *The Teaching of English*, 192 pp. London: Secker & Warburg (Studies in Communication 3), 1959.

59 *Report of the Commonwealth Conference on The Teaching of*

English as a Second Language ('The Makerere Report'), 56 pp. Entebbe, Uganda: Uganda Government Printer; London: Commonwealth Education Liaison Unit, 1961.

60 ROBERTS, Paul. *Patterns of English*, v, 314 pp. New York: Harcourt Brace, 1959.

61 ROBERTS, Paul. *English Sentences*, 294 pp. New York: Harcourt Brace, 1962.

62 ROBINS, R. H. *Ancient and Mediaeval Grammatical Theory in Europe*, vii, 104 pp. London: Bell, 1951.

63 SAPIR, Edward. *Language*, vii, 258 pp. New York: Harcourt Brace, 1921. (Reprint, Harvest Books, 1949.)

64 SAPORTA, Sol (ed.). *Psycholinguistics: A Book of Readings*, xv, 551 pp. New York: Holt, Rinehart & Winston, 1961.

65 de SAUSSURE, Ferdinand (trans. Wade Baskin). *Course in General Linguistics*, xvi, 240 pp. London: Peter Owen, 1960.

66 SCOTT, N. C. *The Place of Phonetics in the University*, 26 pp. London: School of Oriental and African Studies, 1961.

67 SEBEOK, Thomas A. (ed.). *Style in Language*, xvii, 470 pp. New York: Wiley, 1960.

68 SKINNER, B. F. *Verbal Behaviour*, x, 478 pp. London: Methuen (Century Psychology Series), 1957.

69 SLEDD, James. *A Short Introduction to English Grammar*, 346 pp. Chicago: Scott Foresman, 1959.

70 STEVENS, S. S., and DAVIS, H. *Hearing: Its Psychology and Physiology*, xv, 489 pp. New York: Wiley, 1948.

71 STRANG, Barbara M. H. *Modern English Structure*, x, 201 pp. London: Edward Arnold, 1962.

72 ULDALL, H. J. *Outline of Glossematics, vol. 1: General Theory*, v, 87 pp. Copenhagen: Cercle Linguistique de Copenhague (Travaux 10), 1957.

73 ULLMANN, Stephen. *Semantics*, 278 pp. Oxford: Blackwell, 1962.

74 WAYMENT, Hilary (ed.). *English Teaching Abroad and the British Universities*, 63 pp. London: Methuen, 1961.

75 WEINREICH, Uriel. *Languages in Contact*, xii, 148 pp. New York: Linguistic Circle of New York (Columbia University), 1953.

SUPPLEMENT TO BIBLIOGRAPHY

This supplement includes forthcoming books and books which have appeared since the compilation of the main bibliography. Where no date is given, the book is forthcoming; (?) signifies that the title is provisional.

76 ABERCROMBIE, David. *Elements of General Phonetics*. Edinburgh: U.P.

77 BAZELL, C. E., CATFORD, J. C., HALLIDAY, M. A. K. and ROBINS, R. H. (ed.). *In Memory of J. R. Firth* (?). London: Longmans.

78 CATFORD, J. C. *A Linguistic Theory of Translation*. London: Oxford U.P.

79 DIXON, Robert M. W. *Linguistic Science and Logic*, 108 pp. The Hague: Mouton (Janua Linguarum 28), 1963.

80 FIRTH, J. R. *Further Papers in Linguistics* (?), ed. F. R. Palmer. London: Longmans.

81 FIRTH, J. R. *Speech* and *The Tongues of Men* (reprint in one volume). London: Oxford U.P.   1964/5

82 GLEASON, H. A., Jr. *Linguistics and English Grammar* (?).

83 JOOS, Martin. *The Five Clocks*, 62 pp. The Hague: Mouton, 1962.

84 MCINTOSH, Angus and HALLIDAY, M. A. K. *Patterns of Language: Papers in General, Descriptive and Applied Linguistics*. London: Longmans.

85 MACKEY, William F. *Language Teaching Analysis*. London: Longmans.

86 MOHRMANN, Christine, NORMAN, F. and SOMMERFELT, Alf. *Trends in Modern Linguistics*, 118 pp. Utrecht: Spectrum, 1963.

87 ROBINS, R. H. *General Linguistics: An Introductory Survey*. London: Longmans.   1964

88 SPENCER, John (ed.). *Language in Africa: Papers of the Leverhulme Conference on Universities and the Language Problems of Tropical Africa*, vii, 167 pp. Cambridge: U.P., 1963.

89 SPENCER, John, GREGORY, M. and ENKVIST, N. *Linguistics and Style*. London: Oxford U.P.

90 STREVENS, Peter. *The Study of the Present-day English Language: A Triple Bond Between Disciplines*, 27 pp. Leeds: U.P., 1963.

91 STREVENS, Peter. *Papers in Applied Linguistics and Language Teaching* (?). London: Oxford U.P.

92 ZWIRNER, E., GOUGENHEIM, G., *et al*, POTTIER, B. and STREVENS, P. D. *New Trends in Linguistic Research*, 105 pp. Strasbourg: Council of Europe, 1963.

GENERAL INDEX

Where more than one page reference is given, **boldface** numbers indicate the passage where the explanation of a technical term is to be found.

Accent, 84–5, 103–7
Airstream mechanism, 59
Alphabet, 49
  of the International Phonetic Association (I.P.A.), 65, 147
  Initial Teaching (I.T.A.), 290
Ambiguities, 44, 286–7
Ambilingual, -ism, 78, 179
Applications of linguistics, 5, 98, 132, 138–9, 169, 247, 280
  of phonetics, 61, 105–7
Articulacy, 282–3
Articulation, 45, 59, 62, **70**
Arts, 3, 244
Attitudes to language, 75, 98–110, 172, 227–9, 284
Audio-visual aids, 264, 268, 298
Auditory description, 59, 65

Bilingual, -ism, 77–9, 179
Binarity in language, 303
British Council, 188, 278, 293

Category, linguistic, 7, 14, 23, **24**, 39, 62, 133, 145
  theoretical and descriptive categories, 25, 31, 74
Centres d'intérêt, 194
Chain in language, 35
Chinese
  dialects, 76, 81–3
  script, 48–50, 109, 281, 290
Choice in language, 21, 29, 33, 35
  open and closed choices, 22
Citation, 37, 238
Class, **24**, 28–**9**, 32, 35, 38–41
  in phonology, 46
Clause, 25, 38, 41, 237
  in translation, 126–8

Cline, 22, 35, 77, 93
Cohesion, 248
Collocation, **33–5**, 88, 130, 238
Community, dialect, 67, 83, 86, 94
  language, **75–6**, 79–80, 86
Comparison of languages, **111–23**, 132
  transfer, 120–3
Computer, 11, 34, 132–4, 169, 291, 303
Concord, 116, 128
Context, **10**, 12, 19, **37–40**, 75
  contextual equivalence, 115, 123, 266
  meaning, **37**, 124, 151, 240
Contrast, 42–3, 67
Correctness
  see Attitudes to language
Creole, **80–1**, 101, 295

Definition, 9, 37
Delicacy in grammar, **30**, 38
  in phonology, 45, 66
  in varieties of language, 92–5
Diachronic, **95**
Dialect, **76–7**, 81–7
  community, 67, 83, 86, 94
  attitudes to, 102–5
  regional and social, 86–7, 102–5
Dictionary, 22–3, 36–7, 238
Discontinuity, discontinuous item, 27–8
Discourse
  field of, 90–1
  mode of, 91–2
  style of, 92–3
Disponibilité, **195**, 204, 210
Distinctive feature, 301, 303

Element of structure, **28**, 41
Elocution, 105, 229

Method, methodology, 186, **200–1**,
    212–13, 277
  direct, 200, 255
  grammar-translation, 265–8
Methodics, **200–1**, 222, 277
Model, 17, 24, 126, 133, 299
Morpheme, 25, 29, 48, 128
  morphemics, 149, 151, 186, 300–1
Motivation, 182

National language, 83–7, 101
Native language
  see Language, Language learning,
    Language teaching
Negative transfer, 84–5, 112
Neutral term, 30
Nonsense, 238
Normal Voice and Speech, 105–7
Notation, 26, **66**, 165

Observation, 5, 13, 32, 34, 39–40
Organs of speech, 59–60
Orthography (*see also* Script), 49, 128
  English, 51–4, 84, 109–10, 228
  orthographic units, 51, 281

Paralinguistic features, 96
Participant, 92, 246
Pattern in language, 4, 18–20, 22, 29,
    63, 244
  internal and external, **12**, 38–40, 154
Pause, 68
Phatic communion, 91
Phonaesthetic series, 238
Phoneme, 43, 45–6, 49, 68–70
  phonemics, 149, 151, 186, 300–1
Phonetics, 11, 14–20, 47, 56, **63**, 167
  and language teaching, *see* Language
    teaching
  acoustic, 12, 57–8, 65
  applications of, 61, 105–7
  articulatory, 12, 59, 65
  development of, 147
  general, 15, 62
  instrumental, 11, 62, 147
Phonic substance, **10**, 19, 43, **63**
Phonology, 12, 15, 29, 42–7, **63-4**,
    300–3
  phonological item, 282
  unit, 44–6, 51, 68–73
Pidgin, **80-1**, 101
Prescription, 107–9, 171–2, 226–7, 284
  prescriptive teaching, 226–31

Presentation, 212–14
Pre-tonic, 45
Programmed instruction, 213, 298
Proscription, 107–9, 229–31
Prosody, prosodic, **47**, 68–9, 307

Rank, **27**, 34, 51, 126, 237, 302
  translation by, 126–8
  rankshift, 27–9
Reading, teaching of, 225, 227, 236–7,
    242–3
  in English, 289–91
  in foreign languages, 258–9
Received pronunciation (RP), 86,
    105–7, 238, 292
Register, **77**, 87–98
  in L1 teaching, 171, 237, 241–5
  in L2 teaching, 175, 190, 202–5, 263,
    266–7
  literary registers, 97, 130, 171
  scientific and technical, 91, 129–30
Reinforcement, 181, 213, 253
Restricted language, **96**, 174–5, 241–
Rhythm, 43, 46, 71–2
  verse, 72, 248
Russian, 258, 261–3
  examples, 114–17

Sciences, 3, 5, 7–14, 76, 146, 244
  linguistic, 4, 7–14, 56–7
Script, **48-50**, 109, 281–2, 289–90
Segment, segmental, **27**, 47, 69
Selection (in teaching), 199–207, 210
Semantics, 12, 39
  (*see also* Context)
Sentence, 25–8, 158–63, 300–1
  in translation, 126, 131
  orthographic, 51
Sequence (linguistic), 28
Sequencing (in teaching), 207–12
Set (lexical set, open set), **22**, 33, 37,
    238
Situation (linguistic), 13, 16, 79, 87,
    89–93, 95, 194, 245–6
  and language learning, 125, 179
  and language teaching, 204–5, 237
  and translation, 124
Skills, language, 9, 155, 198, 208–9
  acquiring, 178, 225, 252–6
  testing, 215, 219–21
Sound, speech sound, 42–4, 57–60, 66,
    70, 180, 220–1
Spelling reform, 65, 109

INDEX OF NAMES